P9-CNB-614

Chicken Soup for the Soul®

finding my faith

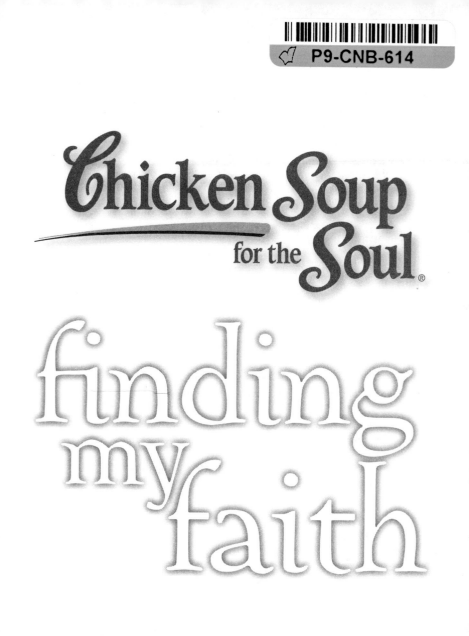

Chicken Soup for the Soul: Finding My Faith
101 Inspirational Stories about Life, Belief, and Spiritual Renewal
Jack Canfield, Mark Victor Hansen, Susan M. Heim

Published by Chicken Soup for the Soul Publishing, LLC www.chickensoup.com
Copyright © 2012 by Chicken Soup for the Soul Publishing, LLC. All Rights Reserved.
No part of this publication may be reproduced, stored in a retrieval system or transmitted in any form or by any means, electronic, mechanical, photocopying, recording or otherwise, without the written permission of the publisher.

CSS, Chicken Soup for the Soul, and its Logo and Marks are trademarks of
Chicken Soup for the Soul Publishing LLC.

The publisher gratefully acknowledges the many publishers and individuals who granted Chicken Soup for the Soul permission to reprint the cited material.

All scripture quotations, unless otherwise indicated, are taken from the Holy Bible, New International Version®, NIV®. Copyright ©1973, 1978, 1984, 2011 by Biblica, Inc.™ Used by permission of Zondervan. All rights reserved worldwide. www. Zondervan.com. The "NIV" and "New International Version" are trademarks registered in the United States Patent and Trademark Office by Biblica, Inc.™

Front cover photo courtesy of iStockphoto.com/creacart (Vetta Collection, © john shepherd). Back cover and interior photos courtesy of Photos.com.

Cover and Interior Design & Layout by Pneuma Books, LLC
Distributed to the booktrade by Simon & Schuster. SAN: 200-2442

Publisher's Cataloging-in-Publication Data
(Prepared by The Donohue Group)

Chicken soup for the soul : finding my faith : 101 inspirational stories about
  life, belief, and spiritual renewal / [compiled by] Jack Canfield, Mark Victor
  Hansen, [and] Susan M. Heim.

   p. ; cm.

  ISBN: 978-1-935096-95-5

   1. Faith--Literary collections. 2. Faith--Anecdotes. 3. Religious life--Literary collections. 4. Religious life--Anecdotes. 5. Conduct of life--Religious aspects--Literary collections. 6. Conduct of life--Religious aspects--Anecdotes. 7. Anecdotes. I. Canfield, Jack, 1944- II. Hansen, Mark Victor. III. Heim, Susan M. IV. Title: Finding my faith

PN6071.F17 C45 2012
810.8/02/0382   2012943520

PRINTED IN THE UNITED STATES OF AMERICA
on acid∞free paper
21 20 19 18 17 16 15 14 13 12   01 02 03 04 05 06 07 08 09 10

Chicken Soup for the Soul®

finding my faith

101 Inspirational Stories about Life,
Belief, and Spiritual Renewal

Jack Canfield
Mark Victor Hansen
Susan M. Heim

Chicken Soup for the Soul Publishing, LLC
Cos Cob, CT

Chicken Soup
www.chickensoup.com
for the Soul

Contents

❶
~Finding Faith Through Family~

❷
~Finding Faith Through Friendship~

❸
~Finding Faith in God's House~

❹
~Finding Faith Through Loss~

❺

~Finding Faith Through a Stranger~

❻

~Finding Faith Through Signs~

❼

~Finding Faith Through Nature~

❽

~Finding Faith Through Fire~

❾

~Finding Faith Through His Word~

❿
~Finding Faith Through Miracles~

⓫
~Finding Faith Through Service~

Chapter
1

finding
my faith

Finding Faith
Through Family

Family faces are magic mirrors.
Looking at people who belong to us,
we see the past, present, and future.

~Gail Lumet Buckley

Finding Faith
at the Run for the Cure

To one who has faith, no explanation is necessary.
To one without faith, no explanation is possible.
~St. Thomas Aquinas

I was afraid to ask the question because I wasn't sure I wanted to know the answer. My sister Deb and I were stuck on a bench outside a public washroom because she did not have the strength to walk back to the campsite. Her breathing was shallow and raspy, and she looked so small in her now oversized jacket. Cancer had taken its toll, and my big sister was fading into herself. The trek had been a mistake. I didn't want the question to be one as well. There had never been boundaries in our past conversations. Deb and I talked about everything. So, how could I not ask the one question that tore at my heart and threatened my foundation of faith? After months of my vision being blurred by hope-filled glasses, I realized there might not be a next time to ask the question.

"Aren't you angry at God for putting you through this again?" The words came out in a hesitant whisper.

I waited for an emotional rant of "Why me?" Here she was losing the fight against inoperable lung cancer after battling through and surviving breast cancer. I would be mad at God. I had lashed out at Him for so much that now seemed so trivial. I was taught that if you were a good Christian and believed, you would be blessed and healed. Deb was a good Christian. She was involved in her church; she dedicated her life to the ministry of leading women to faith-filled lives; she shared her faith wherever she went. She didn't deserve this. She deserved a miracle, and God hadn't given her one.

In the little voice she had left, she answered, "No, I'm not angry at Him."

"What do you mean 'no'? You never once got mad at God? Look at what you are going through. Going through cancer once is bad enough, but now this?" My raised voice tried to bully her whisper away, as if volume were more important than conviction.

As she struggled for the breath to reply, she looked at me defiantly, and her eyes glazed over with tears. My stomach sank. Deb cried more in her lifetime from laughing than from sadness. I knew I had upset her, and that was the last thing I wanted to do. She looked down at her hands cradled in her lap.

"I would never have made it through this without God. How could I be mad at Him?"

I had made the commitment not to cry in front of Deb, for I was her cheerleader. But the grace in that statement, the magnitude of faith, was overwhelming, and I could not stop the flow. On that quiet evening, outside a public restroom, on a bench made for stopovers, not long conversations, I saw the power of faith.

This faith, her faith, was strong enough to carry me through her last breaths, the funeral and the many steps over the past year I have walked without her.

Today, as I stood outside a public restroom, waiting impatiently for my children to join the Run for the Cure, I felt as if this faith, which had carried me through all of the heartache, had run out. I was miserable as the fear of being late for the start of the race wrestled with the anxiety of completing it without Deb. I scanned the sea of thousands, looking for a familiar face, a tether to the oasis of family and friends we were supposed to meet. In the current of pink and white moving past me, I saw a young family go by—a man pulling a wagon with a toddler inside and a woman wearing a pink bandana that didn't quite mask the baldness underneath, holding a little girl's hand. At first, they were just part of the stream of people flowing into the mass gathered at the starting line. Then the "I am running for…" sign on the small child's back caught my attention. It simply said, "Mommy."

The words sucker-punched me, and I struggled to breathe. In that moment, I felt the pain of losing my sister. I remembered Deb walking years before in the same park, wearing a pink bandana that didn't quite mask the baldness underneath, holding the hand of her granddaughter, one of the people she had fought so hard to live for. I saw the hole left in a family when a mother dies and leaves such big shoes to fill. I felt that family's pain.

I sat down and cried. How could God let this happen? As I struggled to regain my composure, I concentrated on the crowd heading to the starting line, trying to distract myself from the pain. Teams danced their way forward, wearing pink from head to toe, topped with strange hats and feather boas. A group of men, who might have refused to wear a pink shirt in their ordinary lives, looked extraordinary in their sequined pink bras. People walked arm in arm, each wearing "I am running for…" signs that listed those who mattered today and every day. And, somewhere in that crowd, my team waited for me. I started to feel the power of hope.

Over the din of thousands of people, I could hear the whisper of my sister. "No, I'm not angry at Him." She had endured suffering I hope I never have to know, yet her faith never wavered. I looked back over the past year, feeling again the anger and pain, the abandonment and loneliness. Then I donned my hope-filled glasses and began to see the blessings. The presence of God shone through new faith-filled friends who carried me when I didn't have the strength to go on. The story, *The Promise*, was a gift that allowed me to have a conversation with God through fiction, one I could never have had in real life. The love of my family was a balm soothing my battered soul. My broken heart had finally healed. I was here, being a witness to and a participant in this incredible display of love for family, friends and co-workers. Faith that a cure would be found was abundant. Hope for the future was infectious. How could God not let this happen?

As my daughters came bounding down the stairs toward me, smiling and laughing, proudly wearing their shirts with love letters to their Auntie Debbie written all over them, I thought, "How can I be angry with God? I would never have made it through this without Him."

~Darlene Gudrie Butts

In the Basement

I am not afraid of storms for I am learning how to sail my ship.
~Louisa May Alcott

Thunder and lightning come and go in our lives but therein lies a lesson. When the sun comes out again, the raindrops on the leaves will sparkle like diamonds. If we stand long enough to watch the last of the clouds blow away, we will also see that the storm had nourished us in a way that we could not predict. It was in such a storm that I learned to have hope.

I must have been four or five years old. My father had died and our mother had to work, so our grandmother came to stay with us one summer. Our home was surrounded by lovely trees, but this terrified my mother whenever a storm blew up. I didn't understand then what I do now—about house insurance deductibles and how much money a widowed secretary with a mortgage and three kids could actually have at her disposal in 1962 to pay for repairs. Impossible numbers must have swirled in her head with every thunder clap. Worse yet, we lived on an island where the waters frequently attracted lightning.

But, oblivious to all these facts, I was standing on a chair by the window really enjoying the sight of the trees fighting against the wind when I heard the phone ring. My grandmother answered it with the shaking hands of someone who'd only ever gotten bad news over the phone. My older sisters sensed trouble, and I recall that a shadow fell across their countenances as Grandma put down the receiver and shepherded us down the basement stairs.

"Grandma, who was it?" they pleaded as we descended. "What's wrong?" It had been our mother calling from work to order us to seek shelter. Grandma, anxious that nothing would happen to us on her watch, complied. At the bottom of the stairs, I stood and watched the old woman pull over a chair and instruct my sisters to drag over the old shaggy pink rug for us to sit upon. The basement, rarely used, was dimly lit with only a bare bulb or two and a pair of cobwebbed windows through which I observed the wind bending the grass flat. I sat by her right knee, my two sisters on her left, and enjoyed the cozy little situation I found myself in for the first time with family members that I loved. As I happily took in the scene, I noticed how peaceful Grandma appeared compared to my sisters.

"What if the tree falls on our roof, Grandma?" they asked. "Who will pay for it?" More pleadingly, "Where will we live then? How will we eat?"

Suddenly alarmed, I looked eagerly to our grandmother. As our father's mother, I held her in high esteem. Touching her, I always felt a connection to him. Today, I know that some family members felt she was a woman of small intellect who, putting everything in the hands of the Lord, unflappably stood her ground. But I was small and looked to her.

She was just smiling and shaking her head.

"Grandma," I ventured, comparing her face to those of my older siblings, "why aren't you afraid?"

She looked up, and we looked up with her. I think my sisters only saw the floor joists and impending doom, but somehow I knew she was focusing her eyes on something farther away than the rough-cut boards, pipes and metal ductwork. "God will watch over us," she declared as the lightning cracked.

My sisters disagreed heartily. Where was God when our father died and left us destitute? Where was God when our mother locked herself in her room sobbing and left us to our own devices? Wasn't it God making the storm? Didn't God grow the trees that were perilously near our eaves, which would take out the hall window if they brushed too close?

I looked at my sisters and weighed their complaints, and then I looked back at Grandma. She sighed a little, folded her hands, and looked up again. And you know what? We were already in the basement. We couldn't hide any deeper from the storm; we had done everything in our power to protect ourselves, and I knew that. When she repeated "God will protect us," making that promise again, I made the first and most valuable decision of my whole life, one I need to remind myself of time and time again. I decided that I liked my grandma better at that moment than the fearmongers. In her seventy-plus years, she had seen many trees felled by storms, watched many loved ones fall around her, but she had still learned, or taught herself, the inner discipline to look beyond the situation at hand and trust that there was something bigger at work than what she could fully understand. I'm just sorry that she never knew how much I needed to see her looking from the basement out at the storm and declaring, against all doubts, that it was going to be okay.

Years later, as I lay in my sleeping bag beside a Rocky Mountain lake with another storm raging around me, I felt the same thrill as that day with Grandma in the basement. I smiled at the power and might of the storm, certain that the sun would shine again in the morning. My tentmates, shuddering in their bags, began to murmur as my sisters had so long ago. "How can you be so calm?" they charged. "We're camped at the highest point on the mountain, and metal poles are holding up the tent! We'll be toast if we take a direct hit!"

I didn't know then how to tell them why I enjoyed the storm, but I do now. When the wind had died, I followed my grandmother up the stairs. I watched her place her hand tentatively to turn the doorknob, not knowing what the storm had wrought on the other side. Then I saw the sun break upon her face and the great relief that rose from her heart. I heard my sisters laugh and saw them jump up with joy. Perhaps I was awfully young to make the decision to follow Grandma's way, but the more I've opened doors and seen the sun greet me in my own life, the more I have hope that there are many more sunny days ahead.

~Kathy L. Baumgarten

Early Mornings with God and Mom

Welcome every morning with a smile. Look on the new day as another special gift from your Creator, another golden opportunity to complete what you were unable to finish yesterday.
~Og Mandino

Growing up, I went to church with my parents, attended Sunday school, and participated in youth groups and service projects. Although these activities supported my faith development, a daily routine I shared with my mother created the foundation for it.

In one of my early memories, a soft glow floated down the hallway from my parents' bedroom when I opened my eyes in the morning. The smell of coffee lingered in the air. During some months, it was still dark outside. I slipped out of bed, grabbed some books from the shelf close by, and padded down the hall in pajama feet.

After Mom saw Dad off to work for his sand and gravel business, she returned to bed. In her housecoat, she stretched out to read her Bible, daily devotions, and Sunday school lessons.

Mom smiled when I entered the room, calling out, "Hi, honey!" I climbed into bed with her, flopping down on my dad's pillow and snuggling up to her side.

While she finished the page and marked her place, I flipped

through a book, my brown hair splaying across the pillow like my mom's wavy locks did on hers.

Mom tugged a thick book from the pile on her bedside table. "Now, where were we?" she asked, as she opened the book of Bible stories for children.

I took out the marker and pointed to the page. "Here, Mom!"

After she finished the story, if we had time, she read from a book of children's prayers or one of the Golden Books I lugged from my room.

As I listened to the sound of her voice and the rhythm of the language, my hands ran up and down the ridges of the chenille bedspread. Words and pictures became stories, and stories became windows to understand a world that sounded different to me, a child with hearing impairments since birth.

We talked about the pictures as we looked at them. Mom listened patiently to my observations. Sometimes, my words didn't sound accurate — a concern greater than typical developmental errors for young children — but she didn't correct me. She simply repeated the word, and then said, "Let's say it together!"

The early morning quiet time I shared with Mom throughout my childhood gave me a significant lifelong routine. Reading together, interacting with Mom, and observing her daily life taught me about faith. She believed, no matter what, that things worked out — though not always in ways we first imagined. I gained confidence in a world understood through language, scriptures and stories of the Bible, as well as through people who acted on their faith. I began to believe that I, too, could live successfully in such a world.

My mother followed her early morning routine until she died. During my college and career years, my quiet time took a less predictable path. Most days, I grabbed devotional time whenever I could and sometimes fell short. As years passed, I gravitated toward early morning again, by then recognizing more fully this piece of my mother's legacy — starting with a calm routine set a positive tone for the day. After life-altering surgery in my late forties, I began writing in the early mornings as well, not waiting to see if opportunities occurred later in the day.

Now, at age sixty—wrapped in a purple prayer shawl—I consistently read the Bible and daily devotions, much like my mother, and follow up with writing reflections. Sometimes, I use her Bible, engraved with her name "Marybelle Parks" on the front, and inscribed by my older sister who gave it to her for Christmas in 1955. The Bible embodies her presence because I left her penciled earmarks and notations and scraps of handwritten notes, prayers, and church programs stuck in it, just as they were when she died more than twenty years ago from cancer.

Mom gave me a foundation in language and faith, but more than that—the lifeline, the routine to anchor me. She lived her belief that faith nourished through all times and sustained through all times. Over my own lifetime, as I experienced handling tough situations, I grew in my understanding of a personal relationship with God—a pattern of ongoing reflection and conversation—and the realization that without it, life could well be chaos and restlessness, with no feeling of safe sanctuary. Whether life seemed happy, mundane, puzzling, or troubled, the comforting routine centered me.

My mom knew a firm faith meant gratefulness, spiritual growth, and willingness to witness by example. By sharing her routine and acting as a model, she gave me the foundation to nurture my faith through the joys and jolts of life. Thanks to her, I keep it growing strong every morning.

~Ronda Armstrong

Life with Ray: A True Adventure

Dear brothers and sisters, when troubles come your way, consider it an
opportunity for great joy. For you know that when your faith is tested, your
endurance has a chance to grow. So let it grow, for when your endurance is
fully developed, you will be perfect and complete, needing nothing.
~James 1:2-4 (NLT)

It was the summer of 1981. Christian Outreach Center in Hillsboro, Missouri was hosting various camps. The family camp I attended in June proved to be a good time of fellowship and Bible study. When I saw the notice about singles' camp, something inside me said, "Go."

Camp consisted of fun activities, Bible study, and meeting other Christian singles. As the week progressed, I found myself spending quite a bit of time with a young man from Wisconsin. Another camper warned me, "It looks like something neurological is going on with Ray. I would be careful about getting too involved."

Ray's last words to me before heading back to Wisconsin were, "We'll see what God will do." As the weeks went on, letters and phone calls became more numerous. I soon realized that even if there were a neurological problem, it could not keep me from falling in love with this man.

Ray's deep commitment to God, his zest for life, and his childlike ways won my heart. His lighthearted, fun-loving spirit was almost a cover-up for this sensitive romantic. Somehow, I knew life with Ray Knudsen would be a real adventure.

I often think back to a poem by Robert Frost entitled: "The Road Not Taken." The last lines of the poem state:

Two roads diverged in a wood, and I—
I took the one less traveled by,
And that has made all the difference.

The road I chose to walk with Ray definitely made all the difference in my life. That road totally reshaped me and actually served to catapult me into God's destiny for my life.

Four years after we were married, Ray was diagnosed with a rare form of cerebral degeneration with ataxia. Always optimistic, Ray took the diagnosis very casually. I was the one who struggled with worry.

My life with Ray was not a typical "happily ever after" story. In most respects, it was just the opposite. It seemed like it was just one hurdle after another. We were not delivered out of the fires, but rather given the grace to walk through them. With God's help, the adversities shaped us into stronger, more determined individuals. We found out that faith in God and a good attitude far outweigh anything this world can throw at you. God stayed our main focus no matter what storm clouds loomed about us. He proved Himself faithful over and over again as we cried out to Him day by day.

Through the years, Ray's example of faith, surrender and trust began to rub off on me. I don't know if I ever achieved Ray's level of acceptance and trust, but I did grow to understand that God was in control—no matter what—and He had our backs.

As the years progressed, so did the disease. Initially, it was weakness in his legs, trouble walking in a straight line, and excessive dizziness. At the onset, he used one cane, then two canes, then crutches, a walker, and finally a wheelchair. But walking was not the only thing taken from him. He also lost strength and usage of his hands to the point that he could not take care of basic daily needs or his personal hygiene. He had some hearing loss. Then swallowing became difficult as he lost muscle tone throughout his whole body. Choking episodes at the dinner table were regular events.

Every loss was devastating, but probably the most difficult was losing his voice. The words he could pronounce came out garbled and hard to decipher. Ray loved to talk, so being stripped of the ability to communicate was quite a blow. The verbal exchanges we had were very limited.

Through all of this, the grace of God continued to lift us above our circumstances. One of our wedding gifts said it best. It was a photograph of a serene wooded pathway. Inscribed at the bottom were the words: "The will of God will not take you where the grace of God will not keep you."

Now I am able to look back and see why Ray was a victor even in the midst of disability. Although he had days when darkness and despair tried to engulf him, he would not allow himself to stay there. Somehow he knew that having pity parties would just make matters worse. Ray's joy seemed to bubble out of him when you least expected it. His smile and laughter lifted up people around him. He made the decision to think about others more than he thought about himself.

Ray never shook his fist at God and wondered why his life was so hard. He offered praise and worship to Jesus Christ with the giving of thanks on a continual basis. His profound love for His Creator was seen by all who knew him, and it never diminished. The last audible words out of his mouth were the song: "Oh, How I Love Jesus."

As I cared for this man and watched this disease ravage his body, I marveled at how the spirit of this man soared even while his physical body was deteriorating. He was the one who lifted me up many times. His joy, love, laughter, and prayers carried me through many dark days.

Somehow, God planted in both of us the tools needed to be overcomers in the midst of adversity. Words cannot completely depict how hard some of our days were. But another reality is also true—mere words cannot begin to express the love, strength, peace and even joy that God richly poured on us.

As I look back now, I would not have changed our situation. James 1:2-4 in the New Living Translation states: "Dear brothers and sisters, when troubles come your way, consider it an opportunity for great joy. For you know that when your faith is tested, your endurance has a chance to grow. So let it grow, for when your endurance is fully developed, you will be perfect and complete, needing nothing."

Through all of the storms, God was in our midst. Was it ever easy? No. Was it worth it? A resounding YES. Was my life with Ray an adventure? Without a doubt. It was an adventure only seen with spiritual eyes.

~Sandra Knudsen

Waiting for Faith

We all walk in the dark
and each of us must learn to turn on his or her own light.
~Earl Nightingale

I unbuckled my seatbelt as my seventeen-year-old brother pulled into the church parking lot. "Hurry," he chided me. I rolled my eyes, jumped out and dashed toward the heavy, wooden doors. Sixty seconds later, I raced back to the car, a smile on my face, church bulletin clutched in my fourteen-year-old hand.

That was the proof that we did, in fact, "go" to church. At home, I dropped it on the counter and headed up to my room so that my mom couldn't question me. I was not a good liar.

Ten years later, I gave birth to my first child. Shortly afterward, my mom asked when the baptism would be. I told her I hadn't thought about it yet. I just wasn't sure what I wanted for my own children where religion was concerned. By the time baby Will had turned one, though, I decided that it was my job to instill some faith in him so that he'd have a basis on which to make his own decisions when the time came. So at fourteen months, I had him baptized. Soon after, he was joined by a brother, and then a baby sister, both of whom were baptized within months of their births. Going to church had become part of our family's way of life. But when Will turned nine, his dad and I divorced. It was a tough time for all of us. I tried to keep a sense of normalcy in our home, taking the kids to church each Sunday, but my heart just wasn't in it. Neither were theirs.

"Why should I believe in God when He did this to our family?" Will said to me one Sunday. His words mirrored my thoughts exactly. And I didn't have an answer. So, church became a holiday-only proposition. The kids attended the parish school of religion (PSR), but our attempts at attendance were half-hearted.

When that nine-year-old turned thirteen, we began preparing for his confirmation. Much as a bar mitzvah signifies adulthood in the Jewish religion, confirmation confirms these newly teen boys and girls as adults in the eyes of the church. Will went along with the rest of his PSR class, selecting his sponsor, choosing his confirmation name, even writing the required letter to our Catholic bishop, all steps toward the big day. But just days before the ceremony, he began to tense up each time it was mentioned.

Finally, late one night, he came to me in tears. "Mom, I don't want to be confirmed." My knee-jerk reaction was anger. How could he back out now? Was he just nervous about his role in the ceremony? All he had to do was stand there and recite a few lines with several hundred other eighth graders. What was so hard about that? This is a tradition in our family, I explained to him. I was confirmed; my mom before me was confirmed; and so were her parents before her. I can't let it end with you, I reasoned. He was adamant. And the more he dug in his heels, the harder I pushed.

We fought about it for days, and finally I called our parish director, apologizing and explaining. She listened to me vent my frustration, and then she explained, "This sacrament is about choice. Typically, kids this age don't raise much of a fuss because it's what they're supposed to do. The majority of them tend to go with the flow of things. The fact that your son is refusing is not a bad thing."

"It's not?" I was incredulous. She explained that this sacrament is meant to be chosen, not demanded. The fact that Will was choosing not to be confirmed meant that he was truly thinking about it, contemplating what it meant, and deciding that he wasn't ready.

I relented, and Will skipped the sacrament. But at the end of his eighth-grade year, as his friends were preparing to head to the public high school, Will had other plans. He wanted to attend a

Catholic high school in our area. Academically, it was a perfect fit for him. Personally, I was thrilled. Carved above the front entrance of the school is a quote from the Bible: "Knowledge has built herself a home." In the center of the two-story building is a round chapel. Standing inside, we looked up to see the library, a circular path around the chapel, filled floor-to-ceiling with books. As a writer, I could appreciate this coming together of hearts and minds. Libraries have always been a kind of chapel to me—the peace, the respect, the endless words. Will simply nodded. He had found his second home for the next four years.

This year, as we stood together as a family for Midnight Mass on Christmas Eve, I watched as Will recited the "Our Father." He followed along, respectfully, throughout Mass, setting an example for his two younger siblings. Maybe he has the same doubts as me. Would he have run into church and grabbed a bulletin—proof of attendance—just like I did at his age? Probably. But does that mean he has no faith? I don't think so. I believe in him, just as I believe in that higher power. I can't always see his faith, but I know it's there. And maybe all those years ago, my own mom knew exactly what I was up to. Maybe she let it go because she, too, knew that I would come around eventually, finding my own faith. Just as my son is finding his.

~Beth M. Wood

My Cherokee Grandmother and My Faith

When you were born, you cried and the world rejoiced.
Live your life so that when you die, the world cries and you rejoice.
~Cherokee Proverb

Grandma was brought up a real Baptist lady, but she also knew about Native religion. I came to find out that although she claimed she was Baptist (on government forms and in front of formal non-native company), she privately told friends she practiced the Native religion her mom taught her. I learned how to worship both ways and the commonality of all religions stuck with me.

My first lesson on the Four Directions came at an early age while gathering plants for healing. Grandma would point at the directions and explain: East was linked with the color red, the power of the rising sun; North was linked with the color white, for strength; West was black and the direction of sundown; and, South was yellow for comfort. These colors made up the medicine wheel and the circle of life, rebirth and unity of the Cherokee tribe. This was a lot to take in at such an early age, and she repeated the wheel many times and expanded on its meaning as I grew.

By the time I was a teenager I also knew that Winter (*go-la*) was the Cherokee connection to the direction of north, which meant cold (*u-yv-tlv*); Spring (*gi-la-go-ge*) and East (*ka-lv-gv*) were linked to new life; Summer (*go-ga*) was linked to the word warm (*u-ga-no-wa*) and meant peace; and Autumn (*u-la-go-hv-s-di*) was west (*wu-de-li-gv*) and stood for the cycle of life.

She explained to me that all life was a circle. A person is conceived, grows, is born, and cycles through the seasons over and over until the transition of death to another place—a good place. Life never truly ends; it continues in a circle. She said that the Cherokee Nation is like this circle: no matter what befalls the Nation, the circle will continue as the Creator intended.

So it came to be that I viewed each season with new eyes. As spring came, I saw that Mother Earth renewed everything, and a rebirth took place among her inhabitants. The plants grew, flowers bloomed, seeds dropped, and the Earth was alive. And so it was with each season, not just a time of frost, snow, cold and warmth, but a part of the cycle that my life was running. In my own life, it was meant for me to be born, grow, repeat the cycles, mature, grow old and transition into death—all in the Creator's time.

We spent many hours discussing the Bible, the Four Directions and the medicine wheel. She did not have much schooling, as her parents had pulled her from school in the eighth grade to work on their farm, but she was wiser than almost anyone I have ever met.

My knowledge expanded through the years, like children's building blocks stacked upon each other, and I was taught the ceremonies of our tribe: of birth, the use of the spirit fire, the pureness of tobacco, reverence for life, and the bonding of the members of the tribe through hardship and happiness.

I remember crying as my great-great-grandmother told of the Trail of Tears, the story that her mother had told her, and of the many along the way who had starved or frozen. At first, I could not believe the hardships and broken promises our Nation had faced, along with broken treaties and boarding schools. Yet the ring of truth was heavy in my great-great-grandmother's solemn words. I learned that wisdom comes with a price.

In Lawrence, Kansas, at the university where I work, there is a full earthworks medicine wheel with the Four Directions marked by granite pillars. Many times, I travel to that wheel and give praise for my blessings and ask for help in times of trouble. How do I reconcile this with the practice of Christianity that I also believe in? It is not hard. The religions have many things in common. They share aims of living the way I want others to treat me; the love of Mother Earth; the belief in the great Creator; the oneness of all things, and their place in the circle of life—all of this flows in my beliefs smoothly and easily. One form of worship honors my mother and her ancestors, and the other honors my father and his ancestors. Both honor life and the spirit and gifts received through the circle of my life.

~Pamela Tambornino

The Faith of a Child

While we try to teach our children all about life,
our children teach us what life is all about.
~Angela Schwindt

I never used to give a whole lot of thought to my spirituality. I grew up attending church and I believed in Jesus, but the subject wasn't one I explored in depth.

Then I got married (in a church) and recited vows that had much meaning for me. Afterward, my husband and I graced the threshold of a church on holidays and during weddings of friends. It wasn't that we weren't religious or spiritual; we simply didn't make it a priority on a daily (or even weekly) basis.

I was in my early twenties and immortal. I thought I could do it all. I was going to be career woman of the century, wife of the world, and mother (someday) of the millennium.

I was comfortable when I felt in control, but if someone asked me to pray for them or said their prayers were with me, I wasn't quite sure how to respond. I wasn't accustomed to praying or surrendering to a higher power.

Then my husband and I were blessed (I now understand) with a pregnancy. It was a joyous time, but I wasn't drawn any closer to a spiritual awareness. We had our baby—a beautiful and miraculous girl—and had her baptized, saying now that we were a family, we'd have to think about joining a church... someday.

Our baby girl blew out the candles on two birthday cakes, and we still hadn't found ourselves a church. As our daughter headed toward her third birthday, our thoughts turned to preschool. I found a program conveniently located close to my work. The teachers seemed superb. They had a proven curriculum and provided plenty of positive feedback to the children. The price was reasonable, and there was an opening. It all seemed ideal.

The school offered one more benefit to students: a Christian foundation.

The whole Christian thing was fine with me. I didn't have a problem with it. After all, I was a Christian myself—albeit not a very active one. Because the program had so many desirable features, we decided to enroll our daughter.

About a week after starting at the school, our little girl came home singing the familiar "Jesus Loves Me." We took it in stride and thought it was cute. One night at supper, she stopped us from eating because we hadn't said grace. We paused and listened as she sang us the "Johnny Appleseed" song.

Still, the religion and spirituality thing was something our daughter did in school. We were going to get to it someday—when we had the time. After all, we worked all week, and Sunday was really our only day to sleep in.

Easter rolled around, and our daughter came home with joyous news: "Jesus is alive!" More and more, her spirituality and love of God crept into our daily lives. When she was nervous about something, we'd say a prayer, and she'd feel better. When she was happy, she'd want to give thanks. She observed God's miracles in every moment of every day. He made the rainbow, the clouds and even the puddles. To her, spirituality was as integral, necessary and basic as eating, breathing or rolling out of bed.

At first, I felt self-conscious about praying, especially out loud, but my little girl showed me how natural and easy it could be. Prayer with her was a joyous, satisfying and spontaneous event, so I began practicing on my own, with the same results. We started attending a church and recognized how much it added to our lives.

Because of my young daughter's ease and openness, my husband

and I discussed topics of faith and spirituality we'd never ventured to before. As I watched him listen to her bedtime prayers or explain the miracle of Christmas, I saw him in a whole new light, and I loved him in a whole new way. We'd been a family before, but now we were something even better.

I used to think I could do it all. Now, I know I can; it's just that my definition of "all" has changed as my faith has grown. I no longer feel the need to be in control. I've relinquished that and have never been happier, more at peace or more fulfilled.

It took the innocence of a child's faith and some of God's own intervention to remind me of the importance of my own spirituality. I'm lucky. God gave me the gift of a daughter to show me the way toward His perfect love. I now recognize the importance of my own spiritual journey and realize that some people never get around to making the trip. Still others go through hardship or tragedy before finally turning to God.

And then, there are those who come to the idea as small children and grow up just knowing. For them, God's love is as integral, necessary and basic as eating, breathing or rolling out of bed.

~Jill Pertler

From Selfish to Faithful

A whole human life is just a heartbeat here in heaven.
Then we'll all be together forever.
~Chris Nielsen, What Dreams May Come

"I got the job! I'm going to be a camp counselor this summer!" Zach, my then-boyfriend, now-husband proclaimed the second I opened the front door to find him standing there, beaming.

"That's great news!" I exclaimed, giving him a big hug. We'd been dating for a year, and I knew he loved God, kids and sports. This gig at T Bar M, a Christian sports camp in the Texas hill country, was absolutely perfect for him.

There was just one thing: What was I supposed to do all summer long? My happiness quickly faded to disappointment.

"Wait. Just how long will you be gone?" I quizzed him. With my boyfriend out of the picture for potentially weeks at a time, my summer was beginning to look bleak.

"Well," he began softly, "it's an all-summer kind of thing. But you can visit me!" His eyes pleaded with me to see the good in this opportunity, but all I could think about was myself.

What would I do when my shifts were over at the restaurant where I waited tables? I'd grown so accustomed to hanging out with Zach that I didn't know what I'd do without him. It was my junior year in college, and, quite honestly, I just wanted to have fun. I didn't think much about God.

Zach, on the other hand, grew up a devout Catholic. God was a very big part of his life. While my family attended the occasional Mass, we mostly slept in on Sundays and rarely, if ever, said prayers.

Maybe that's why I was instantly drawn to and inspired by Zach's faithfulness. He invited me to join him at Mass on Sundays, and soon it became part of our normal weekend routine. As much as I would have preferred to stay burrowed under the covers until noon, Zach gently made it clear that going to church on Sunday morning wasn't optional—it was mandatory.

I loved this about Zach, but standing there in the sunshine-soaked entryway of my mom's house, his faith made me angry.

"What am I supposed to do while you're gone? Do you know how boring my summer will be now? It's like I don't even have a boyfriend. I can't go weeks without seeing you," I fumed.

Undeterred by my bad attitude, Zach grabbed my hands and guided me to the couch. "You know that movie, *What Dreams May Come*?"

I immediately recalled the movie; we had watched it together in his dorm room just a few weeks ago. It made me terribly sad when the husband in the movie left heaven to rescue his wife from hell.

"Well, the reason I want you to go to church with me, read the Bible and invite Jesus into your heart," he said, holding my hands in his, "is so that I can see you in heaven."

Those words changed my life. A spark had been struck somewhere deep within my soul, and I, for perhaps the first time in my life, felt true love.

There was a great love sitting in front of me, and there was the love of Jesus. I only needed to invite Him into my heart.

"How do I ask Him?" I murmured softly, tears welling up in my eyes.

Zach gave my hands a squeeze and said, "Just invite Him in. There's no wrong way to do it. He just wants you to ask."

I dropped to my knees right there at the side of the familiar cream-colored couch, pressed my hands tightly together, closed my eyes and asked Jesus to come live in my heart.

The rest, you could say, is faith history. Zach and I got married in 2005 and had a precious baby boy in 2010. I count my blessings every day. And when the Lord calls me home, I'll tell Him Zach helped me find the way.

~Audrey Sellers

In His Hands

It is not flesh and blood but the heart which makes us fathers and sons.
~Johann Schiller

At twelve years old, I had no faith in God. I believed that He was our creator, and I had memorized plenty of Bible verses, but I did not trust His plan for my life. Already it seemed that I had struggled through so much, and I often felt like God had forgotten me and my family. Thankfully, God blessed my life with patient and loving people who taught me that unconditional love is really possible. The support and guidance of two generous families showed me the love of Jesus and brought me into His arms.

My mom left our family when I was four years old to move to another state with a new husband. I missed her, and sometimes I felt like I hated her. I wanted to be with my mom while my dad worked, instead of at daycare, and I wanted a mom to brush and braid my hair in the mornings. I wanted my mom to hold me in her arms again. Part of me couldn't believe that she had ever loved us at all, and I felt like I had been thrown away. I felt lonely and out of place, and I acted out with tantrums that strained my relationships with caregivers and friends.

Over the next few years, home became a place of secrets. I learned to tell lies or to avoid questions. My big sister went through so much hurt that I stopped praying, feeling sure that no one was listening. When I was twelve, she reached out for help. On the day that I was taken away from my dad and my home, I felt more broken and abandoned than I had ever felt in my life.

Now I can see just how much God held me up during that time. Thankfully, my brother and I were placed in the same foster home, and we were able to stay together during our entire stay in foster care. Our foster parents, the Corders, agreed to keep both of us until we were able to move onto our permanent home, though they had originally signed on to keep us only for the night. It was the first gift of kindness that we received from them, unasked for and unearned.

My foster parents had their work cut out for them with my brother and me; we were used to watching the shows that we wanted, eating what we wanted, and looking out for ourselves. The first few weeks in a home with firm boundaries and set rules was a tough adjustment for us, and a tough time for everyone. I tested them, waiting for them to turn on us in anger and turn us out of their home.

The Corders had built their family on love and faith, and they shared both with their foster children. I settled into a routine that included church every Wednesday and Sunday. Going to church wasn't new, but for the first time in my life, I attended one church regularly and got to know everyone who attended. There were always friendly faces to greet me, and Sunday school was a place where I could get real answers instead of canned expressions. I had a lot of questions that year: I wanted to know why God let bad things happen to kids, why some people had so much and others had so little, and why some people were so mean to others. The answers were not always what I wanted to hear, but my Sunday school teacher and my pastor took me seriously and tried to help me understand that God had a plan for me, too.

I was saved through God's grace while singing a hymn on a Sunday morning. Every Sunday we sang "Just as I Am," with every voice joined to lift the words to heaven. I sang along as always:

"Just as I am, without one plea, but that thy blood was shed for me."

Suddenly, the words wrapped around my heart and squeezed hard, and for the first time I felt the truth in the song. Even though I had lied and hated, even though I was just a poor girl from a broken family, Jesus loved me, too. I didn't have to do anything to earn it; I only had to walk into His waiting arms and give control of my life into His hands. I began to cry with joy and relief. My foster mom looked into my face and knew that I had opened my heart. She hugged me and cried with me, and then I walked to the front of the church and turned to face my family with a smile.

Of course, life did not become an easy stroll after that day. There were still times when my faith faltered, and I doubted my worth in the eyes of God. At sixteen years old, I became an emancipated adult. I struggled to prove that I didn't need anyone to help me, and I sometimes felt that I could only trust myself. But again God blessed me with supportive guides who bolstered my faith through their unconditional love. My boyfriend's parents, the Kendalls, opened their hearts and home to me, and showed me the unwavering support and acceptance of true parents. They forgave every harsh word and mistake, and expressed their love even when they were disappointed in my behavior. In times of doubt, my father-in-law reminded me to look to God, and his unfailing faith reminded me to look to my blessings. The entire Kendall family of aunts, uncles, cousins, and grandparents accepted me into their number with sincere warmth, and I saw a reflection of God's love for his children in their support.

In order to find lasting faith, I had to accept the truth: God is the one in control, even if we think otherwise as we're struggling or succeeding. It was hard for me to trust in God, but the acceptance and love of the Corders and the Kendalls made it possible for me to believe in His guidance and unconditional love, and to return that generosity of heart into the world. They taught me that all of us have an opportunity to do God's work on Earth, just by loving others. As a mother, I've been blessed with the opportunity to set my two children on God's path. Each day I teach them about trust and faith through my patience and steady devotion, and in time they will be able to do the same for their children.

~Miranda Kendall

Heaven's New Star

Watching a peaceful death of a human being reminds us of a falling star;
one of a million lights in a vast sky that flares up for a brief moment only to
disappear into the endless night forever.
~Elisabeth Kübler-Ross

At the age of forty-seven, my sister, Char, had already endured ten months of breast cancer and chemotherapy. She was in remission for two months when she noticed a persistent stiff neck and a new lump in that area. It was diagnosed as the same aggressive cancer that had now spread. Chemotherapy was to start again.

Another chemo treatment was scheduled for the Thursday before Christmas. A body scan indicated a new area of concern; her liver was now affected, too. Despite not feeling well, her family drove five hours north to share Christmas with us. My sister looked thin and pale. Her bright and shiny eyes were dulled by a yellow hue. We fixed all her favorite foods, attempting to make this our best Christmas ever. She picked at everything and had to leave the kitchen because the smells we loved were nauseating her. She slept a lot and seemed in a fog most of the time. She seemed so small and helpless. Their vacation was cut short when my sister noticed the yellowing of her eyes had worsened. She called her physician, who suggested she come home immediately for testing. She left with tears in her eyes, trying to be brave for everyone. The lab testing showed some increased liver functions, but nothing to be alarmed about.

Char continued to teach her preschool class and help out at Sunday school, but she got weaker as the days went on and eventually developed ascites, a pooling of fluids in the abdominal region. She had to have the fluids drained weekly with a huge needle that pierced her abdomen. As the ascites progressively got worse, a permanent tube was placed so she could drain herself at home. Neuropathy settled into her feet, and they were swollen and tingling all the time. She began using a walker for balance.

When I called my sister, she said weakly, "I wish I could eat. I miss food. I'm so thirsty all the time. All I do is drink water—hot, cold, and ice cubed. You know in the Bible where they say hell is an unquenchable thirst? I'm there. I'm in hell, and I don't want to be here anymore. I know where I am going someday when I die. It will be heaven."

It wasn't long before laboratory results revealed that Char's liver had failed. She looked at the doctor and simply asked, "Am I going to die?" She was told she had only one to three days left, and any family should be notified immediately. Char lovingly cupped her hands around the doctor's face and looked deeply into his eyes. She said, "I know you did everything you could for me. God is good."

She was taken by an ambulance across town to a cancer hospital, accompanied by her loving husband Brad. With heavy hearts, members of her family awaited Char's arrival. Tears drenched each person's face as she entered the room. She looked around at everyone and exclaimed, "Chop-chop! Get the tears over and done with. I'm going to heaven to be with Jesus. God is good."

Meanwhile, my husband and I picked up Dad and Mom and searched for answers on our five-hour journey to the hospital. Where was God in all of this? The trip seemed like a lifetime. We arrived at the hospital around 10:30 P.M. to find Char still awake. She smiled and called to our parents. "You're here! I'm not afraid to die. I'm going to heaven. God is good." She had so willingly accepted her fate and was consoling us instead of us consoling her.

Throughout her stay at the hospital, the morphine drip eased her pain so she could talk to us while taking short naps in between.

She had so much to tell us and so little time left. Her sense of humor never ceased. She had asked our sister, Mindy, to clean out her closet and take whatever each of us wanted. She said, "I only need one outfit where I'm going. Just make me look good." Char also informed all of us that she was going first to prepare our rooms for us in heaven. She looked at me seriously and asked, "What do you want your room theme to be?" I sputtered out, "How about a spa theme? Clean and crisp and very relaxing." She loved to decorate, clean and rearrange. She de-cluttered all of our houses and souls.

I looked at my dying sister with such awesome respect. She actually made dying seem like the ultimate exciting adventure. There was no fear. She explained that a priest had been in and anointed her forehead and hands. She was wearing our father's blessed scapular around her neck and another one pinned to her hospital gown that my brother-in-law had brought in for her. It is said that if you die wearing the scapular, your soul goes directly to heaven.

My hero never stopped amazing me. She remained so composed and aware of everything around her. She even asked me if I'd stop by her house and scrub her tub because she didn't have time. We sat in silence sometimes, just watching her breathe and sleep. She called me toward her when she woke and pointed to the ceiling. "Do you see those stars up there?" I looked up. She continued, "They keep calling my name." I asked, "Do you want to go with them?" With a big smile and a little giggle, she said, "Yes." She rolled to her side toward our mother and held her hand, falling into a peaceful sleep.

The next morning, her young daughters, Ashley and Ava, were coming to see her at the hospital and were going to be told that their mother would soon be in heaven. Char had thoughtfully asked that two of her favorite necklaces be brought to the hospital and gave one to each daughter. They were to think of her and her great love for them when they wore them. Ashley and Ava entered the room with tears streaming down their faces and ran into the loving embrace of their mommy's arms. She kissed their faces and reassured them that Jesus was waiting for her. She would see them again in heaven.

As the afternoon wore on, she became increasingly restless, but still managed to smile at the nurses and any visitors. Around 4:00 P.M., she was slipping into a coma. We all said our final goodbyes, and I whispered in her ear, "I believe in you. I know you are going to heaven. I'll never let your girls forget you. I love you." Her husband spoke these gentle words to her, "Char, it's okay. Jesus is waiting for you. Take His hand." And she did.

At 5:01 P.M., her journey was finished. We knew where she was and that God was in that very room. Prayers from family, friends and people we didn't even know comforted us. It was like a blanket of love was placed over us and lifted our hearts and eyes to Jesus. Our star, Char, was in heaven. Our tears fell, but our faith soared.

~Yvonne Riozzi

Chapter
2

Finding Faith Through Friendship

If instead of a gem, or even a flower,
we should cast the gift of a loving thought into the heart of a friend,
that would be giving as the angels give.

~George MacDonald

The Friend I Needed

If you give a man a fish, you feed him for a day.
If you teach a man to fish, you feed him for a lifetime.
~Chinese Proverb

With my oversized handbag dangling from my elbow and brimming with beauty products, I elbowed the doorbell, shifted from one aching foot to the other, and found the friend I needed—dressed in denims and a red-checkered shirt, hair windblown, eyes seeming to dance behind her horn-rimmed glasses, and a leaping pup at her knees. The second she smiled, I wondered if I'd ever seen anyone so radiant. As she flipped through my catalog, I noted her face glowed despite her lack of make-up. Inhaling the pot roast fragrance drifting from her kitchen, I admitted—but only to myself—that her home felt welcoming, while the one I lived in did not. Not only that, her King James Bible—lying open on a nearby couch—was falling apart, while mine still looked as new as the day my husband bought it.

We'd only just begun to talk about possibly placing an order when her youngest darted into the room and threw his arms around his mother. She grinned, mentioned her name was Betty, and told me about the rest of her family. Then she asked about mine.

"Mine?" I uttered, pressing my fingers to what had suddenly become my tear-streaked face—and within minutes I was sharing all the worst about me, my life, and my past. When I had finished, Betty asked if I would come back. She didn't need my beauty products, but she wanted to talk.

"No!" I blurted, shaking my head. "Really!" I shook my head again.

Desperately, I tried to collect my wits and samples and apologized for taking up too much of her time. But as I crammed catalogs into my bag, I heard Betty say, "Okay, I'll come to your house instead."

Unnerved, I could only nod and spin toward the door and my "getaway car." Without looking back, I drove home as fast as I dared to the seclusion that had, for more than a year, been my only comfort.

The following day, Betty made the first of many visits. She never seemed too busy for me; she came as often as I would allow. I'd share, quietly weep, wail, complain, and question—and she would listen, read from her Bible, and then bow her head even when I adamantly announced I would not be praying. I'd had Christian friends in high school and even as a young adult. I'd actually believed—once upon a time—that I was one. I'd joined Young Life, attended Sunday school, and went to camp. In my former life, I'd even sung in a church choir, directed the youth, taught Vacation Bible School, and joined a group of supposedly Christian women. When there were babies in my home, I sang "Jesus loves you, this I know…" because I did know Jesus loved them; I just didn't know He also loved me.

Betty never once said, "We'll pray for you at our next scheduled meeting" or "Maybe our pastor could come talk with you sometime." Instead, she said she understood about my life seeming beyond hope after years in a fear-filled marriage and the loss of two of my children to divorce, while the "good" women of the church and their pastors began to make a point of turning their backs on me. When Betty visited, she did say she'd pray for me—but she also prayed with me. She suggested Bible verses and devotions we could read together and even recited those that had become most significant and special in her life.

Several weeks into our friendship—after listening to her chide me almost daily—I purchased a newer translation she promised I would understand. She even set my radio to a Christian station and gently ordered, "You better leave it there, too." She then suggested I attend a Bible study. When I balked, she drove me to the church, enrolled both of us, and announced she'd be picking me up.

Eventually, Betty realized I needed professional counseling, and she said so. I told her I would call a counselor soon, but on our way to lunch, she stopped at a Christian counseling center and introduced me to the staff. When I wasn't certain I could handle the fee, she offered to pay. At the end of my final session, she casually mentioned she had tickets for a luncheon where a "special" speaker would share with us and pray. "And," she said, "you are going."

"Okay, this is absolutely the last straw!" I wanted to say aloud, but I didn't.

My counselor felt I was much better, but that there still seemed to be something that hadn't completely surfaced. Midway through lunch, the speaker began to talk about inner healing and being done with anger-filled memories that too often caused great pain. And after weeks of counseling and prayer, I discovered I was ready to give up the hatred and unforgiveness I had harbored for so many years.

For several months, Betty and I continued our weekly study together—until I was hired to teach in a Christian school and Betty resumed her personal ministry. Coveting the few minutes we could spare, we'd meet for lunch or coffee. Even when I traveled, I always knew she would be there at the other end of the phone line, ready to listen and pray—until the day the leukemia she'd dealt with for years but seldom mentioned became too much for her. She might have raged or completely withdrawn when the doctors began to prepare her for what so many call "the worst." Instead, she continued to pray and study, even sharing her faith from her hospital bed. Then God called her home.

Because God had changed my life through my beautiful friend, I found I could finally walk in faith and accept Betty's death. She was gone from family and friends, but she'd been God's handmaiden, and through her He had made it clear that He is always with us.

Today, I write, teach, speak, and help build Habitat for Humanity homes beside my godly second husband because "If you give a man a fish, you feed him for a day. If you teach a man to fish, you feed him for a lifetime."

Betty taught me to fish.

~Nancy Hoag

Am I Jewish Yet?

I believe in God, but I'm not too clear on the other details.
~Bill Veeck

A few years ago, I was sitting across the restaurant table from my best friend Susan eating my usual Sunday breakfast of scrambled eggs, tomatoes and toast.

Susan popped a bit of bacon into her mouth and then turned to me. "So, time to discuss this year's menu."

I stared at her blankly. "Menu for what?"

"Rosh Hashanah," she said, waving her fork in the air. "You know, the High Holidays. Jewish New Year." She sighed as she speared another piece of bacon. "And you call yourself a Jew."

I shrugged. "What can I say? My mother usually reminds me at least two weeks ahead. She's late this year. Besides," I said, staring at her fork, "I'm not the one eating bacon."

She laughed, and we decided on that year's dinner: chicken, asparagus, salad and tsimmes.

"Don't forget the prunes in the tsimmes," I said. "My mother always put in prunes with the carrots. But if you want to put in sweet potato like last year, that's fine. In fact, I prefer it with sweet potatoes, but don't tell my mother."

After the High Holidays, I usually shelve religion until the next Jewish holiday rolls around. This time was different. A couple of weeks later, I came across a quiz on the Internet titled "What kind of

Jew are you?" I couldn't resist, especially when the answers labeled me in terms of food. You can't get more Jewish than that.

According to the quiz, I fit into the haroseth category, named after a Passover fruit and nut mixture. As haroseth, my Jewish identity blends tradition and innovation, and revolves around holidays and lifecycle events, rather than religion.

The next Sunday, I told Susan about the quiz. "I guess I shouldn't be surprised. It's not like I attended parochial school. I went to a regular public school that was mostly Protestant. Jewish students were allowed to take off the Jewish holidays, giving us twice the number of holidays the other students got, although you'd never find a single dreidel among the Christmas decorations or a Hanukkah song at the Christmas concert. For the most part, Jews were invisible."

"No wonder you turned into a WASH."

"A what?"

"White Anglo Saxon Hebrew."

I thought about Susan's comment. My mother kept kosher in that solid North American tradition: meat and dairy, with a special set of glass dishes for non-kosher food. As a kid, I went to synagogue on the High Holidays and spent most of the time bored to death by our rabbi's long sermons. I was far more interested in seeing who wore the ugliest hat than in learning anything about my place as a Jew in the world.

As I grew older, I drifted further away from religion. When I left home to attend university, I lived in an ethnically diverse area, and my friends reflected that diversity. The thought of joining a synagogue never crossed my mind—that was for families.

Suddenly, it was twenty years later. I had a house in a nice but overwhelmingly Protestant area of the city and was the only person on the block who didn't put up Christmas lights. I still remember a neighbor's astonished face when I said I didn't celebrate Christmas. She automatically assumed I was too mean-spirited. It never occurred to her that I wasn't Christian.

That Sunday, in the restaurant, I realized Susan was my only

Jewish friend. If she didn't invite me over for Hanukkah and Passover, I would probably ignore both holidays.

After our conversation, I went back to being a WASH. But something had sparked in my mind, a small flame that grew as I began to read more and more newspaper articles about religious violence. That flame prompted me to write several letters to the editor and ultimately a full-page newspaper feature in which I argued against fundamentalism of any type.

Two weeks after the feature came out, I got a phone call from a small Unitarian Fellowship congregation that wanted me to speak at one of their meetings.

"But I'm Jewish," I said. "Well, sort of Jewish."

Assured that my religion or lack of it wasn't a problem, I agreed to speak. I also persuaded Susan to go with me. "Just in case they try to convert me," I joked. "My mother would kill me."

I spent days researching and writing, distilling everything I thought about religion and God into a forty-five-minute presentation, with an emphasis on what I disliked about organized, fundamental religions.

That Sunday, I introduced myself as half-Jewish, half-agnostic, and then launched into my topic. During the question-and-answer period, one of the members of the congregation asked me if I ever felt a need to believe in God and religion.

"No," I started to respond and then stopped. That answer simply didn't feel right. I started again, feeling my way as I spoke. "I may not be ready to believe in God with a capital G or religion with a capital R, but I do feel a need for a connection to something greater than I am. I just don't know what that is yet. I'm stumbling around in the dark, looking for the light."

After my presentation, I drank tea and chatted with the congregation. But part of my mind was still mulling over my answer about God and religion. Putting my half-formed thoughts into words started me on a path to learn more. I began to buy books, both on Judaism and religion in general.

A few weeks ago, I was walking along a busy street when

something caught my eye: a small sign in the window of a non-descript building. All it said was: "If you want to learn more about Judaism, call this number." For a minute, I felt as if the universe was shining a light on me.

I wrote down the number, but I haven't called. I've kept it, though. As a Jew and wavering agnostic, I'm still stumbling toward an ill-defined something beyond myself. Who knows? One day soon, I might be ready to take a leap of faith. When I am, at least I'll know who to call.

~Harriet Cooper

Lost and Found

Man can live about forty days without food, about three days without water,
about eight minutes without air... but only for one second without hope.
~Hal Lindsey

"I brought you something." It was the middle of the afternoon on a bright sunny day when my best friend Penny
decided to drop by for a visit. She lived in a house one
yard away, so we saw a lot of each other growing up. But for the past
year we hadn't seen each other as much because I was in some sort of
blue funk that wouldn't seem to let up. At twenty, the age when my
friends and peers were already in college or working, I read books all
night long, slept all day, had no interest in finding a job, and no real
plan for my life except a desire to, at some vague point in the future,
become a social worker so I could help people.

I was living a nothingness with which I'd grown too comfortable.
My teenage years had been spent on finding myself, to no avail. All
the hundreds of books and documentaries and people I'd consulted
had left me empty. I hadn't found the answers to my questions—Why
am I here? What is my purpose? What does it all mean? How do I fit
into the world? Does my life mean something? My search for truth
had yielded only a page full of question marks.

On this particular day, I had an agonizing toothache, so my
family was off doing fun things without me. Penny sat down at the
kitchen table and placed a book in front of me. My left hand held my

aching jaw, while my right shielded my eyes from the happy sunlight that beamed through the window.

I read the title aloud: "*The Late Great Planet Earth*?"

She nodded. "You'll like it. It's about Bible prophecy."

She knew I was always asking "why" and seeking answers to world mysteries.

"Did you read it?" I asked.

"Some of it."

Penny wasn't a big reader, but she had read enough of the book to know I'd be interested.

Her family had taken me to Sunday school with them since the third grade. It was just about the only exposure to faith I'd received while growing up. While other kids were giggling or talking during class, I listened intently, hanging on every word having to do with Jesus Christ—this Savior and Son of God who made miracles and taught peace and kindness.

Since my father and mother had divorced when I was a year old, and I had had stepfathers I wasn't close to, I secretly longed for a father figure. Jesus seemed like the perfect one for me. Whenever I saw a picture of Jesus with children sitting on His lap or gathered around, I imagined I was there, too, and He was talking to me.

But as I grew up, I put such childlike yearnings aside. Reality wasn't a Bible picture. It was a landscape in stark relief, of the rocky hills of divorce, dark valleys of a broken family, and the dry, cracked creek bed of a broken heart. As a child, I carried my Bible around with me on the farm, finding a place to lie back in the musky hay with my dog to read about the things Jesus did and said. But I had put away my Bible when I grew old enough to question Jesus's existence.

"Something happened to me at church the other night," Penny said with a smile.

"Really? What was it?"

"I was saved."

"Oh."

I remembered the word from Sunday school.

She continued. "I gave my heart to the Lord, and I feel... different.

Better. I'm a Christian now. I think you'd feel better if you became a Christian, too."

Here we were, both twenty, both adults, and we were relating to each other again like the two little girls we had been in Sunday school class. Simple little words. It couldn't be that easy.

"I'm not sure about any of it," I confessed. "I've read so many books...."

It was true. I'd consumed books on different religions, New Age movements, the occult, meditation, yoga, Transcendental Meditation, and more. I had looked for happiness in boys, alcohol, drugs. I had looked everywhere for truth.

"Just pray about it, Tammy. God won't turn anyone away."

She left me with the Hal Lindsey book a few minutes later. I took two aspirin for my toothache and took the book to my bedroom to read.

How could this book, which wasn't even a Bible, help me?

As I read the book, certain passages prompted me to check out some Bible verses. I was on my quest again; my curiosity was renewed.

After I finished the paperback, I decided to read the Book of Matthew to find out if my questions could be fully answered, not just addressed by some religious writer. By the time I reached the end, I was crying so hard I could barely breathe or read the words. I closed the Bible, feeling that the Holy Spirit was dealing with my heart, drawing me to Him, and softening the heart of the little girl who had longed to be with Him so long ago.

At the next church service, I could scarcely wait for the altar call. As soon as the preacher invited "whosoever will" to give their life to Jesus Christ and invite Him into their heart, I walked—no, nearly ran—to the front of our little country church and knelt down, pouring myself out to Him and asking Him to forgive my sins. I begged Jesus to come into my heart.

I arose from the altar a changed person. Smiling and crying at the same time, I felt new, clean, alive—actually born again. Just like Penny and the Bible had described.

Penny and her family hugged me. All I could whisper was, "He's real."

I finally had The Answer I'd been looking for. I did have a purpose — to serve Him and others. God had used my best friend to light my way home. No longer was I lost, but found.

~Tammy L. Ruggles

Facebook and Faith

The Internet is becoming the town square for the global village of tomorrow.
~Bill Gates

My daughters were less than thrilled when I told them I was setting up accounts on any social media websites they visited. Like so many young people, they felt that these sites were for teens, and that Mom was simply too old to be tweeting or on Facebook. They didn't want their mom "spying" on them, either. I assured them that was not my intention.

Truthfully, I was a little concerned about some of the negative stories I had heard about the Internet. I wanted to make sure that my girls weren't giving out improper information over the Internet or "friending" anyone they shouldn't. I figured I would check their accounts weekly, but I wasn't really interested in doing anything else with my accounts.

After the first few weeks, however, this began to change. People from my past began asking to be my "friend"—my best friends from kindergarten, my high school guidance counselor, and my long-lost pen pal from England. A whole new world opened up to me. I reconnected with so many people who had impacted my life in a positive way, and I was glad to find out what was going on in their lives. Hearing about their careers and families, and seeing pictures of their children—all of these things were special to me and truly brightened my day.

One of the happiest days was when I reconnected with my

friend Beth from high school. Her mom had been my sixth-grade teacher and had encouraged me in my writing. I was glad to let her know that her mom's encouragement had helped me pursue short-story writing. The more we talked, the closer we became. We bonded through our mutual interest in charity work, and after a while, we planned a visit to see her second cousin, Mary, and her family, who ran a Christian youth camp in Kentucky. They were in need of clothing, kitchen equipment, and financial contributions, and we began to gather these items in anticipation of our trip.

Several months later, my daughter Blakely and I pulled up to Beth's house in Memphis, Tennessee. Even though we had not seen each other in thirty years, the time flew away as soon as we saw each other. We packed my car to the brim with our donations and headed out to rural Kentucky. I don't think we stopped talking, laughing, and catching up during the entire thirteen-hour drive.

When we finally arrived at the camp, Beth's family greeted us with open arms. Tired but happy, we unloaded the car and were touched by their excitement at seeing our gifts. I was thrilled to have so many new friends.

Our weekend flew by with an auction to benefit the camp and a delicious dinner. Mary and her children sang, played musical instruments, and gave us a tour of their town. We were sad to leave, but felt enriched and blessed by the experience. I gained many more Facebook friends as a result of my visit.

By that point, Facebook had become more to me than just a social site. I realized how much of an impact it had had on me and the people I knew. The power of faith had reached the digital age. Whenever someone in my circle needed prayer or had a sick family member, I began to send messages of support. I decided to spread love, positive quotes, and uplifting comments on my profile on a daily basis—hoping to share my faith in a higher power with my friends. Faith had ceased to become just a personal experience. It had become amplified when shared with others. I was truly surprised to connect with people via the Internet on such a spiritual level.

The greatest blessing I witnessed online happened while we

were planning my high school class's thirty-year reunion. Two best friends from school found each other via Facebook. One was in need of a kidney transplant, and the other was a perfect match as a donor. I was privileged to assist them before and during their surgery by providing food, babysitting services, moral support, and prayers. Our entire high school class held a fundraiser to assist with the costs of the surgeries. Facebook literally saved a friend's life! The bond we all established gave strength to my friends, and the positive messages posted online gave them much needed encouragement and aided in the recovery process. We truly bolstered each other with faith.

I originally got on Facebook to keep my daughters from becoming victims of the dangers I had read about. And while negative experiences can occur, I almost overlooked the blessings of the Internet and social media to enlighten people in a spiritual way. Friends who might have felt alone now have a family of faith to help them when they are in need, hurting, or lonely. The positive energy I have felt and sent through social networks has become invaluable to me and others, offering encouragement, and giving us all strength, love, and hope. It is not organized, nor dependent on a particular belief or denomination, but its effect on us all has been truly divine.

The Internet has become a place where I can encounter God through others. It is a place where I can teach and be taught, provide and receive counsel, and facilitate conversations, share experiences, and worship. When life pulls us in different directions, connecting online makes it harder for us to be pulled apart.

Facebook and faith might seem like unlikely partners, but I have truly become a believer.

~Melanie A. Hardy

The Faith Seed

Don't judge each day by the harvest you reap but by the seeds that you plant.
~Robert Louis Stevenson

"Kathy, will you walk to the altar with me today?" my friend Karen asked.

I was thirteen and shy. I'd never have walked down front to pray by myself, but I followed Karen.

Karen continued to nudge me from time to time in the next two years. If the teens had a rally with several churches involved, Karen would take me by the hand. She faithfully shared with me about God, how Jesus died on the cross, how no matter what happened in my life, God loved me. I wanted to believe her, but then I went home.

We lived in the most rundown house in the neighborhood. My parents squabbled, and my dad cursed every car he worked on. He never hit me or my siblings, but he didn't laugh. And if we were too silly, his bad language increased. I generally ran to my room upstairs where I couldn't hear it.

Many times, Karen encouraged me to read my King James Bible at night, but it was so hard to understand. I soon set it aside. My Sunday life and weekday life were so different. During the week, I tried to remember the Bible stories from Sunday school, but I couldn't quite grasp what being a Christian was all about.

Then a handsome young man came into my world. It was love

at first sight. We were "steadies" at fifteen and married when I turned seventeen.

Wise, no. But we were both raised in the same church. I was in love and had visions of a fairy-tale marriage with a happily ever after ending. What I didn't know was that my husband, at seventeen, had felt the call to preach. He didn't tell me because he was afraid it would scare me away. He also didn't tell me about his home life. His stepfather was an alcoholic—a mean drunk. Gary married me to escape.

We moved a hundred miles north, and Gary took a job in a mill. The mill workers often stopped off at the bar after work, and Gary soon joined them. I hated alcohol. Between a crying baby and the alcohol, I wondered if I'd make it that first winter. If I said anything, though, Gary just drank more.

One night, I didn't bother to get out of bed when I heard Gary stagger into the house. I lay in bed crying, afraid he'd hear me and get mad. But Gary surprised me. He came into the bedroom and said, "I can't live like this anymore. I've poured out all the booze and gotten rid of the cigarettes. Will you kneel and pray with me? I truly want God's forgiveness."

We knelt beside our bed, and Gary asked for forgiveness and God's guidance in our days ahead. When we crawled back into bed, I said, "What do we do next?"

"When I was a little boy, my mother took me to a Church of the Nazarene in Beatrice, Nebraska. Last week when I drove through Washougal, I saw they were building a Nazarene church. Let's try that first."

"What if it's not a good church for us?"

"Then we'll try a Baptist or a Methodist or… we'll find one. Don't you worry."

That night, another mustard seed of faith was planted in my heart—just like the ones that Karen had planted so many years before. It was a tiny seed, but it said, "God is in your marriage. Trust Him." Gary held me and told me how sorry he was for all the things he'd done. He wanted to be a good husband and father.

The next Sunday, we did attend that Church of the Nazarene. After a few weeks, we joined the church and were members for fourteen years before we took our family to Nazarene Bible College in Colorado Springs, Colorado. Gary was finally ready to answer the call he'd heard when he was seventeen. After he graduated from NBC, he served as senior pastor in four churches.

I'd like to say our lives have been perfect, but we are human, and humans do fail. We struggled through major health issues and marital difficulties where we almost divorced. The good news is, when we knelt by that bed in prayer, we both committed our lives to the Lord.

Our faith grew through the trials and the lack of finances. When Gary was burned all over his body and couldn't work, when he tore a tendon and couldn't work, when he fell off a motorcycle and couldn't work—we learned the art of gracious receiving.

When the doctors diagnosed me as legally blind, I lived in fear of the unknown. But because of my faith, I survived the cornea transplant journey, and today I can see. Then an oncologist diagnosed Gary with a rare cancer of the appendix. Our faith assured us that Gary would see heaven, but he didn't die. He was one of the few who beat that type of cancer. Seven years after his cancer diagnosis, he died of a heart attack. We had been married almost fifty-one years.

Last year, I met my friend Karen again. Fifty-six years had passed since she first started planting and watering faith seeds in my heart. When I saw her across the room, I raced to her side and hugged her. "You know, you are a good seed planter."

She looked at me as if to say "What?"

"You don't remember all the times you grabbed my hand and dragged me to the altar?" I made it sound really dramatic. "Seriously, Karen, many times you asked me to go to the altar and shared the gospel story with me. And those little seeds of faith you planted did blossom. Gary and I were blessed to serve in ministry, and my parents also accepted the Lord. Isn't that the most awesome blessing?"

I don't know if Karen asked others to the altar or not, but I'm so grateful she asked me. And because of my faith, I too have planted seeds in other lives. I've learned that when you plant a faith seed, be prepared to watch it flourish.

~Kat Crawford

The Radical Difference

*Christ is the head of this house, the unseen guest at every meal,
the silent listener to every conversation.*
~Celtic Saying

"You've been pretty quiet on this trip," I said, glancing over at my husband, Dick. We were returning from an overnight visit with my parents.

"Yeah," he murmured absently. "Neither of us has said much the last three hours."

As a pastor to three small churches, Dick had been feeling dissatisfied lately. We had discussed leaving the ministry and drove home to break the news to my parents that weekend.

My mom had recently started attending a local Wesleyan church. She was forever talking about the Lord and people getting "saved." Dick and I decided that she had gone overboard and become some sort of fanatic. Although we felt people should try to please God, we were uneasy about getting so personal with Him.

The church that Mom attended had a new pastor. "You just have to meet Bill and his wife, Peggy," Mom urged us during our visit. "I know you'll really like them."

Dick and I reluctantly agreed, although we thought with a shudder, "If Mom is so gung ho, what will her pastor be like?"

We pulled into their driveway and got out. Dick looked at me over the top of the car and whispered, "Fifteen minutes—just long enough to be polite."

I agreed. Even fifteen minutes would seem like an eternity if these people were anything like we were expecting.

Thankfully, they weren't!

That evening, we visited with Bill and Peggy for two hours. We came back the next day and spent six more hours! It was the start of a very special friendship, and more importantly, the beginning of our relationship with Jesus.

We had much in common—even our last names—Williams! We were the same ages. Their daughter, Rachel, and our son, Seth, were both eight months old. We were serving our first pastorates and leading the youth in our churches as well.

There, however, the similarities ended. Bill and Peggy were content and satisfied with their ministry, while we were discouraged and unfulfilled.

Over iced tea in the living room, Bill asked when we had become Christians. We explained that we had grown up in the church and felt that we had always been Christians.

However, Bill and Peggy's lives as Christians differed radically from ours. They talked about the Lord and how He was leading them—as though I should be able to look over and see Jesus sitting on the couch!

Their relationship with God was so personal that Peggy even consulted Jesus when she cooked. It was as though she had a running conversation with God! "Pray continually" (1 Thessalonians 5:17) was a description of her lifestyle, not just a quote from the Bible. Dick and I felt disconcerted and a bit overwhelmed.

Perhaps that is why we were so quiet on the trip back to our home when we would usually have talked for hours.

"I've been thinking about Bill and Peggy," I finally said. "Their lives seem very similar to ours—but there is something different."

Dick nodded.

"Did you notice the plaque above the dining room table?" I asked.

"Notice it? I memorized it!" Dick said. "'Christ is the head of this house, the unseen guest at every meal, the silent listener to every conversation.'"

"That's the radical difference," I stated, comprehension dawning. "For me, God is far away—a distant being in heaven that I try to appease with good works. For Bill and Peggy, Jesus is right there with them—in their decisions, in their conversations, in their home. He's not in our home."

Dick agreed. We were quiet the rest of the trip, giving what we had seen and heard over the weekend a lot more thought.

Our church organist had arranged for a gospel singing group to lead worship that Sunday. Songs of praise and challenges to commit your life to the Lord filled the service. The Good News that Jesus can deliver us from our sins was made very clear.

I had known about Jesus's death on the cross for the sins of the world, but the thought had merely flickered through my mind and never pierced my soul. When the group invited people to the altar to pray, I yearned to go forward, but Seth fussed and squirmed in my arms.

I thought, "Lord, if you want me to go up there, you will have to quiet Seth."

Instantly, he fell asleep. As I knelt at the altar rail, Dick joined me. That morning, we asked Jesus to come into our lives and our home. We wanted Him to be with us, just like He was with Bill and Peggy. It was the beginning of a whole new life for us, with Jesus as the head of our home.

Many people would have thought that Dick and I already had a relationship with Jesus. As a family in ministry, our lives revolved around the church. But though we knew that Jesus had lived and died a long time ago, He was more like a figure from the pages of history than someone we could know today. Neither Dick nor I had realized that we needed to believe that Jesus died to forgive *us*.

We thought we needed to please God and earn our way to heaven by being good and helping others. At last, we understood the words of Ephesians 2:8-9: "For it is by grace you have been saved, through faith—and this is not from yourselves, it is the gift of God—not by works."

The very next Sunday, Dick preached his first sermon straight from the Bible. A lady in one of our churches came up to him after the service and said, "I've been praying for this day!"

That weekend was thirty-four years ago. My husband felt God calling him to remain a pastor. But the radical difference is that Jesus is right here with us—in our home, in our decisions, in our conversations. Jesus promised that He would always be with us (Matthew 28:20). And we have found that God's Word is true.

~Pam Williams

Never Too Late

You are as young as your faith, as old as your doubt; as young as your self-confidence, as old as your fear; as young as your hope, as old as your despair.
~Douglas MacArthur

Usually, my "other mother," eighty-four-year-old Mollie, is full of confidence and energy. She can accomplish things during the course of her day that tire women half her age. Mollie strides fast, drives confidently, and speaks her mind directly. She can make blintzes from scratch, appraise a nineteenth-century antique, chair a fundraising meeting, and beat you at bridge. She can also beat you at computer games and has e-mail correspondents across the country. She's up on the latest television, theater and scientific discoveries.

"I keep going forward and never look back," Mollie says.

Except once. When she was eighty-one years old, Mollie decided to do something she had always wanted to do and never had the time or the nerve: She wanted to be bat mitzvahed, a Jewish coming-of-age ceremony, normally performed at age thirteen.

Mollie had been talking about it for years, tossing comments casually into the conversation.

"If I weren't too old," she would say, "I'd love to be bat mitzvahed."

"I wish I weren't too busy to study Hebrew," she'd say.

Every time she went to a friend's granddaughter's bat mitzvah, something sighed and stirred inside her.

In Mollie's day, coming-of-age ceremonies were reserved for boys. Besides, Mollie didn't need a ceremony to tell her she was a young woman: At age thirteen, she was already caring for her invalid mother, driving a car around the mountain roads of Colorado, and working a part-time afterschool job. She was the one who cooked the meals, lit the Sabbath candles and said the prayers. She listened eagerly to stories of her ancestors, a long lineage of religious Jews, going back to fifteenth-century Poland. She felt she, too, was part of that lineage, even though she didn't get to learn and study the way she secretly wanted to.

As Mollie grew up and got married, she tucked away her strong religious feelings. Her husband was an agnostic, her sons restless in Sunday School. Though Mollie diligently raised money for the Sisterhood and temple, and went to High Holy Day services, she felt like a concert pianist relegated to "Chopsticks." There was music her soul longed to sing, words she yearned to chant, a proclamation she needed to make.

When Mollie turned eighty, the idea of a bat mitzvah came more frequently into her conversation. Her son Ron and I encouraged her. We knew she could do this.

In the beginning of her eighty-first year, she began her classes. Every Tuesday night for two years, she was to study Hebrew and Jewish history, thought and philosophy. She would have homework and extra assignments.

"I am the oldest one in the class," she told us after her first session. Four women, ages forty to eight-one, were taking the training.

"It's too hard. I will never learn Hebrew," she wailed.

Each Tuesday night, she went to the classes. Sometimes, she took homemade mandel bread to share with her class. Other times, she baked a batch of brownies. The cantor made a tape of her Hebrew portion. She listened when she walked on the treadmill and when she lay down, sleeping with her headphones on, the tape crooning through her dreams. Though she studied hard, she was still worried about her ability. The others, she told us, were so much better. The Hebrew melted on their tongues like manna.

Though Mollie suffered and worried that she wasn't good enough, we could see her thrill and pride in learning about her religion. And we knew that once Mollie decided to do something, she would succeed.

One Saturday in May, Mollie's family and an array of friends of all ages gathered in the auditorium of B'nai Jehudah Temple. Some of her friends had never been in a temple before, and most had never witnessed this type of ceremony. I held my breath as the class took the stage. Mollie looked both radiant and nervous.

When Mollie finished her portion of the service, she looked at all of us and smiled. She had done it. She had been even better than "good enough."

At the end of the service, the audience stood and applauded. As I stood, crying and clapping, I realized all the things that Mollie had taught me during her time of commitment and study. She showed that to truly live your faith, you have to stumble, to fail, to try again, to prevail. You have to be willing to stand in front of people and proclaim yourself. You have to believe that God is truly guiding you. You have to let go of some of your deepest fears and see what is beyond them.

Mollie taught me that it is never too late to follow your heart.

~Deborah Shouse

How Faith Got Me Through

Faith is a passionate intuition.
~William Wordsworth

We all make choices in life. At times, those choices are in accordance with God's will for our lives; at times, they are not. My most important choices, I came to find out, were to walk on stepping stones that God had placed on a path He'd chosen for me—a path that would lead me to victory over breast cancer.

When I was in my twenties, like many young adult Catholics, I set aside my religion, neglecting my spirituality and ignoring my faith. Things slowly changed when I had children. My husband and I baptized our kids, started attending Mass again, and even sent our kids to a Christian preschool.

I turned thirty-five years old the September my oldest son turned three and started at that preschool. Early in the school year, another mother named Lorraine approached me about a play date for our boys. I didn't jump at the idea, but each day I saw her, I'd think about her offer. I couldn't get the idea out of my head that we should get together. (That was God talking to me; I'd soon discover that meeting Lorraine was part of the plan.) Halfway through the school year, I finally invited Lorraine and her son to our house after school. They accepted. God must have smiled that day because I took the first step down His path.

As the boys played, I discovered that Lorraine and I had much in common. We both had September birthdays and loved to go camping. I felt a connection with her, like she was an old friend rather than a new acquaintance. Two weeks later, she had us over to her house. Unbeknownst to me, my spiritual journey was continuing.

That day at Lorraine's house, she told me that her mother and her mother-in-law had died within six months of each other the previous year after battling breast cancer. It was unimaginable to me how she had endured that heartbreak. But Lorraine made a statement that would change my life. She looked me square in the eye and said with certainty, "My faith got me through."

Lorraine went on to talk about the community and fellowship she found at her church, and while I heard her words, I kept repeating in my head: "My faith got me through." I knew I did not have that kind of faith. I wanted to have it, but I did not know at the time that I'd need it.

I noticed a *Life Application Study Bible* on the countertop and told Lorraine I'd always wanted to study the Bible. She told me about a women's Bible study at her church called "Joy in the Morning." They were reading a book by Donna Partow called *Becoming a Vessel God Can Use*. Spiritual self-help—exactly what I needed. The church provided babysitters to care for little ones, and the women prepared coffee and brought in baked goods. It sounded wonderful. But I had a naïve concern: Could I, as a Catholic, attend a Bible study at a Protestant church?

Lorraine's opinion was quite simply evangelical: The God she knew wouldn't care what kind of building I was in as long as I was in His word. Logical, I thought, but I was skeptical. I went home and talked with my husband. Since the opportunity to study the Bible had never before presented itself so clearly, he believed that perhaps it was God's will. Possible, but I was still uncertain. I decided to search the Internet (of all places!) for some insight. I found a website called OnceCatholic. org, and on a webpage called the Reading Room I read an analogy that went something like this: "If you lived in Italy, you could dine in Greece on Saturday night yet return home to enjoy breakfast in Rome on Sunday morning." I had my answer! I could study the Bible at Lorraine's church and still remain faithful to my religion.

I joined the study in January of 2003 after purchasing a *Catholic Women's Devotional Bible*; I thought I'd learn more about my religion while learning about God and the Bible. There was so much more to God than I knew. I pored over my Bible and remembered things I'd learned as a child about Catholicism and its traditions. Within weeks, I was praying daily, getting more out of Mass each week, and gaining conviction in my personal beliefs. I began to acquire the kind of faith Lorraine had told me about—and not a minute too soon. (God's timing always proves to be perfect.)

The study wrapped up at the end of the school year before breaking for summer vacation. About that time, I felt something in my left breast—not a palpable lump, but a sensation, a tenderness, like an internal bruise. It wasn't sore to the touch, but it just wasn't right. One night, I asked my husband, "Do you think I have breast cancer?" He thought I was crazy. Breast cancer didn't run in my family, and I was only thirty-five. But he said that if I felt something was wrong, I should call my OB/GYN. I kept thinking about Lorraine's mother and mother-in-law. In fact, I couldn't shake them from my mind. The next morning, I called my OB/GYN and talked to a nurse practitioner.

She suspected I'd pulled a muscle lifting one of the kids. She also told me that my insurance company covered baseline mammograms beginning at age thirty-five, so I could schedule one if it would ease my mind. I thought of the brochure I had picked up at the gym the week prior for a radiology and mammography center. I was five years away from the recommended age for a mammogram, but I grabbed the brochure just the same and tucked it away. I wondered if God had placed that brochure within my reach for a reason, and I scheduled the baseline.

Although the discomfort had subsided, I kept my appointment. My initial mammogram required a follow-up. The follow-up showed an abnormality in my right breast—not my left where I'd had the feeling that brought me there! I scheduled a core needle biopsy, and within a few days of the procedure, I was diagnosed with breast cancer: ductal carcinoma in situ (DCIS), Stage 0, treatable with surgery, radiation and hormone therapy. One hundred percent curable. I didn't need a full mastectomy, only a partial. I would not need chemotherapy. I was so blessed! If I had waited until I was forty to get my first mammogram or until there was a more pronounced lump... Well, early detection was going to save my life, and save me from a prolonged and ugly battle.

My doctors wanted to know what had led me to schedule the mammogram. They recognized I had no reason to suspect breast cancer. They called it intuition—listening to my body—but I knew it was God. He sent me a message, but not until He had taught me how to hear His voice. He made sure that when He spoke to me, I would hear Him loud and clear.

That realization stayed with me throughout my treatment. I continued to feel blessed. My children were young and had no preconceived notions about cancer; they had no fear, no idea that people with cancer could die. My family, friends, and neighbors supported my husband, the children, and me with countless acts of kindness. I knew I would survive because God wanted me to live. I realized that my faith was strong and would get me through.

I often reflect on the way God worked in my life prior to my diagnosis. He brought me to a location where I'd meet Lorraine, who showed me the importance of faith during times of trial related to breast cancer. He gave me a longing to grow my faith, but He also gave me a way to do so. He brought me to a Bible study that helped me acquire the kind of faith I saw modeled in Lorraine. He laid information about mammography before me. And then He spoke to me. He gave me a physical sensation in my healthy breast to get my attention. Then He told me that I needed a mammogram to get an official diagnosis. I felt so close to Him, so blessed that He'd go to such lengths for me. I was special to God... and that was all the strength I needed.

~Karen M. Lynch

I Resisted, God Persisted

God gave burdens, also shoulders.
~Yiddish Proverb

My son was three months old when my journey of faith began. Until then, I had pretty much avoided the big questions in life. I was too busy having fun, and I didn't see the need for God. Growing up, I never went to church—only the occasional Vacation Bible School. As I got older, what I witnessed of "Christianity" was not anything I wanted to be a part of. Whenever I did feel a pull toward God, I would resist it. After all, I only had myself to think about. But that all changed when I became a mother.

As a new mom living hundreds of miles away from family and friends, and with a husband who worked long days, I was left on my own with a new baby. With this new 24/7 responsibility, coupled with isolation, I sometimes felt as if I might lose my mind.

One afternoon after I had put my son down for a nap, I began searching through the Yellow Pages. Don't ask me how or why, but I knew I needed to find a church.

There was no answer at the first church I called, and I remember thinking "Perfect!" sarcastically, but I persisted. I will never forget the sweet voice that answered at the next church. The secretary welcomed me to the area and invited me to join them that week.

That Sunday, my son and I arrived early at the church. This was his first experience in a nursery, and the grandmotherly women in attendance were wonderful. Assured he would be just fine, I headed to the sanctuary.

That morning marked what would become my faith journey. I immersed myself in this new life. Three times a week, I had somewhere to be. There was church, Sunday school, Tuesday Bible study and even a women's circle. In the beginning, it was just a place to connect; I was no longer lonely.

But the tide really turned for me after a young moms' group formed at the church. Wow! For the first time since becoming a mother, I was hearing real stories; it wasn't someone on the television or in a magazine. These were women just like me.

Here was a safe place to share my concerns and fears, and celebrate the joys of being a mom. There was no judging, just support.

One young mom who had recently given birth was being pressured by her husband to return to work. Sobbing, she told us, "When all this 'breastfeeding stuff' was done, he said I had to go back to work." Exasperated, she added, "He just doesn't get it." Each of us understood exactly what she was feeling. God's love flowed that morning, and for the first time I witnessed the true meaning of Christianity.

Since then, those women and supportive saints just like them over the years have made my life richer and my faith and family stronger. I was baptized into God's family, and with His help I have raised my children, who know God as their Lord and Savior.

I remember how skeptical I was when I first started out, but my marriage withstood the rocky times and has flourished as our faith has grown. None of it would have happened if I had not taken that first step.

~Deanna Baird

A Child's Perspective

Drugs are not always necessary. Belief in recovery always is.
~Norman Cousins

I t had been a rough week. I was worried about getting a new computer with a different software program. A personal concern troubled me, and, for the first time in years, I began to doubt myself as a writer. Between writing assignments, I usually have an idea that begs to be written. But this time, my mind was blank. I started to wonder if my writing made any difference to my readers anyway. Did anyone even read the material I wrote for Sunday school papers? With all the stress, a chronic ailment flared up big-time.

Then I began to worry about worrying. Since the Bible says not to worry, was I even living out the faith I professed?

During lunch, I shared my anxiety with my friend Wilma. I expected her to offer encouragement. Instead, she said, "I want to tell you a story."

On Sunday morning, Wilma had received a call from Heidi, who lives next door to Wilma's church. As she did most weekends, Heidi had her grandchildren with her.

"Will you pick up some yogurt and bring it when you come to church? Gage is sick and can't keep anything down. Maybe yogurt will help."

When Wilma agreed, Heidi also requested that Pastor Malbone come to pray for Gage after church.

Not only was Heidi concerned about Gage, but five-year-old

Gavin touched her heart when he laid his head on his older brother's chest and cried.

Gage's mother had taken her son to the doctor Friday afternoon. The doctor prescribed medication, but there had been a glitch in getting the prescription filled. Fortunately, the yogurt stayed down.

After church, Pastor Malbone came to the house. He knelt beside the couch and touched the boy on his head. The pastor said something like this: "Gage, I want to tell you about my sermon this morning, which I called: The Doctor Is In. When you're sick, you want the doctor to be in. But there's another kind of doctor who is always in. His name is Jesus. Jesus can help you when you're sick or when you're sad, and He will be with you all the time. So I'm going to pray that Jesus will help you feel better."

The pastor prayed and left. A short while later, Gage's mother arrived with the medicine. She took one look at her son, and then the surprised woman said, "Why, Gage, you look so much better, and you haven't even had your medicine yet."

Gavin spoke only two words, but they packed tremendous power. He simply said, "Jesus came."

The mother looked at Heidi for an explanation. "That says it all," Heidi said. "Jesus came."

That said it all for me, too. My faith was restored. My anxiety melted away. A child's perspective of a sacred moment filled my heart with many blessings that continue to bubble up every time a negative thought threatens to steal my joy.

~Esther M. Bailey

Chapter
3

finding
my
faith

Finding Faith
in God's House

"For where two or three gather in my name, there am I with them."

~Matthew 18:20

21

Just One More Time

The church is the great lost and found department.
~Robert Short

Back in the 1980s, I found myself very frustrated with God and church in general. Nothing seemed to be going right. What was the use in believing in a God who never answered prayers? Was He really out there at all?

After much soul-searching, I decided to forget the whole religious idea and just get on with life. I decided that work and family were the important ingredients for life. Things continued to go wrong, but at least I wasn't depending on an unseen God to direct my future. I was in charge and would plow on alone.

By 1986, I had muddled along on my own just fine and was sure I had made the right decision. But one day, as Christmas approached, I felt a sudden nostalgia to attend one last Midnight Mass. The feeling lingered all week long and gradually became an obsession, so on Christmas Eve I decided to go to confession and attend the Midnight Mass at the local parish. I knew I had to confess my sins to participate, and so off I went that Saturday to make my first and what I thought would be my last confession.

When I arrived at the parish at the appointed time, which was listed on the sign outside the church, there was no one around but a lone workman. He asked if he could help me, and I told him I was there for confession. He gave me a very strange look and said they didn't have confessions on Holy Days. They had done general confessions the previous Wednesday.

I was very embarrassed since my ignorance indicated how long I had been absent from church. Quickly sputtering that I was sorry to have disturbed his work, I turned to leave as fast as I could. Suddenly, I found myself running out the door and straight into another man. I almost fell over from the collision. The man steadied me on my feet and asked if he could help me. By this time, I was so embarrassed, I just wanted out of there. I stammered that I had mistakenly come thinking there would be confessions, to which he replied: "No problem. I'm Father Mike, and I can hear your confession." Then he whipped out the Roman collar from the back of his overalls. Egad! Now I would have to go through with it, so I followed him to the confessional and began my first confession in over twenty years.

It wasn't easy as I forgot how to go through most of the prayers, which I admitted to Father Mike. So, he led me through the process and all went smoothly—until I told him I had just come to attend one last Mass before I left the church for good. Suddenly, he let out a chuckle and said, "Well, we are glad you came for one last Mass, but we hope you'll decide to stay!" I told him that wasn't very likely, but thanks anyway.

With that ordeal over, I went home and got dressed up in my finest Christmas attire. I was supremely confident in my decision, and all was well with the world. Back at church for Midnight Mass, the old childhood memories flooded in. The sights, the smell, the magic of it all seemed to return as it had in days of my childhood. I chuckled to myself, remembering how I had fallen out of the pew fast asleep when I was five years old. I remembered how we used to have a chili supper after Mass and then open our gifts.

When the time came for communion, I panicked a bit as things had changed drastically since I had last received communion. Gone were the altar rails and kneelers. Now everyone just formed a line and went up to receive. I kept trying to peek around to the front of the line to see what they were doing. As I got closer, I could tell they cupped their hands and said "Amen" as they received the host in their hands.

When my turn came, I confidently stuck out my cupped hands and said, "Amen!" But the instant the host hit my hands, it felt like it weighed one hundred and fifty pounds. I hit the floor on my knees, so embarrassed I wanted to crawl under a pew. As I got back up with help from Father Mike, I saw he was grinning from ear to ear—for the second time that day! I quickly went back to my pew and sat down, utterly befuddled. Then all of a sudden I heard Christ's voice speak to me: "It was I. I am truly present in the Eucharist, and I am here for you. Welcome home!"

Needless to say, I came home to my faith. Christ set me back on the road to belief in Him. It is a decision I have never regretted. And even though I have not heard Him speak to me since that day, I know He is real and loves us all. I was lost and He came to find me, just as the Bible says.

~Christine Trollinger

The Morning After

When you do things from your soul, you feel a river moving in you, a joy.
~Rumi

Worse than the killer headache and nausea was the total humiliation. I was in a hotel room in my beautiful seaside hometown with friends. We were staying in a hotel, as my childhood home was in the process of being sold. We had headed down for the final fun-filled trip of the summer.

But when I awoke early that morning, all I could focus on was what a fool I had made of myself the night before. On the scale of barroom breakdowns, the scene I caused probably didn't even register. But I wasn't someone who drank too much and caused scenes. I hadn't had that much to drink since the summer I turned twenty-one. I was a responsible local girl in town for a visit with responsible friends. Friends who had to pick me up and pull me away from an ex-boyfriend who no longer wanted me and who I had dramatically pleaded with not to leave with the girl on his arm. I cringed as I thought of how I had followed him out of the bar, my friends chasing me and telling me to pull myself together. In my inebriated state, I told them I knew what I was doing.

"Let go of me!" I cried. "He is making a huge mistake, and I have to tell him. It is me he really wants to be with!"

"If he wanted to be with you, he would be with you. Wake up!" they shouted.

I managed to catch up to him, only to have him ignore me and leave with the unknown woman. My friends dragged me to the car, took the car keys and drove back to our hotel, all of them shocked and embarrassed by the drama. The emotional outbreak was probably accelerated not only by the drinking and the prolonged breakup, but also by my grief over the recent death of a friend, an older woman who struggled greatly in life but was strong in her faith. I had been deeply moved by her eulogy and the hymns she had chosen herself upon learning of her untreatable illness. The last time I was home was for her funeral, and the words we had sung for her had really touched me.

The morning after the scene outside the bar, with shame and a killer hangover, I sat in front of my hotel door, smoking cigarette after cigarette, looking at the sun rise across the bay. So many emotions swirled in my head along with the thought that it would have been better if I had blacked out the night before. At least then I wouldn't remember.

Suddenly, it occurred to me that I might find comfort in hymns. I went back into the room, dressing quickly and quietly so as not to wake my tired and annoyed friends, and slipped out the door for the morning service at the local church. I was in such a hurry that I didn't take the time to leave them a note.

This was out of character for me. My parents were not particularly religious. The exposure I had to church and Sunday school had come at the hands of my Portuguese grandmothers, for whom faith was a constant companion. As a teen and an adult, I moved away from religion without giving it a second thought. I believed in God, but in a distant sort of way, and attended church only for weddings and funerals. This inclination to find comfort in forgotten hymns was unexplainable. But it was very strong.

The church was over a mile and a half away. It was 7:25, and the service started at 8:00. As I walked, I picked up speed, feeling like I just had to be there. It was as if the humiliation of the night before would fade only if I made it to this particular service. I moved as fast as my hangover and post-drinking cigarettes would allow, determined to make it before the service started. I reached my destination at 7:55 and was surprised that there weren't any cars in the parking lot. I read the sign out front—Mass was at 9:30. There hadn't been an 8:00 A.M. Mass in years, probably since my grandmothers had dragged me with them as preparation for my First Communion. How could this be? Why this intense desire to come to church, only to find out Mass wasn't for an hour and a half?

I sat teary-eyed in the grotto depicting Our Lady of Fatima and her visit with the three shepherd children in Portugal. While thinking of my grandmothers, the loss of my childhood home, my recent breakup, my local friend who had just passed away, my friends who had to babysit me the night before and how my actions were so out of character for me, another strong inclination took hold. A voice in my head told me to try the church doors. I ignored the voice at first, as listening to my thoughts had gotten me nowhere the previous night. But it continued and was adamant.

I tried the doors and was shocked that they were open. There would be no music, but at least I could read the hymns. As I did so, I started to cry. Almost instantly, the cries turned to sobs. I cried for all the emotions that were swirling within my sad, weak, and confused state. I sobbed as I had never sobbed before. For more than an hour, I poured my heart out in tears.

At one point, a local gentleman who was an usher in the church walked in to light the altar candles. He promptly left, seeing that I needed this time alone with God. Something big was happening. As the tears dried, an immense peace filled me. I felt stronger than I had in a long time and I believed that everything was going to be okay. I was going to move on from this bad patch, and someday my friends and I would laugh at how badly I had lost my usual composure. Mostly, I felt at home. Suddenly, I understood that there was a reason my grandmothers wanted me to take part in religious services, for they knew faith would always bring me home. From then on, church became my place of refuge, God my Savior.

I'm not sure why God used that sequence of events to call me back. Perhaps He had been constantly calling, and I had been too complacent to hear. But I was listening now, and for the first time I was hearing Him loud and clear. I soon headed out into the day to meet up with my friends before they began to worry. The walk back to the hotel was much happier than the walk from it. Finally, I knew that no matter what, God wanted me and would always welcome me home.

~Yvonne deSousa

The Silence Sings

... and, as we waited upon him in pure silence, our minds out of all things, his heavenly presence appeared in our assemblies, when there was no language, tongue, nor speech from any creature.

~Francis Howgill

This warm Sunday morning, sunshine flows into the old meetinghouse through its many small windowpanes. Light brushes across the rows of dark wooden benches, spills onto the floorboards, illuminates the still faces that greet me, eyes cast inward, ears tuned to silence, as I tiptoe into Meeting for Worship. Without a word, I take my seat on the bench.

A whole hour of silence. It intimidates me, even as it calls to me. Silent worship is especially challenging for me in this modern world of constant stimulation. Without the soundtrack of iPod, Internet, radio and TV, without even the constant buzz of conversation and thought, I struggle to fill the time. And yet I need that stillness.

In the Protestant church where I grew up, music filled Sunday morning service. My father was the church organist and choir director. My brother and sister and I each did our time sitting on the big organ bench, turning the pages while Dad wrapped his arms around organ preludes such as Bach's Toccata and Fugue in D Minor. Hymns and psalms surrounded me and provided a kind of vocabulary of prayer.

As an adult, I learned other kinds of sacred music. Through my Jewish husband, I discovered the grand simplicity of the Shema,

"Hear, O Israel, the Lord our God, the Lord is One." I was moved by the Mourners' Kaddish, a response to death that does not even mention death or sadness, but praises "the name of the Holy One, blessed be He, beyond all blessings and hymns..." From other cultures, we learned to love Indian Kirtan music, Buddhist chants, gospel music, and so much more.

So perhaps it is ironic that at the same time we started attending Quaker Meeting, in which there is no music, no minister, no prayer book, no planned service. In the Friends' tradition of unprogrammed Meeting, we gather in silence, listening for "the still small voice," until someone is moved spontaneously to speak. The first time I attended Meeting, I knew this simple form of worship held depths of meaning. Over the years, I've learned that the silence calms me, helps me center, gives me back that equilibrium that I sometimes lose sight of in the anxious busy-ness of my days.

That's right. The Quakers, the Society of Friends. Think William Penn, founder of Pennsylvania. Think the guy on the oatmeal box. When our Meeting was founded in 1698, Friends actually resembled that familiar Quaker on the oatmeal label, with his simple gray clothing and his "thee" and "thou" speech. Today, Quakers wear modern clothes, and I have met only one who uses "plain speech."

But we still follow the practice of the English mystic, George Fox (1624-1691). Although we have no specific creed, we express our trust in the Inward Light, or "that of God in everyone," and follow six basic testimonies: Simplicity, Peace, Integrity, Community, Equality and Stewardship.

Our interest in the Friends tradition was first sparked years ago when our son attended a loving little Quaker preschool. We were struck by the solid values expressed every day to the children. Later, friends invited us to attend Meeting with them. Very gradually, that "still small voice" called us. My husband and I were both drawn to the unprogrammed meeting — its open-endedness and the sincerity of spontaneous messages, and, of course, the people. Our involvement grew over the years to membership. Last summer, I chaperoned a group of twelve high school students to England, to the beautiful "1652 Country," where Quakerism began. We visited simple old meetinghouses that echoed with the voices of those courageous early Friends. We climbed Pendle Hill, where George Fox had an important epiphany, and visited Firbank Fell, site of one of his first messages.

Today, those memories reverberate with me in the hushed meetinghouse. Visitors often find Meeting confusing. There is a story about a visitor who waited the entire hour in silence, then asked the Quaker next to him, "When does the service begin?"

"When the Meeting is over," came the answer.

Outside, cicadas chirp. I listen to the sounds of people shifting in their seats, the shuffling of feet. After the first twenty minutes, there is a general rustling as the younger children leave for child care in the playground.

I settle into the silence, let go of thought, still my mind. I wait for someone to rise, to share a message, a personal story or surprising metaphor that fills the silence with meaning. When someone does rise to speak, it is as if the silence adds weight to their message.

A man clears his throat. I wait, but he does not rise to speak.

The ceiling fan whirs. The breeze lifts my hair from my forehead. Children whoop in the playground. The space of the hour seems so wide and vast. It seems to vibrate with the breaths of generations who have sat here before me. Inhale, exhale, inhale, exhale. Outside the window, a bird weaves a piece of straw into a nest she is building in the rafters of the meetinghouse.

And then I hear it. The silence itself, breathing. I inhale, and when I exhale, the silence vibrates like a psalm. I hear echoes of my father's organ music and voices chanting the Shema, Kaddish, Gospel and Kirtan. In the silence, I touch a place of calm within, the Source of the music, "beyond all blessings and hymns."

With a start, I realize I am no longer waiting for someone to speak. The silence is no longer absence of sound. It is alive and vibrant with a message just for me, and the message is that silence is to music as inhale is to exhale. That music vibrates on the edge of silence. I just couldn't hear it, until I sat still enough — and long enough — to hear the silence sing.

~Faith Paulsen

Journey's Beginning

As you start to walk out on the way, the way appears.
~Rumi

Our pastor, Paul Robinson, writes
on a large white board.
Welcome to Trinity Church
Membership Classes.
Underneath it he writes:
Name.
Where you live.
What brought you to Trinity Church?
How you've come to be a Christian.

My mind drifts to six months ago.
My nine-year-old asked, "Can we go to
church? I've never been."
"Neither have I," I replied.
"Do you believe in God?" he asked.
"I don't know," I replied.

So we talked. Which church to go to?
About the commitment involved.
About the change it would make to
our designated family day.
We picked a Sunday and started.

I was nervous. I busied myself
with the hymnal and marking songs.
I was relieved they handed out a program.
We watched others and followed their lead.

In a few weeks I knew the routine.
Song. Announcements. Offering.
Greeting. Song. Sermon. Song.
Farewell. I became somewhat comfortable.
I began to listen.

The choir touched me first.
Eyes closed, I was sometimes taken
to another place. The tollers' bells, though
rarely played, touched a chord deep inside me.
My soul maybe? I didn't know.

We borrowed a children's book of Bible stories.
It took us the full summer to read it out loud.
We smiled at each other during a sermon
when we recognized a story we'd read.

Paul's sermons taught the Scripture
and with his calm voice and dry wit
he managed to relate it to my daily living.
I left church with a good feeling.

"Do you believe in the story of creation?"
my son asked one day over breakfast.
"I don't think so," I replied, "but I don't
know the teachings of the Bible well enough.
Maybe I'll take an adult Bible class
when you start Sunday school in the fall."

Bible 101 begins and I find myself
for an hour every Sunday morning before
church, reading the Bible, starting at page one.
This class will continue for a year.
My son and I compare what we think and feel
about what we've learned in our classes.

At times in church, a peace settles within me
I find hard to explain.
I begin to wonder about the Trinity, and that
Sunday it is explained in the sermon.
My brothers both go for surgery within a
week of each other. I ask the church congregation
for prayers, and feel a weight lifted.
Is this God?

I become more aware of myself.
Of the relevance of honesty and fairness.
Forgiveness and temperance in my
everyday life. Is this God?

"Do I have to believe it all?" I ask my husband.
"Faith is a journey," he tells me. "Not a
destination."

Paul still stands next to the
large white board. "The hardest thing,"
he says, "in looking for faith, for God,
is the fear that you won't find anything."

There are twenty-one of us in the
membership class. At my turn I
answer the questions on the board.
"My name is Amy Morgan.
I have lived here all my life.

I was married in this church and our
son was baptized here."

My throat closes up now. My eyes fill
with tears. I don't understand why.
I sit staring at the next question.
I don't know how much time passes as
I silently read it over and over.

How have you come to be a Christian?
This room, full of people who have given their
religious histories brimming with family memories
and traditions, positive and negative experiences, all wait.

I have nothing to offer them. No history.
No religious upbringing. No basis for faith.
Without warning a calming presence
settles within me.
I look up and meet eyes with Paul.
"I've come here to become a Christian," I say.

~Amy E. Morgan

Heartbreak and Faith

It is only when we silent the blaring sounds of our daily existence that we can finally hear the whispers of truth that life reveals to us, as it stands knocking on the doorsteps of our hearts.

~K.T. Jong

On a November night in 1983, my father tried to break down my bedroom door in a fit of rage. For most of my twenty-three years, my silence and refusal to take part in the sparring wars that took place daily in our household had made me an outcast. I had survived many nights by escaping to my attic room, shielding myself from the insults. When my mother—my protector—had lost her battle with cancer and was called home by God the previous year, I knew my continued existence in our Richmond Hill house was fragile.

My father told me to leave the next day. I found some shelter with a friend until he left to go home. I sought aid from a few other college buddies, but they couldn't help. On Thanksgiving Day, my aunt on Long Island said I could stay with her. But when I called the next day to see if they could pick me up at the train station, my uncle said, "Your father really lashed into your aunt. I'm sorry, but we can't help you."

Weary from the begging, I gave up and made the E train in New York City my home at night. I continued to seek employment, even landing a job interview. But I had nowhere to take a shower. I tried a nearby university, but the showers were being renovated. I had no other choice but to wash my hair in a toilet.

While riding the trains at night, I reflected on my motives, my goals, and most importantly, my faith.

Who was Jesus Christ to me?

I knew from rigid classroom teaching how history viewed Him. But what did He mean to me, huddled at the end of the subway car, warming my feet? I didn't know. I remember looking around the train, avoiding eye contact whenever possible, embarrassed over my dirty appearance and fighting off a nauseous feeling after truly comprehending that this was now my bedroom. I had nowhere to go. Nowhere.

And I asked the question over and over again: Where are you, Jesus?

Then I did what came naturally. I pulled a notebook and pen out of my green garbage bag of belongings and started to write. Was there something more to my relationship with Jesus than just reciting the Lord's Prayer?

On New Year's Eve in 1983, as I walked through the streets I had biked as a kid, I started to cry. It was frigid, and the wind rammed its force into my face, fingers, and toes. I didn't want to spend another night on the dangerous subway. I walked quickly to a familiar church in the neighborhood. I got there before the last service of the evening ended, and hid in the back under a pew. I waited anxiously for everyone to leave, hoping no one would notice. They didn't. I felt a sense of relief as the doors were locked.

I was alone. The wind creaked eerily in the old church, the slightest sound echoing loudly, causing my heart to skip a few beats. But was I really alone?

I walked to the front of the church. There was a makeshift manger with the baby Jesus lying in a wooden cradle. I knelt beside it and said a prayer for my mom. Then I wrote and wrote and cried. I looked at the innocent baby; His life lay ahead with promise, hope, and dreams. I spoke softly, telling the baby how sad I was. I even picked Him up and kissed His cheek. He was so beautiful, with the dim light from above shining proudly on His face. I sat there for a couple of hours and reflected. This is who Jesus is. He was there for me whenever I needed Him. And in a dark moment, I discovered the nature of our relationship.

That spiritual conversation so long ago is what helped inspire me to send my characters in my novels, *Everybody's Daughter* and *Necessary Heartbreak: A Novel of Faith and Forgiveness*, back in time during Christ's life. Like me, the characters struggled with their faith and received an opportunity to truly understand what Jesus means to us all. It was a chance to understand God's greatest gift—the gift of time, the gift of each new day.

It wasn't long after that night that my aunt and uncle defied my father's wishes and gave me a place to stay. Later on, I married, and after helping raise two daughters, time allowed me to revisit the memories of my homelessness and my search for what Jesus really means to me.

Two years ago, I received an e-mail from Simon & Schuster requesting the publishing rights to my book. Since its publication, I have been fortunate to receive emotionally charged letters, phone calls, and e-mails from clergy, widows, a woman who lived in a car, those struggling with their faith, and those whose faith knows no limit. And just think—it all started with those three weeks on a train, and one incredible night alone in a church.

~Michael John Sullivan

A Heart Full
of Questions

The important thing is not to stop questioning. Curiosity has its own reason for existing. One cannot help but be in awe when he contemplates the mysteries of eternity, of life, of the marvelous structure of reality.
~Albert Einstein

My family's assorted Christmas decorations sparked my first big inquiry into faith. The scent of Douglas fir filled the air while we unpacked ornaments in the living room by the tree. My brother retrieved his favorite decoration from a cardboard box. Perched atop a world globe sat a silver biplane flown by none other than Santa. But it was me who always set out our tiny nativity.

It looked like a three-sided horse stall made of brown plastic dusted in gold glitter. The people and animals stood no bigger than my pinky. Each December when I unwrapped the nativity, a feeling of peace and hope swept over me.

My first attempt to push open that doorway to faith came when I asked my mom, "What does the little stall with the people have to do with Christmas?"

"It's just a thing we do," she said. Her nervous response clued me in that she did not want to talk about it, or maybe she didn't know the answer, either.

The second question arose during summer vacation from school.

"What religion are you?" my nine-year-old friend, Becky, asked me as she looked over the rim of her glass of Hawaiian Punch. Janice crunched into a Snickerdoodle and stared. I looked at the tiled kitchen floor and shuffled my feet, not sure what to say. An uncomfortable silence hung between us while my neighborhood playmates waited. Then I smiled, stood up straight, pulled back my shoulders and pronounced, "I'm Irish."

Janice gave Becky a weird look and stared back at me.

"No," Becky said. "I mean, are you Baptist, or Lutheran, or Catholic?" All words I had never heard in my nine years of living.

"I don't know anything about those," I said. "All I know is Mom's Irish and Daddy's French." They gave each other a puzzled look and shrugged, and we ran back outside to play.

The question gnawed at me all afternoon. What did Becky mean by religion? When I returned home later that day, I asked Mom what my friends meant.

"How rude. Don't those girls have better manners?" she said. "If they ask you again, you tell them you're Episcopalian."

I stumbled over the foreign word, trying to repeat it. "What's that?" I asked.

"That's what your dad's family is, so you tell them you're Episcopalian," she snapped.

Startled by her response, I grew quiet and thought it best to never bring up the subject again. "Okay," I said, unsure of what I was agreeing to. And the door slammed shut on any further discussion.

My friends didn't ask me any more about religion. And with nowhere to find answers, the questions piled up in my head.

Fall came, and I went back to school, my mind occupied with fractions, world geography, and U.S. history. That is, until Halloween arrived.

Dressed like a scarecrow, I raced across my friend Lenora's yard and onto her front porch. The house stood dark. To the left of the door, a bowl of apples sat on a table with a note that read: "Gone to church. Please help yourself."

I paused for a moment in the glow of a single porch light. Why didn't Lenora and her brothers dress up and trick-or-treat like the rest of the neighborhood kids? Instead, they went to church. I didn't get it. Wasn't church just for weddings and funerals? Each question that lingered was like another swipe at a cobweb that veiled me from the truth.

The one constant was Christmas, that magical season of flying reindeer, Santa and his elves. Each year, like welcoming an old friend, I reached into the boxes of decorations to reclaim a wad of aged tissue sparkled with gold and unwrapped the nativity. My brother set out his flying Santa. Elves dressed in red and green felt took their usual place as sentries on the console stereo. And alone in the background sat my beloved decoration. However, it just didn't seem to fit with the rest of my family's Christmas theme. Year after year, my heart stirred with more questions about the brown plastic stall that I felt so drawn to and loved so much. Maybe it was the couple looking at the baby, or maybe it was the animals gathered around them. I didn't know or understand the significance of the manger or the Savior it represented. I only knew how the scene made me feel, and because of that I treasured it. The plastic people and animals told a story, one I wanted to know.

The mystery lived tucked away in my heart until a boyfriend invited me to church when I was in high school. I wasn't sure about all the God talk, but my curiosity was piqued. When Christmas came, we attended the children's program. I watched while the elementary kids took their places on the stage. The lights dimmed, and a spotlight shone on a young couple. As the play continued, the children formed the same scene that was in my nativity. In awe, I leaned forward on my chair and listened to every child's line. It was as if the door had been flung open, and I finally understood.

My stall was a stable, the couple was Mary and Joseph, and the shepherds had received a special invitation from heaven's angels to come and worship the new baby. And the baby had a name: Jesus. The Prince of Peace. Emmanuel. God with us.

Now I knew the reason for the peace and hope that washed over my soul each year. God wanted a relationship with me, to be an active part of my life, and He was extending to me a special invitation to be His child forever.

That Christmas, I accepted God's invitation. I not only discovered my faith, but years of questions were wiped away, and I finally knew the story behind my treasured Christmas decoration.

~Kathleen Kohler

A Monastic Heart

*True silence is the rest of the mind, and is to the spirit what sleep is to the
body, nourishment and refreshment.*
~William Penn

My two worlds were about to collide. I needed help,
and I needed it fast. My deepest fears and insecurities were rising to the surface and I felt lost. With
the responsibilities of a high-pressure executive position plus an
overwhelmed wife and rebellious teenage children, I had reached an
impasse. I searched for answers to the perplexing questions clamor-
ing in my head. They all boiled down to the worst questions of all:
"Can I save my family? My career? Myself?" I didn't have the answers.

My corporate position required international travel; I spent fifty
percent of my time in the jungles of southern Mexico, sometimes
out of touch for days. My children reacted to my absence by acting
out. My wife was snowed under as a part-time spouse and a full-time
mom. I slipped into depression.

My circumstances required action, but what action? My advi-
sors, both personal and professional, formed a committee of empty
voices offering biased solutions.

The Protestant faith of my youth taught me that God is always
with me. I believed it, but the chaos in my life blocked His voice. A
friend suggested I make a silent retreat—at a monastery. A Catholic
monastery was a stretch for me, born and bred Southern Baptist, but
my need overpowered my apprehension. I decided to go.

The monastery, located in North Central Georgia, was an eight-hour drive from my home in Florida. As my expedition began, I wondered, "How can four days of isolation resolve a situation requiring action?" The urge to act almost ended my journey. I drove and listened to spiritual music to eclipse the internal voices asking the seemingly answerless questions. The landscape lay flat and green along the highway until it gave way to brown, rolling hills with occasional patches of snow. I prepared myself for an awakening—uncertain of how it would happen. A sense of contemplation washed over me. A transition had begun; even the landscape whispered, "Be still."

Turning through the monastery gates, my eyes followed the long drive climbing the gentle rise to the church. The trees stood naked above the tan grass, fallen leaves swept into every nook and cranny. Thousands of pieces of colored glass adorned the majestic windows of the church. I felt a glimmer of hope in the dreary landscape of my life.

A lonely, tattered sign directed guests to the Retreat House at the back of the church. I found my way to the rear entrance, wondering if my seedling of optimism would be nurtured in this place. Stepping from the car, the cold surrounded me like a monk's habit. Quickly entering the lobby, I inhaled the warm scent of the antique radiators. An elderly, silent, robed monk sat behind the counter. Tilting his head, he pointed to an envelope with my name on it. Inside were a room key and a page of instructions. I walked up the stairs to my room and found a single bed, a small desk and a chair. No phone, no TV, no radio.

I sensed the intensity of the quiet. Nothing made a sound. No traffic noise, no music playing in the background, no voices in the hall or next room, no phones ringing. Stillness seeped into my spirit.

In ancient times, the monks referred to their rooms as cells and spent most of their time there. In the cell, there is no place to hide from oneself. There is no external stimulation providing an escape from self-examination. Neither can you avoid His voice, for, in the quiet, it is only you to whom He whispers. His soft words give strength to your inner voice, which begins to silence the chatter in your head.

Day by day, His gentle words spoke with authority. Discarding the questions regarding time, space and circumstances, I was able to interrogate myself about who God intended me to be instead of what He wanted me to do: "What do you live for?" "What do you value?" "Does the life you are living reflect the values you hold most dear?"

In the solitude of this place, I realized my life did not reflect the character principles I desired. The choices I made created a chasm between me and the things I loved most. The dark clouds of confusion rolled back, and even though my problems were not yet resolved, I discovered the central question, "Do my choices reflect my values?" It was a question only answered in the internal cloister where God speaks.

Leaving the comfort of my childhood faith to explore the ancient traditions of Benedictine monasticism added a new dimension to my spiritual walk — stillness. Ending my days in retreat, I returned to my car to find I had released the heat-generating friction in my mind to the cool tranquility of God within.

The trip home was a pleasure — eight hours of solitude to contemplate the beginning of a new life. No longer plagued by questions, I focused on solutions. The overcast sky gave way to a cloudless sky, alert with sunshine. I rode in silence with a song in my heart.

Upon returning home, I started each day by meeting God in the sanctuary of my heart. He queried, "Will your choices today reflect the values you cherish?" As my choices changed, my life changed. Sometimes, the choices were simple — "Son's ballgame or corporate event?" But sometimes they were complex — "How will 'no' sound to my boss?" Or, more importantly, "Does my career contribute to the fulfillment of my love of faith and family?" By reconnecting with the ideals God set in my heart, the answers came easily, but the implementations were complicated.

No longer deadlocked by fear, I was able to make complex changes. A career change, repenting of negligence as leader of my home, and submission to God became simple choices. Pricked by the thorns of change, I navigated my way through life's thicket, discarding everything that interfered with the fulfillment of my role as husband and father, including the career change I feared. The scratches and scrapes of altered external circumstances did not compare with the joy of the internal transformation. Broadening my Protestant world by embracing the stillness of Benedictine monasticism, I avoided a cataclysmic collision of my personal and professional lives.

Years later, with faith and family intact, I spend time with God each morning, weighing my options against the values I hold most dear. His influence gently nudges me toward correct choices. Living in the stillness of a monastic heart, peering out through the window of His will, leads to easy choices followed by confident implementations.

~Dan L. Cosby

Christmas in July

How silently, how silently, the wondrous gift is given.
~Phillips Brooks

On a summer afternoon motorcycle ride along a familiar route, we stopped for a red light. My roving gaze stilled at the crest of a circular driveway where, behind a log fence, rested a small white building shaded by large, overhanging tree limbs. My heart simply stood still. This place was calling out to my spirit.

"What is that place?" I asked my husband.

"I don't know. We'll go look."

He drove the motorcycle over to a small sign: Alexandria Friends Meeting (Quakers). I had learned a little about the Quakers in my studies and teaching, but had never seen a Quaker meetinghouse. We both sensed we were being nudged to discover more.

This fortuitous encounter came at a time when I was experiencing a deep, aching longing for "something more." In my sixty years of life, I had experienced many traumas, including a divorce after thirty years of marriage, but also many blessings that included three wonderful children, grandchildren, and a very successful teaching career. At this point in time, my life was on an uphill plain. My career was going well. I was married again to a wonderful man with whom I enjoyed weekend and vacation travel on our motorcycle, days on our boat, and having family and friends visit or gather at our home for meals. Yet, at this happy time in my life, I began experiencing that deep longing that had become an aching reality. My lifelong religious commitment made me aware that this longing was spiritual in nature, but I hadn't a clue how to go about satisfying it. Obviously, nothing in either my religious life or the wonderful blessings of my material life was adequate to the task.

I was sure that our sighting of this meetinghouse was no chance encounter. It was as if some inner force were urging me: "Come and attend worship here."

So, on the Sunday of a July 4th weekend, dressed in our nicest "go to meeting clothes," we drove into the yard of that little white building and parked among the other cars. A covered porch extended the full length of the building and curved around one side. Green wooden benches resembling church pews were spaced along the walls. A few people dressed in jeans and shirts stood talking on the porch and greeted us with smiles as we approached. We entered the doorway, and several men in the hall, also dressed casually, greeted us warmly with handshakes.

"Have you ever attended a Quaker meeting?" one man inquired.

"No."

"Well, go on in. It's different!" the man said with a smile.

We stepped through the door onto a floor of wide wooden planks in a very old room. The building dated from 1854. Three rows of wooden benches lined the walls. In the far end of the room stood a small, ancient wood stove, its pipe rising and curving to an outlet in the wall. Cutting the room in half was a waist-high panel above which were sliding panels that could be pulled down to divide the room. These were used in earlier days to separate the men's meeting from the women's meeting. On one side of the panel stood an antique folding table barren of any decoration. Except for the table, the center of the room on both sides of the panel was clear space.

We sat down on one of the benches and watched as about twenty other people entered quietly and seated themselves around the room. Then there was silence. Heads bowed, and eyes closed. I knew enough about the Quaker way to know we were entering silent, waiting worship. The next hour in silence passed as though it were a moment. I cannot really explain what happened. It was as though a soft veil settled over the room. All was hushed and still. I felt held in a timeless silence, a holy stillness. A palpable sense of God's presence filled the room. He reached out and wrapped His arms around me with love, His Love.

When an elder reached out to shake hands, signaling the close of meeting, my spirit surfaced with the assurance that I had come home—not to a place, not to a group of people, but to God. It was for this my spirit longed! Christmas in July? For me it was! Immanuel had reached down to fill the emptiness in my spirit and make His home there.

"How silently, how silently, the wondrous gift is given." These words of a Christmas carol express vividly the experience with which God graced my life that morning. A warm glow seemed to fill my whole being, something I can only describe as joy. I confess that I even wondered if other people could see me glowing.

"That was the most powerful experience of God's presence I have ever known," I said, finally breaking the silence in which we were driving toward home.

"I feel the same way," my husband responded.

From that moment, our lives were completely changed. For me, it was like falling in love. I could not quench my thirst for the things of God. Silence became the garden in which I nourished my relationship with Him. Cultivating that "garden" became the top priority in my life. It was in silence this sought-for relationship began, and the Spirit helped me understand it must be in silence that the relationship would be nurtured.

We began attending the silent waiting worship of Quaker meeting. My very early morning hours, before work, offered time to read and listen for God's voice and guidance. After thirty-plus years of gathering dust, my Bible came off the shelf. Reading it felt like the love story I was now living, the aching love of God for me, His wayward child. In an amazing way, the words seemed to lift off the pages to challenge, to guide, and to offer comfort and hope to my newfound faith. I felt I had suffered through years of spiritual starvation, and now the "bread and water of life" were being offered in abundance in this garden of silence. And I was feasting.

God continually set "new tables" before us to nourish our growing relationship with Him in the form of a spiritual formation program that led us further into the ways of silent listening; a test of faith to give up my beautiful clothes and adopt plain dress; twice-a-year silent retreat weekends where we also formed deep and lasting spiritual friendships born of the silence; and the new quality of our motorcycle trips. Riding in silence, we became attentive to God's presence in the beauty of His Creation. My journal entries began to fill with how waterfalls, trees, canyons, sunsets, and the sea spoke messages that challenged and informed my spirit's quest. This led eventually to the Lord's calling us to become full-time traveling contemplatives.

Beginning with that Christmas-in-July experience, not only did our lives change, but through the grace of His Spirit, God began the difficult and lifelong work of transforming us, tendering our hearts, making us more loving and generous, and filling us with His Peace.

~Judy Ceppa

Pay Attention

You learn something every day if you pay attention.
~Ray LeBlond

It's not because of any one event that my faith is so ingrained in my life, but if there was one lesson that constantly nourishes my faith in God, it came from Father Paul Waldie when I was a parishioner at St. Benedict Church in Seattle.

Father Paul was not a typical priest. He was of retirement age, yet he preached with the energy of a child and the wisdom of an observant philosopher. Like any good homilist, he brought real life to the gospels. He told textured stories with real people in real situations, and lo and behold, he unveiled God in the midst of the tale. And whacked his congregation over the head with it!

Probably the most significant lesson I learned from him was in two words short enough for a bumper sticker: Pay attention.

If you think God has abandoned you, pay attention. If you feel like you don't have anything to be thankful for, pay attention. When life gives you a reason to cry, a reason to laugh, a reason to lose your hair, pay attention. Because just like one of his engrossing narratives, God is in there somewhere. Not in some magical twist of fortune. Not in some mystical encounter with an apparition. Instead, Father Paul taught, God's conduit is much more organic. God is in our own hearts and minds, and in those of the people around us. Any people around us. Complete strangers convey God to us every day.

But none of that begets faith unless we pay attention.

Since I chose to weave Father Paul's lesson into the fabric of my daily life, little miracles have been happening left and right, and truly, it takes a person of faith to make the leap from coincidence to divine presence. Not divine intervention, but presence.

The first time I traveled alone, that presence seemed to elude me. I ventured out more than 5,000 miles from home to the epicenter of my faith—Rome. I was nineteen years old and had lived a very sheltered life. I was a mama's boy, and boy did I want my mama when I arrived, fifty hours deprived of sleep and desperately wanting to find a cab to take me to the convent where my mom had made accommodations. Every person I tried to speak to couldn't understand what I was saying, nor could I comprehend their broken English. Even their gestures seemed foreign to me. When I finally arrived at the convent around one in the morning, I settled in and stretched out on my bed. I'd never felt so alone in my life. Always surrounded by family and friends, there I was in a country where even the nuns couldn't understand what I wanted to communicate: an aching loneliness.

There, I cried until the physical need for rest evaporated the emotion. The next morning, I didn't even want to go out. The sadness had done its worst, and fear was the outcome. Fortunately, it was a weak fear easily conquered by boredom. After sitting in my room for three hours, I could no longer take the solitary confinement and decided to venture out. I followed the map to St. Peter's Basilica. On my way there, I learned a few local customs like how to greet people in the morning and how to cross a six-lane road one lane at a time.

Then came something I wasn't prepared for—my first glimpse of the monolithic columns of St. Peter's Square. Never had I seen their architectural equal. Perhaps what instilled the most awe in me was the way they stood—tall and confident. Time-tested and unwavering, they were everything I wasn't at that moment in time, and I admired them with a deep respect and excitement. They brought me in, and I could feel my despairing loneliness cracking under these white marble giants.

The exhilaration didn't end there. In fact, it was elevated when I walked into the basilica. Some people comment on the extravagance of the church. That wasn't my impression. What I felt was an over-whelming sense of humility and inferiority—not a negative inferior-ity, however. It was one that said in no way could I possibly be the center of the universe because here I was in the presence of some-thing much more profound. And though I felt small, the place didn't treat me that way. At God's house, I belonged, even though my home was on the other side of the world.

Finally, in one of the chapels of the basilica, a priest and a small congregation celebrated Mass. It was in Italian. I had no idea what they were saying, but I knew exactly what they were doing. I partici-pated, albeit in English, but still I was a part of something in this city I had felt no communion with not so long ago.

It was during this Mass that I remembered Father Paul's words: Pay attention.

All of a sudden, the sequence of the last twelve hours was put into a greater context. The lack of sleep, my inability to find any-one to share my thoughts with, that painful feeling of loneliness and homesickness, and then the incremental joy I had just experienced were all part of God's plan. Because it certainly wasn't my plan.

It was on this day that I finally understood what Father Paul meant. As I grew older and farther removed from my first time in Rome, I began to pay attention to even the smallest interactions and feelings in my life. After a while, I began to see a design. Hardly one I could grasp or foreshadow, but always one of purpose.

You could say that what happened to me in Rome was merely life unfolding, but as a man of faith, I believe God was paying very close attention to me that day.

~J.C. Santos

A Journey to Faith

It is Jesus that you seek when you dream of happiness; He is waiting for you when nothing else you find satisfies you.
~Pope John Paul II

My parents didn't teach me from a Bible. They instilled in me their no-frills guidelines for making the right decisions as an honest, caring and ethical adult. To them, it was simple: "Treat others as you want to be treated," as in the Golden Rule, with emphasis on "Thou shalt not steal, kill or lie."

Attending church is something we just didn't do when I was a child—for what reason, I'm not sure. Mom and Dad had steel woven into their fiber when it came to the difference between right and wrong; perhaps they thought what mattered most was teaching me to be a decent and honest person. I'm thankful for inheriting their strong constitution and strength of spirit.

I did attend weddings and funerals with my parents so I got the gist of what it was like being inside a church. On those infrequent occasions, I learned to behave myself, close my eyes and fold my hands to pray, and to be respectful to everyone. I recall feeling so intimidated and overwhelmed by the foreignness of church that I was nearly speechless. We had friends and some relatives who lived far away and attended church, so I knew other families regularly attended church and drew from it some kind of spiritual value.

The no-frills basics I was taught by my parents must have been sufficient because I grew into a secure, worthwhile and productive woman who adhered to the rules and tried to do what was right by others. There were times as an adult, however, when a small voice inside kept saying, "There's more out there spiritually." If that was true, where could I find it?

Those longings occurred mostly when life handed me not-so-pleasant situations. Occasionally, I'd venture out to mainstream Protestant churches, usually during the more bumpy times or when I was lonely. Ultimately, I'd feel out of place in church and would quit attending because I was managing just fine on my own.

Then in 2005, my mother, who was in seemingly good health, suffered a massive brain hemorrhage. She collapsed on a Monday at noon and was gone within twenty-four hours. She was seventy-seven years old and had survived my dad by fifteen years. I began to realize that Mom was the only common link between me and my already small circle of close relatives. Her death had driven us apart rather than closer. It turned out that Mom was the family glue, and we'd stayed connected for her sake alone. We all went to our respective corners to grieve.

I was thankful for the support of my husband and children, but it felt as if the basic no-frills guidelines for living I'd practiced since childhood had died with Mom and Dad. For the first time in my fifty-seven years, I felt a vast emptiness, and I needed something more powerful to hold me together.

A strange and scary phenomenon started taking place as my clear black-and-white guidelines started changing to fuzzy gray lines. My religious and spiritual practices, such as they were, began undergoing a transformation of which I was only mildly aware; I found myself thinking more about Christianity.

I started digging up all the information I could find from religious television, the Internet and book studies. There was a hunger within me to explore the meaning of faith and what it was like to walk with God's love, support and guidance. It was a spiritual love I'd never experienced, and I hoped it would be a way of putting the steel back into my fiber. This time, too, I wanted to find a church family.

I felt it was time to swing open the doors and invite God in. I was floored when it was Pope John Paul II who accepted the invitation and walked through my door with outstretched arms.

Faith and belief are difficult to explain logically, but my mother and Pope John Paul II died within months of each other. It was after their deaths that all of my spiritual and religious soul-searching started to take place. As I sat intrigued by the pomp and circumstance of the Pope's funeral proceedings on television, a curious spark lit up within me. It was as if Pope John Paul II had filled me with a light, leading me toward the Roman Catholic Church.

In the weeks to follow, I was a woman on a spiritual mission who was clueless as to where she was going. What had touched me was difficult to articulate, but I felt my spirit had shifted in a way that made me want to develop a relationship with the Holy Spirit.

I enrolled in the Rite of Christian Initiation of Adults (RCIA) classes to learn about the faith. Three years later, I was confirmed into the Catholic Church. The entire process felt right to me; I knew in my heart that everything was going to fall into place right down to the smallest detail, and it did.

The Catholic Church was a mystery to me, and it still is in many ways, with its endless number of creeds, prayers, artifacts, incense and rituals. It's a church that's slow to change its doctrines, regardless of social pressures from a constantly advancing, fast-paced society. The religion is two thousand years old, and I found it to be a faith-based blend of the tangible and the intangible.

In looking back, I think the Catholic faith was the ideal fit for me because of its structure; once again, the guidelines were black and white. I was drawn in part, too, because of its solid history and age-old doctrines. Broadly speaking, Catholicism is a foundation with no frills, although it may not appear that way to non-Catholics observing a Mass.

Would I have sought out a faith, a religion or a church family if my parents were still living? I'm not sure, but probably yes, because I'd been testing the spiritual waters since my twenties. Besides, so much of life is timing, and it was time.

Now I can see that the centuries-old traditions of Catholicism lit the path toward me finding my faith. I believe it also took the divine intervention of a soon-to-be saint to walk through the door and introduce me to my church, my church family and my growing faith.

~Cynthia Briggs

White as Snow

"Though your sins are like scarlet, they shall be as white as snow..."
~Isaiah 1:18

"Maybe," my young husband said, "if we find a different church, we'll be okay."

We'll be okay? Not likely. I ran my fingers along the nubby tweed of our sofa. Picked at a loose thread. Then I looked him in the eyes. Hard.

"I don't know what 'okay' means anymore. Or if this marriage is worth the effort." I blinked back tears. "And I can't imagine how changing churches would help. We've gone to church our whole lives."

But then our one-year-old little boy came around the corner. His blond hair was rumpled from afternoon sleep. He padded across the room in warm, wooly socks. Michigan winters were cold.

Just like my marriage.

Lonny opened his arms for his son, and Logan snuggled deep into his dad's chest. I wished that Lonny and I could love one another that way.

"Well, I guess it wouldn't hurt to try," I finally said. "Pick one from the Yellow Pages."

Lonny nodded to seal the deal.

I looked away.

Just the day before, he and I had sat on an overstuffed leather sofa in our marriage counselor's office. Classical music wafted through the cavernous room. Lonny drummed his fingers on jean-clad knees. I tapped my foot against the leg of the sofa, deep cherry wood sculpted to the sharp talons of a bird.

"The two of you," Jaclyn said from behind a dark, mammoth desk, "have different values. Different ideals. You are driven by different things. Lonny, your focus is on your career. Shawnelle, for you, family comes first."

I twisted my wedding ring around my finger and wondered why we were paying someone to tell us what we already knew.

"After this time of evaluation, I believe that it is best for you to terminate your marriage. The differences are too great."

I looked up to meet her eyes. Surely she wasn't serious. We'd gone to her in a desperate move to salvage a sliver of hope.

But her cool brown eyes offered nothing of the sort.

Lonny and I listened to the remainder of the verdict and left, feeling like our world had gone black, the last flicker of light snuffed right out.

The two of us had married young, before he'd graduated college. I worked while he'd finished, then we moved to Michigan for his first engineering job. A year or two passed. We bought a house. Had a child. All the while, our individual ideas of family carved a vast, deep chasm in our relationship. Lonny believed the best way to care for us was to succeed at work. I wanted time and affection. Before too long, we lived in opposite camps, and resentment became the common ground.

And after our counselor's appraisal, I'd wanted to take our son and move out. But I decided we could wait one more week. Give the church thing a try. We were already members of a Christian church, but I didn't want to leave without trying anything that came to mind.

Even if it seemed impossible.

The next Sunday morning brought snow. By the time the daylight peeked through our bedroom curtains, the winds had gone quiet, but a thick covering of white left everything buried deep. It took Lonny an hour to shovel a path from the driveway. Then we bundled up

Logan, piled in our van, and crunched over snow-packed roads. The church we had chosen was just on the other side of town, but after forty-five minutes, we knew that we were going to be late.

"Maybe we should pull over," I said. I groped for the phone book under the seat. "Let's look for a church with a later worship time."

Lonny eased the van alongside the curb. I tugged my gloves from my fingers and flipped through the Yellow Pages. Lonny peered out the window.

"What about this one, Shawnelle?" he asked. He nodded in my direction.

I looked out my window. We'd pulled in front of a red brick church. It was tiny and capped with great mounds of snow. There were only a few cars in the parking lot.

"I hear music," Lonny said. He rolled down his window. There it was. A steady beat of bass and drums.

I shrugged. Logan needed to get out of his car seat, and I didn't see much sense in further travel through the snow.

A few minutes later, our tiny parade shuffled up the freshly scraped, narrow brick walkway. And when I wrapped my hand around the handle and pulled that arched wooden door wide open, I knew that something was different.

The worshippers stood while they sang. Some raised hands. There was joy in that room. People weren't there on that snow-hazard morning because they had to be. The people in that church were there because they wanted to be. There was peace. A presence.

And the Spirit of God was so powerful and strong I felt as though I could reach out and touch it. It wrapped around me and moved through me in a way I'd never experienced. Then the pastor spoke. He shared about Jesus. I'd learned about Jesus all my life, but not like this. Here He was spoken of as someone to have a relationship with. A personal Savior. Redeemer. Lover of our souls.

I had never been so moved.

Or scared.

Lonny and I re-bundled Logan and left before the message was over. We were uncertain. But on the way home, we talked. About what we'd heard. About what we'd seen. And about what we'd felt in the deepest parts of our hearts. We talked all afternoon.

And I didn't leave with our little son.

Whatever was in that church, I wanted it. I wanted to go back.

Lonny and I visited that church for many Sundays. We learned about having a relationship with the living Jesus, and faith in Him began to transform our lives. We understood, for the first time maybe, about His redemptive gift on the cross, and it was personal, personal enough to flow into our marriage. And the more our love of the Lord grew, the more our faith motivated and directed our lives and priorities, and how Lonny and I treated one another.

We began to look at our own hearts instead of each other's mistakes.

And life was no longer about my way. Or Lonny's way.

It was about Jesus's way.

It wasn't easy. The pastor of the church spent time with us, and the congregation prayed for our family. We began going to Sunday school and reading our Bibles daily. One Sunday, I went forward to be baptized, and Lonny was by my side. He was baptized, too, while a friend held our little son.

Now it's almost twenty years later. Lonny and I have four more sons, and our home is built on our faith in Jesus.

He gave His life to save us.

He saved our marriage, too.

And it all began one sweet, stormy Sunday, when our faith began to grow, and we first understood that though our sins were like scarlet, He made them white as snow (Isaiah 1:18).

~Shawnelle Eliasen

Becoming a Bat Mitzvah

*There are always three speeches, for every one you actually gave. The one
you practiced, the one you gave, and the one you wish you gave.*
~Dale Carnegie

My heart was pounding. I clenched my fists. I had been preparing for this day for months. All the practicing, volunteering, and singing myself to sleep would finally add up.

I walked down the aisle in our small sanctuary to my seat on the stage. I looked out at all the people, more people than I had imagined. Some talked quietly, while some eyes wandered around the room, not knowing what was about to happen.

When the rabbi walked up to the bimah, it was as if someone had hit the mute button. I could barely hear him starting to give the opening prayers and introductions.

"Now I would like to welcome our bat mitzvah, Rayni Lewis, to lead us in our prayers this morning."

Everyone's eyes were on me.

"If you feel nervous, grab onto the side of the bimah and squeeze it," I could hear my aunt repeating in my head.

I latched onto the bimah like my life depended on it and opened my prayer book.

"Please open your prayer books to page 77 and follow along," I squeaked. I could hear the fluttering of turning pages. "Don't let me fall…" I stumbled over the words.

I finished the first English readings, calming down a bit, until I came to the first prayer in Hebrew. Then the butterflies started swarming in my stomach again. When I started, all I could hear was my voice echoing off the stained-glass windows. Then the congregation joined in, our song mingling together in an out-of-tune harmony.

At the time, it went on for what seemed like hours, but looking back, all I can remember seeing was a blur of faces and words. When my parents gave their speeches, I saw people getting teary-eyed. The speeches were beautiful, bursting at the seams with love, compassion and thoughtfulness. As their final thoughts came to a close, we embraced and went to open the ark.

I took the Torah in my arms. Thousands of years of stories, history, commandments, prayers, and songs rested on my shoulder. The weight of the words burdened me, making what I had done and what I had seen look like nothing.

Cheerful songs and clapping erupted as I brought the Torah around the sanctuary. Hands reached out toward the Torah as they touched their lips and prayer books to the sacred document, now sleeping like a child in my arms.

Then it was laying on the bimah, and I was standing over it, trying to make sense of the scribbles I had spent the last ten months learning. Aunts and uncles gave the prayer, giving me permission to start reading. Without realizing it, I had started singing.

At the end of the first aliyah, I struggled to stop, worried I wouldn't be able to resume when I needed to start again. But after the translation, I continued through the rest of the portion successfully. When the Torah was raised, I let myself focus on the people I loved so dearly. Smiling faces glowed, blinding me. I had to tear my gaze away and begin the Haftorah.

My tone dropped an octave, and I commenced the beautiful song that is my favorite part of the service. When I heard the congregation join to sing the final note of "amen," I smiled with relief.

The rabbi beckoned me to the aisle to start a sweet future. I took the first step, and a noisy wrapper hit my arm and thumped on the floor. As if that was the signal, candy hard and soft, big and small, was thrown from all corners of the rooms, soaring through the air, people cheering as they hit my head, back, and feet. I have always enjoyed our community's little tradition.

As the service came to an end, we gave blessings over the challah and the wine, which made my face scrunch up. At the end, my family came up to the bimah, and we all sang "Lean on Me." As we hugged, sang, and swayed, all I could do was smile. Ten months dedicated to this one day, and it was more than I ever imagined.

When the song came to an end, the crowd was drawn to the delicious food outside. I wanted to collapse. People swarmed me, offering congratulations. I would never forget this day. I had never felt more connected to the things around me: friends, family, recognized faces, or strangers and, most importantly, my faith. My faith and my religion are important to me. It makes me who I am, and I will never be ashamed.

~Rayni Lewis, age 15

Chapter 4

finding my faith

Finding Faith Through Loss

Unable are the loved to die. For love is immortality.

~Emily Dickinson

Six-Foot-Three Angel

"… Be strong and courageous. Do not be afraid or terrified… for the LORD your God goes with you; he will never leave you nor forsake you."
~Deuteronomy 31:6

I have never been a particularly religious person. I was raised as a Lutheran, was baptized, confirmed and went to Sunday school and youth group. My family went to church, but all the while, religion was more of a side note than an influencing factor growing up.

In college, faith took an even further back seat. I was focused on the normal things — classes, grades, friends and socializing. My roommate, Sarah, was a different story. From the start, she was everything a follower of God should be — faithful, selfless, dedicated and kind. She grew up with a strong presence of religion in her life, and she carried her faith with her to college and held firmly to it. I always respected her for that.

Sarah and I never really discussed religion or our respective faiths, even though she joined a campus youth group and I tagged along for a meeting or two — not until something happened that would change both our ideas of faith forever.

Tuesday, December 7, 2010, was an exciting day. It was my half-birthday — something I like to make a big deal of for the pure irony of it not being a big deal. Our housemate got engaged and texted us a picture of her beautiful new ring, and my mom sent us a huge package with Christmas gifts for all our roommates. Sarah and I were sampling the chocolate we'd been sent when her phone rang.

Two days earlier, Sarah's younger sister, Leah, who was eighteen and a freshman at Indiana Wesleyan, had been rushed to the hospital with appendicitis. She had been feeling crummy for months, and despite going to the doctor several times, they had not determined what was wrong with her. The doctors who removed her appendix found several masses on her liver and ran tests on them. Sarah got the call midway through a box of peppermint bark: Stage IV colon cancer.

In an instant, our day changed. Everything happened so fast, but looking back on that night, it seems like slow motion. I had no idea what to do or what to say to Sarah to make things better. There were literally no words. Her family was coming to pick her up, but as we were lying on my bed waiting, we exchanged our very first words on faith.

"Try not to think the worst," I told Sarah. "God always has a plan."

"You know, I've never really talked about God with you," she said.

"I guess we've never had a reason to."

The next few months were a flurry of activity. Leah was taken to the Mayo Clinic to receive chemotherapy and treatment, and the doctors there fell in love with her friendly spirit and unshakeable faith. She was pulled out of school due to all the traveling and treatment, but she never complained. She made visits back to IWU as often as she could manage to see her fellow basketball players—both her teammates and her family. She should have been finishing her first year of college, but instead she was enduring terrible pain and constant medication. Yet, she never said a word.

The faith surrounding Leah and her family was incredible. A group started on Facebook on her behalf grew to thousands of members within days. Strangers prayed for her across the globe, adding to the IWU community, her friends and neighbors in her hometown, and others who had only just heard her story and recognized her incredible spirit.

And I prayed for her every night. I—who hadn't said a prayer in years—prayed every night for Leah to recover, for her family to remain strong, and for God to be there with them every step of the way.

For her part, Sarah juggled finishing her final year of nursing school with making trips home to be with her family. I don't know how she did it.

In August 2011, things took a turn for the worse. The clinical trials in which Leah had been participating weren't having the desired effects. There wasn't much the doctors could do. They gave her two weeks to two months.

Leah and her family kept their amazing faith. They put everything in God's hands, knowing that His will would be done. Throughout her journey, Leah's proverb was Deuteronomy 31:6, "'Be strong and courageous. Do not be afraid or terrified… for the LORD your God goes with you; he will never leave you nor forsake you.'" Even during the hardest, most emotional days, Leah was always strong and always courageous. She accepted God's will with unwavering faith. She knew He would not abandon her.

On Tuesday, August 16, 2011, I had to go to work. I checked my phone and got in the shower. When I got out, I found several missed calls and text messages. Leah had passed away.

As much emotion as I was feeling that day and the days following, I cannot even begin to imagine what Sarah and her family were going through. My heart was breaking for them.

At Leah's funeral, her basketball coach from IWU spoke. He told the large crowd that had gathered to mourn the loss of a beautiful, unselfish, caring nineteen-year-old that when most people asked, "Why—why Leah? Why now?" She asked, "Why not? Why not me? Better this happen to me than someone else."

That amazing example of the person Leah was each and every day stuck with me. Though I was still asking why, I was learning. I learned that faith is a powerful thing, and that it is real. Leah knew that. And she taught me. Through the girl who was an entire foot taller than me, with the most beautiful blue eyes and glowing smile, I learned that faith and love are what life is really about.

And while I miss her each and every day, and I wish I could ease the pain that her family still feels from losing her, the lessons she taught me make everything just a little bit easier.

I know that we all have a six-foot-three angel looking after us, challenging anyone in heaven who will listen (including Jesus) to a game of one-on-one and watching over us with those big, beautiful blue eyes.

~Kate Allt

My Easter Awakening

Let the resurrection joy lift us from loneliness and weakness and despair to strength and beauty and happiness.
~Floyd W. Tomkins

While waiting for the church service to begin that Easter Sunday, I tried to chew my gum without being caught by either parent. We'd arrived early enough to sit in one of the front rows, all five of us kids spiffed up for the holiday. My three sisters and I wore new Easter dresses, while my little brother's blond hair was slicked back so his cowlick didn't show.

I was twelve years old, and early arrival for church at that age feels like a preview of eternity. My older sister and I weren't even on our best behavior because we'd sneaked sticks of Juicy Fruit into our mouths. We didn't get away with it for long before Mom pulled a tissue from her purse, passed it to us, and mouthed, "Spit it out."

I thought more about my gum that morning than about heaven and faith, even though it was Easter. I was eager for church to end because that's when we'd go home for our family celebration. Relatives were coming from all around. Aunt Fran would be bringing a delicious apple pie. Aunt Anne would arrive with her fantastic "strawberry goop." And Grandma always brought her homemade rolls. There would be ham, deviled eggs, jelly beans, chocolate bunnies... And I was still young enough to take part in the Easter egg hunt. Before church began that day, this was what Easter meant to me.

The choir finally walked in, singing "Morning Has Broken." Our minister, Reverend Jim Angell, followed behind, walking with the woman who served as lay minister that day. The entire congregation stood and sang along with the choir. After we were seated, the lay minister went to the podium, gave the call to worship and read the day's scripture. She was having a hard time talking, her voice occasionally breaking. I didn't really catch on that something was wrong until she walked over to Reverend Angell. She patted his arm and started to cry. It was all very odd.

Reverend Angell rose from his chair and momentarily gathered her in his arms. As he stepped to the podium, he paused, and then began.

"I had prepared a sermon for today, but an event happened last night that changed it. Many of you know that our daughter, Susan, arrived home yesterday on spring break from her freshman year of college. After visiting with us, she went for a ride with friends to Mt. Baldy. Our phone rang in the middle of the night, waking us. It was the police. On the way down the mountain, the car that Susan was in went out of control. Susan was thrown from the car and killed. Fortunately, the others in the car weren't seriously injured."

Gasps and then silence fell over the congregation.

Reverend Angell continued. "Nothing prepared us for that sort of phone call. The death of a child is an untimely and terrible shock. Many of my friends and relatives urged me not to come here today; the Bible says there is a time to mourn. Some of you might be wondering why I'm standing here this morning giving a sermon. When we got the news, I realized that it was Easter Sunday, and overcoming death is the true meaning behind Easter.

"Everyone who knew Susan knows that she was a Christian. Today's the day we're reminded that Jesus gave His life so that we can have eternal life. It is God's Easter promise to us! And it is because of Jesus's resurrection that I know we will be with Susan again in heaven someday. I am here to give you the good news that Christ is risen! Hallelujah!

"Our family and friends will miss Susan, and we grieve her

loss here on Earth. But we await the day when we will join her in heaven."

As I listened to Reverend Angell continue, my understanding of Easter and heaven both changed. People talk about their faith, but seldom do you witness it in action. Reverend Angell's faith had given him the courage to declare victory over death even in the midst of what should have been despair. While I'd been chewing gum and dreaming of candy, Reverend Angell was using his faith to handle the death of his beloved daughter. I knew right then and there that I wanted that same strength, too.

When the services ended, I remember people hugging and crying. I don't remember much else about what happened later that day. I was just a kid. I hadn't gone to church expecting to find faith. But the power of that Easter message has stayed with me always.

Reverend Angell passed away some years ago. I believe he is with Susan now.

As one of my younger sisters battles amyotrophic lateral sclerosis (ALS), and my parents have reached their twilight years, I often gain strength from remembering the promises I heard on that Easter Sunday when I was twelve.

~Ronda Ross Taylor

The Body Beautiful

It is not love that is blind, but jealousy.
~Lawrence Durrell, Justine

I was fourteen years old in 1953, and my best friend, Judy, and I counted the days until we would be off to church camp on the shores of Lake Geneva, Wisconsin. This would be our second time, so we were seasoned campers. We traveled by train from Chicago to the lake resort area feeling very grown up to be on our own.

The rustic cabins had room for eight girls or boys. Ours rocked with the squeals and giggles of young teens and loud music. One girl stood out. I thought of her as The Body Beautiful. At fourteen, Natalie had the lush curves of a much older girl, putting pencil-slim me to shame. Natalie's brunette curls and big brown eyes took center stage wherever we went. The boys watched her with open mouths and silent thoughts of conquest, which made the rest of us envious, disdainful and sometimes angry. We watched her flirt, wishing we knew how to do the same. I was jealous.

At night in our cabin, Natalie shed her outer clothes and pranced around in her always-matching underwear. Her long, slim legs and bare feet seemed better than anyone else's. The outfit I both coveted and resented most was her leopard-skin bra and panties. It was exotic, looked absolutely great on her, and left me feeling like a child of eight. My white cotton Sears specials could never stand up to leopard skin!

We swam, played games, had songfests around a campfire and attended Bible classes all week. When there were only a couple days left, all the campers gathered for a night rally around a crackling campfire. The leader spoke eloquently about God and Jesus and what fully trusting them could mean in our lives. "Accept the Lord into your heart," he said, "and you'll walk a path of faith forever."

That evening, under the starlit summer sky, with the aroma of wood smoke in the air, I felt something different, something new. It wasn't the first time I'd been in a group like this, with my cabin mates and the rest of the campers and leaders seated around the campfire. But I'd never felt such warmth and a love so strong that it made me shiver with anticipation of the good things ahead.

"If you accept Jesus into your heart, He will be with you always." The leader spoke in a soft but firm voice, and I listened carefully. "Make a commitment," he said, "and you'll never walk alone."

Emotion welled up, and I felt God's love around me. Suddenly, faith was mine to have and hold as long as I wanted it. I closed my eyes and made a vow to repeat the Lord's Prayer every single day for the rest of my life. As a young girl, I didn't know what else I could do to show my acceptance.

We returned to our cabins, and the magic of the moment was lost as we all got ready for lights out. Natalie cavorted in her leopard-skin undies. I rolled my eyes at Judy as Natalie pranced in and out of our room. We finally got settled down for the night. My last thoughts centered on the campfire rally and the commitment I'd made.

Early the next morning, just as the sun was about to make its appearance, I woke to shrieking and crying from somewhere in our cabin. Something was wrong, but I was afraid to get up and investigate. Soon, one of the counselors stuck her head into our room and told us that Natalie's mother had died during the night. She was leaving to go home. The tragic news shocked Judy and me into silence.

At fourteen, losing my mom had never entered my mind. Natalie had everything. She was The Body Beautiful. She had special underwear. She had lush curves and boys drooling over her. But her mother was suddenly gone. I lay in my bunk and thought of my own mother back in Chicago caring for my dad and my two younger brothers. What would life be like without her? As I listened to Natalie's wails, I clutched my blanket and turned my face into the pillow to muffle my crying. Suddenly, I had so much more than the girl I'd envied. I had my mother, and I had my newfound relationship with God.

I silently repeated the Lord's Prayer to fulfill the commitment I'd made the night before. The short prayer eased my sadness. I wanted to tell Natalie how sorry I was for her, but I couldn't make myself leave the security of my bed. Instead, I asked God to comfort her. I hoped Natalie would turn to Him in the days ahead, that she had enough faith to hold her up. I'd envied Natalie, but now I pitied her and prayed for her, a big turnaround in a matter of hours.

Occasionally, I've wondered what happened in Natalie's life. Did she, too, make a silent commitment to God that long-ago night? Did her faith allow her to be strong as she went through her teen years without her mother? I hope so. Never again did I wish for matching lingerie. I had so much more.

~Nancy Julien Kopp

My First Ebenezer

Then Samuel took a stone and set it up between Mizpah and Shen. He
named it Ebenezer, saying, "Thus far the LORD has helped us."
~1 Samuel 7:12

There are moments in my life that I remember with perfect clarity: the moment my boyfriend proposed, holding the ring out in the front seat of his Trans Am; the snowy afternoon I pulled a letter out of the mailbox and viewed my acceptance into my first-choice college; and that snowless, dreary February day when I reached the first real turning point in my faith.

February 12, 2000 was an unseasonably warm Saturday in the suburbs of Chicago. I sat on the couch, probably doodling as I was wont to do. The phone rang. I looked out the window to the sleepy neighborhood. The grass was brown, with the snow long melted but spring still far off. I suspected I knew who was calling. Then Dad came in and told me in a mercifully direct way that Tim had died. I let him wrap me in a hug while I cried, my tears dampening his shoulder.

Later, upstairs in my bedroom, I turned on my late-nineties Christian music and leaned against my tall dresser, allowing myself to mourn. I opened up my journal—a spiral-bound notebook that still bore the colorful traces of girlhood—and wrote what had happened. My mascara-tinted tears stained the page.

In May 1998, I was about to graduate from the eighth grade, leaving the friends with whom I'd spent nine years of my life. I was to enroll in a new high school, full of beautiful, tall, blond, images of near-perfection—and I didn't know a soul. As if that weren't frightening enough for a fourteen-year-old, my parents had dropped a bomb on me: We were leaving the church in which I'd grown up. This was the church where I'd met my closest friends, been involved in a children's group for years, and created countless memories. We were leaving, and I didn't understand. My whole world capsized, and to a fourteen-year-old, this was unbearable.

We started church hunting one Sunday, beginning at a local church... and we never left. Immediately, I was welcomed into the youth group. Smiles, laughter, warmth—they showed me the love of Christ. This youth group and its leader ignited something in me that would change the rest of my life. Tim Yetter was a young grad from the Moody Bible Institute with a wacky sense of humor and a deep love for the Lord. I'd never seen someone so young be so on fire for the Lord. He inspired the whole youth group to be "fully devoted followers of Christ." The lessons I learned as I entered high school were the building blocks of my true faith, and little did I expect that I would soon need to rest on those blocks when the storm came.

One day, we sat on sweltering, peeling vinyl seats in a bus that was falling apart. We were at a youth retreat in Minnesota, and Tim mentioned some fleeting health concerns. We made fun of him, put Anbesol in his fake Billy Bob buckteeth to make his mouth go numb, and forgot about it on the eight-hour ride home in an un-air-conditioned bus. But just a couple of months later, he was yellow—jaundiced because of a rare liver disease. By winter, we knew he had liver cancer. He was twenty-seven. His ministry was thriving. How could this be happening?

His name went on the transplant list. One night around Christmas, youth group was canceled because Tim was on his way to potentially get a transplant. We gathered anyway in the sanctuary that was lit with twinkling Christmas candles. We prayed and we sang. We made the choice to trust God rather than blame Him.

The transplant didn't pan out. A month or so later, we had an all-night church lock-in. Tim fed us words we'd heard him say before:

"'He must become greater; I must become less'" (John 3:30). He was weak, yellow, dying. But words of praise, not words of pain were coming from his mouth. Two weeks later came the day that Tim's faith became sight, and he went to be with Jesus.

And that's where you meet that girl, crying in her room on a dreary February day. I say "that girl" because I am no longer "that girl." Through my tears, I knew I had a decision to make: I could choose to not trust this God who had allowed something so terrible to happen to such a wonderful leader and teacher... or I could choose to trust that this God was sovereign and good, with a purpose so beyond me that I could not understand. And here I raise my Ebenezer: I trusted Him. And that test of my faith grew me more than I could ever have imagined because I (and the rest of the youth group) was forced to depend on the Lord, and trust and hope that good would come from this painful situation.

It wasn't easy. I remember going to bed each night, fighting tears and praying that God would make me not miss Tim as much the next day, that it would hurt a little less. I thought I'd never heal. But I did. Years passed, and the series of events that have played out in my life are sovereignly connected to Tim's impact on my life. I attended Moody Bible Institute, which forever changed my relationship with the Lord. That education led me to move to Florida where I now have my own ministry to young girls whom I teach to be fully devoted followers of Christ.

I pray that as you read this, you will think about your spiritual legacy. I pray that you will remember that God is sovereign and good. And I pray that you will strive to be a fully devoted follower of Christ, as Tim so wanted us to be.

And God, the next time you see him, please tell Tim "thanks" for me, and let him know that "I'm keeping the main thing the main thing."

~Amanda Arbia

Dying Faith

God is closest to those with broken hearts.
~Jewish Saying

I turned away from God the day that man killed my sister. The details of her death aren't important here. Suffice it to say it was a cruel and violent end to a strong and beautiful woman. A woman who should be here now, full of life and irreverent wit. A tiny wisp of a woman with a big heart.

Throughout her life, she embraced the weak and the small, the daft and the needy. She laughed at the pompous and stood up to the bullies among us. She smoked and drank and always fell in love with the wrong man. Because of these things, she had reason to cry far too often. Her passing ripped a hole in my heart, altering my world.

I knew from harsh experience, long before she was taken, that life could be cruel. Babies, including one of my own, are conceived and not born. Children cry from hunger, and young men go off to fight in distant lands, never to return. Life is fragile. But this was far too much to bear.

"How dare you?" I cried, shaking my fist toward heaven. Ironic since I no longer believed in God, don't you think? I railed at this nonexistent being for failing her, for failing me, for taking her away when I wasn't ready to let her go.

"Damn you!" I told Him. "You could have saved her if you tried. Why didn't you try?"

When He didn't answer, didn't bring her back or bother to

explain Himself, I closed my heart against the pain. I wrapped my grief in anger and slammed the door on faith. God didn't listen to my curses. He paid no mind to my tirades accusing Him of being a fraud, a sham, a made-up being created by the weak-minded and the gullible.

Apparently, He wasn't ready to let me go. He kept tweaking me, reminding me with my own words that He was there, waiting for me.

"Oh, for God's sake!" I said when I dropped a plate while emptying the dishwasher.

"What in God's name are you doing?" popped out when I came upon one of the kids bathing the cat in the sink.

"Goddamn you!" I yelled when the speeding car cut me off at the intersection.

"Good God, girl!" was my exclamation when my best friend told me some delicious gossip.

"God bless you," I said when the grocer sneezed.

"One nation under God," I recited, leading the Pledge of Allegiance with the kids in their classrooms at Open House.

Words, meaningless words, I tried to tell myself when I heard them coming from my own mouth. Even at night, I'd catch myself falling into my lifelong pattern of prayer as I drifted off to sleep.

"Our Father who art in heaven…"

I'd make myself stop. Force myself to think of something else. The car needs new tires. I forgot to put five dollars in Kelly's lunch bag, and she needs it for the field trip. What time is it?

"Hail Mary, full of grace…"

That's enough of that, I'd say, and pull the pillow over my head, only to go on thinking. The mortgage is due, and I'm short again. Why can't the support check ever be on time?

In spite of the pain, I smiled in the dark, remembering the time my sister had that same sort of problem with her rent, and we all pitched in and helped her out. I see her face, remember how she laughed and cried and promised that as soon as she got back on her feet, she would help the next person who might need it. And she did, often.

I would talk to God. "She won't get back on her feet this time, will she, God? Stop it! Get out of my head and leave me alone. Isn't it bad enough you let her die? Let me sleep, please just let me sleep. Oh, my God, I am heartily sorry for having offended thee... No, I'm not sorry for anything. I did not offend this time; you did! You offended me by taking my sister away. You offended my mother by taking her child. You offend me today by being a fake and a liar. You promised you would answer our prayers. You promised to watch over us. You promised us life everlasting. I know she must have prayed that night. In the fear and confusion of what was happening to her, she would have asked for your help. How could you turn away and leave her to her fate? Tell me. How could you turn your back on your child?"

Tears stained my pillow every night for months. I was so tired and worn out that I could barely function. I had no place to find comfort, no faith to carry me through the unending days of darkness. I was failing my children, sleepwalking through my job. Life had become mere existence.

Finally one night, out of sheer exhaustion, I forced everything from my mind and drifted off to sleep. That night, there were no dreams to disturb my rest. No memories of two little girls playing house or running through the grass. No recollection of silly teenage fights over clothes and make-up. And, blessedly, no nightmare imaginings of her final moments. Finally, I slept.

The next morning I woke up feeling refreshed for the first time since the funeral. There was a hint of clarity to the world once again. I began to think I might survive this. I was altered, diminished by my loss, irrevocably older, but I would live on and carry her spirit with me.

Looking at her picture on the dresser, I could feel her love. Hear her insistence that I continue to live.

Eventually, over a great deal of time, after much soul-searching and months of questioning, I began to see the truth. God didn't do this. He didn't allow it to happen. A man did this. A broken justice system failed to protect her. And since God didn't want to see His child suffer, He was there, easing her fear, enveloping her in His love. When the time came, He took her home, fulfilling his promise of everlasting life. He then began to focus His attention on healing those left behind. What I failed to see in my grief, what I turned away from in my anger and fear, was the vision of His everlasting love as God turned toward me the day that man killed my sister.

Our Father who art in heaven, hallowed be thy name...

~Bobbi Carducci

You Are on My Road

Hope is like a road in the country; there wasn't ever a road,
but when many people walk on it, the road comes into existence.
~Lin Yutang

I am a school psychologist, and I deal with many children during a typical school day. Throughout the years, I have worked with many grieving children who have lost siblings and parents. I've listened to their stories of anger, guilt, hope, and despair. I've cried with them and laughed with them. We have shared stories about our faith and the anger we sometimes feel toward God for the loss.

One child always comes to my mind when I think about the many children I have worked with in my grief groups. For confidentiality reasons, I will call him Mike. I met Mike during his three-year re-evaluation for special education services, which was kind of ridiculous when you consider the emotional state he was in. Mike had lost his father the year before to cancer, and he lost his last remaining grandparent that same year. This particular year, he was about to lose his mom to cancer as well.

Before we began the evaluation process, I asked Mike about life, his goals and dreams. He could not think of any. I asked him if he had thought about entering a grief group that I had started. He smiled at me, but said, "No, thank you."

I decided not to proceed with the evaluation process. Instead, I called his dying mother and talked to her for what seemed like hours. She talked about Mike the whole time, never about the loss of her husband or her own fight against cancer. She talked about Mike's kind heart, his love for her and hers for him. She talked about her hopes for him and how God would help him find his way. She stated repeatedly that "God puts certain people in the middle of the road that you are walking on, in order to help you." I never forgot those words. To this day, I use those words with the children I counsel.

Weeks later, Mike's mom lost her battle with cancer. Mike did not grieve the way I expected. He did not speak or cry. The school staff started to see him giving up in school and isolating himself from others. He no longer cared. He had lost so much in just a short time—a loving father and mother, and his only grandfather. He was, in fact, alone.

After the funeral, I ran into Mike at school and made an excuse that I needed to see him to finish testing. He reluctantly came to the testing room, not so much to help me out but to get out of the class-room. His head was down, and his eyes were on the floor. I knew this was my chance to stand in the middle of the road. I called Mike's name, and he reluctantly looked at me. I told him that we weren't going to test, but that I just wanted him to listen to what I had to say. I talked for two-and-a-half hours about life, faith, memories, and the power of love. Tears ran down his face from time to time, but he never uttered a sound. I had no idea if my words had made a differ-ence to him or if I did anything to help him. For the first time in my life, I felt so ineffective.

Years later, as I sat in my office at the end of the day, I received a surprise visitor. It was Mike. A sophomore in high school, he looked happy, strong, and peaceful. He seemed so confident standing there in front of me. He told me about how well he was doing in high school, and how he had made the swim team and joined various other clubs. I was pleased to hear that his aunt had stepped in to take care of him.

I smiled when he began to talk about his goals and dreams. He saw me smiling and said, "I listened to every word you spoke to me that day. Thank you."

We talked on, laughing and crying, until he finally got up to leave. He turned to me and said, "God put you in the middle of my road, you know."

I replied, "No, I think God put you on my road."

~Manny Patla

Epiphany

Tears are God's gift to us. Our holy water. They heal us as they flow.
~Rita Schiano, Sweet Bitter Love

"You'll never believe who just died," said one of my friends at our coffee break. We always stopped for an hour after our daily walk. As seniors, we vowed to keep as fit as possible for as long as we could.

The news wasn't surprising as we had all read the obituaries. "Did you ever think we'd reach this stage of our lives when we wouldn't miss reading the obits?" said another. "Remember when we were more interested in fashion and the newest shade of lipstick?"

The conversation then fell into a familiar pattern of who else was sick, or what the doctor said, or who was experiencing arthritis in yet another joint.

"Good heavens, that's all we seem to talk about," I said. "Doesn't anyone have any happy news?"

We all seemed to be thinking as we looked at one another, and then we simultaneously broke into peals of laughter as the silence lengthened.

This would have been an opportune time to tell them about my happy, unbelievable experience. But I was afraid they might think I had imagined it, or worse, that I was losing my mind. So I said nothing. I didn't want to see the doubt in their eyes.

Back in August 2001, my husband and I had just returned home, driven by friends, after a lovely dinner at our favorite restaurant. As

I was unlocking the door, my husband somehow missed a step, and all I can remember is seeing, in my peripheral vision, flailing arms and the sickening sound as his head hit the pavement. My friends dashed out of their car, and then the rest was a blur—the call to 911, the ambulance, the waiting at the hospital, the hurried flight to a hospital out of town that dealt with head traumas. Two weeks later, my husband, who never came out of the coma, died.

Then on September eleventh, the world came to a complete stop due to the unbelievable news of the destruction of the terrorist attacks.

The retail gift business I ran also came to a complete stop as everyone was glued to their TV sets. My sales plunged alarmingly. A scant three weeks later, my mother died.

I managed to keep the business going for two years after my husband's death, but the big box stores moved in, and I could not compete with their prices. I was advised by my accountant to finally close the doors, so after thirty years it was another death.

As time passed, it became evident that I could no longer keep up with the expenses of my big house. Again, I was advised to sell and get something smaller. I moved into an apartment.

It is said that the biggest trauma one can experience is death in the family. The second is losing a home, and the third is losing one's job. I always prided myself on being tough and resilient, but I hit the trifecta on traumatic events, and it did me in.

My days were empty, and I was lonely. Although my friends and family were supportive, I felt I had become invisible. I missed my productive, happy days. I fell into a deep depression and was forced to seek medical help. The tranquilizers helped a bit, but I hated being dependent on them.

My daughter, understanding my distress, insisted I stay with them for an extended visit. She lived in another city. Being with my grandchildren and helping with the cooking and babysitting helped, but I could not stop my brain from reliving past events, so I was often in tears (which I hid from them) and angry with myself for being so weak.

After a few weeks, and countless counseling sessions with my daughter and son-in-law, I declared I wanted to go home. But nothing had changed. I was still sad and crying all the time.

A friend called one day and asked if I would join her and her husband at church. I had fallen away from my religion with the excuse that I was too busy with my business. I was also angry with God about my misfortunes, but I reluctantly said I would go.

Sitting in church, I let the organ music and hymns wash over me, but the beautiful music again brought the ever-present tears to my eyes. I closed my eyes and fervently beseeched the Lord to help me.

The priest was finishing with the communion preparations and intoned, "Happy are those who are called to his supper," and the congregation replied, "I am not worthy to receive thee, but only say the words and I shall be healed."

With eyes closed, I repeated those familiar words from the bottom of my soul.

It is difficult to describe what happened. I opened my eyes, and the room seemed to be bathed in an unnaturally bright light. I felt like I was in a trance as I walked up the aisle to receive communion. And with the blessing and taking the Host, my heart seemed lighter. I was infused with the warmest feeling. I felt a happiness that had been so long absent. I wanted to shout out my feelings of joy.

That feeling has stayed with me to this day. I truly felt I had been healed, and I could face life again. Now if I shared my secret with my friends in the coffee group, they might think I'd lost my mind. But in my heart, I know my faith was restored that day—and I can only describe the event as an epiphany.

~Virginia Funk

40

I Will Be Your Father

We love because he first loved us.
~1 John 4:19

As we entered the home, my mother gave me some crayons and pieces of notebook paper and sent me to an adjacent sitting room to busy myself with coloring. A number of men and women were all surrounding the kitchen area. Soon, my mother had gathered some women around her, and as they huddled together, I heard some disturbing chatter.

As a traveling salesman, my dad was gone a lot, but it seemed from their conversation that he was not going to be coming home to us anymore. The youngest of five children, I was only five years old at the time. I didn't understand. What did this mean? My little head was trying to comprehend what I had just heard, and I became fearful. Before I could think of running to my mommy for reassurance and comfort, I felt a strong presence enter the room beside me. I looked around the room, but no one was there. Then I became aware of something like the warmth of a strong embrace surrounding me. Immediately, I felt my fears melt away, replaced with an unfamiliar peace.

I was so moved by what I experienced that I decided to make something special. Folding my paper like a fan, and then folding it in half, it looked like it would make a fine bookmark. I colored it with flowers and put my name in cursive on the front. Then I put a secret message in one of the folds. I wrote, "I Love God." It was my response to this event and a memento that I still possess. How true the verse is in 1 John 4:19, which says, "We love because he first loved us."

My parents divorced soon afterward, and I vividly remember the day my mom went to court. I watched as she put on a green dress suit and leaned in toward the mirror to put on a pretty pair of earrings. As I lay looking up at the seagull mobile she put above the bed so I could go to sleep at night, I asked her if Daddy would ever be coming home again. "No," she said. I lay there quietly and wondered. Was my mom not pretty enough? What could have driven our daddy away? Was it my fault?

The gaping hole his absence made, the sense of security, value and direction that a father's love brings, were replaced with the gnawing sense of being rejected and abandoned, and a belief that we must not be worthy.

My siblings were deeply affected, but I felt the pain of it more acutely for my three brothers. They had to borrow someone else's dad, or maybe an uncle for father/son events, which made us more aware of our loss. I never saw my mother loved by anyone. I never saw her hugged or kissed by anyone beyond her own children.

A five-year-old can hardly put into words such an experience as I had that day, or be aware of its effect to alter one's life. But now I can describe what it spoke to me then. God was declaring to me, "I will be your Father."

That first encounter with the Lord would be the beginning of my new Father's care over my life. It would take years before I would really know the One who had embraced me, but He placed a hunger in my heart that would eventually lead me straight to Him.

Throughout every challenge I would face and rebellious road that I would take, I often heard the voice of my Father speaking to me, "Teri, this isn't want you want."

I thank Him for His guidance and discipline, His pity and compassion. His love healed this little girl and made this woman His own. And when I see the admiration and praise on the faces of earthly fathers toward their children, I can see my Father there, in my mind's eye, taking delight in me.

~Teresa Hanly

41

Giving Thanks with a Broken Heart

Gratitude is an art of painting an adversity into a lovely picture.
~Kak Sri

My Methodist church has always co-sponsored a community Thanksgiving Eve service with the local Baptist church. For many years, I sang in the choir during the services when my church was the host, and I had simply thought of the service as part of the holiday routine. We sang the traditional hymns, "We Gather Together" and "Come, Ye Thankful People, Come," and heard a sermon, and the choir sang a Thanksgiving anthem.

After the death of my nineteen-year-old daughter in a car wreck, nothing about church seemed routine. For a while, I continued to accompany my husband to services as usual, but in a few months, I shut down. Everywhere I looked in that church, I envisioned my daughter. The memories were not soothing; they were painful.

I turned to the Crystal Cathedral on TV for my Sunday morning worship time, and my husband went to church alone. This went on for a year or two. One time I tried going to church but the hymn was "Majesty," which my daughter used to accompany with her friends in a praise dance. I broke down in the pew and quickly left. I tried again in a few months but the opening hymn was "It Is Well with My

Soul." Well, it wasn't well with my soul, and I didn't feel like being a hypocrite. I left again. My husband got a ride home with his sister.

The second year after the car wreck, I found myself sitting in church on Thanksgiving Eve, next to my sister-in-law. The church was almost empty. I looked around at the bare pews; there were almost more people in the choir than in the congregation. Why were my sister-in-law and I, of all people, sitting in this church on Thanksgiving Eve?

My sister-in-law and her husband had also lost a child. Their thirty-two-year-old son had died two years before my daughter. He had been diagnosed with skin cancer on his neck a few years earlier. He went to the doctor and had it removed, but never went for additional follow-ups. Their son had led a tortured existence for several years, unable to shake his addiction to drugs and alcohol. His friends had mistaken his bizarre behavior for alcoholic rage, and when someone notified my sister-in-law, he was beyond help. His skin cancer had metastasized to his brain, and the brain tumor was inoperable.

The only help that could be given to my nephew was medication to relieve his pain. My husband and I helped take turns sitting by his side in the hospital. He was coherent enough to talk about his childhood, and my husband and he would talk of Little League baseball, hunting, and fishing—all of the pastimes my nephew had loved. He died just a few weeks after the diagnosis, leaving behind two young sons.

During that Thanksgiving Eve service, I wondered why these pews weren't filled with the people whose families were whole. I thought, rather meanly, of the number of people in my church who could have filled the pews with their children, their sisters, brothers, aunts, and uncles. They should have been the thankful ones. What in the world were my sister-in-law and I doing at this service?

As the service continued, it dawned on me. Perhaps it was because we were so painfully aware of just how precious life is. Is it possible I am more thankful than those people who have never suffered a tragedy? Certainly, many of them thank God for their families and their many blessings. No, I just think we are more aware. Perhaps we live a little closer to the eternal, knowing that our children are already there. Perhaps, having known great grief, we are more eager to seek out joy.

I have heard others say that you cannot be healed unless you have been broken. This broken heart of mine will never be fully healed; there will always be an empty place there that I fill daily with memories of my lovely daughter. But such a loss has made me more eager to experience joy, to embrace the blessings of this day, and to seek the good things life has to offer with as thankful a heart as I can muster. "Come, Ye Thankful People, Come." I am coming, and I am trying. Create in me a thankful heart. Amen.

~Kim Seeley

Losing to Gain

To win you have to risk loss.
~Jean-Claude Killy

I stood in my kitchen and stared at the note my sixteen-year-old daughter had left while I was at work. She was taking a bus from our home in Florida to somewhere in Colorado. She left no contact information and she had no cell phone.

My heart sank, which had happened often over the past few months. Just weeks before, my heart had ached when my beautiful, strong-spirited daughter had dropped out of high school. The decision was made without my consent or knowledge. Instead, she had convinced her dad to sign a permission slip, and since her dad and I were separated, I found out about the school decision after the fact. My very bright, artistic daughter would not participate in high school activities or graduate, and that saddened me.

The separation from her dad had been an earlier heartache. After nearly twenty years of marriage, mine was dissolving, and there wasn't anything I could do about it. Now, standing almost paralyzed in my empty house, that hopeless out-of-my-control feeling overwhelmed me. Would my daughter be safe? Who was this boy she was meeting in Colorado?

There was only one thing to do: fall to my knees and cry out to God. So, like I had already done many times during the previous weeks, I knelt in front of a living room chair and sobbed. When I could sob no more, I wiped my tears and talked to God. And when I could no longer think of new pleas, I read from His Word.

The comfort came. I had put my faith in Him as a young child. Then in college, my relationship with Him grew stronger once I understood about making Him Lord of my life. During that time, a friend of a friend explained the difference between simply believing God existed and knowing Him in a personal, intimate way. That realization was life-changing. And over several coffee-time chats with this woman, I learned to trust the Lord in all areas of my life.

But now as I grieved for my daughter, I knew this was one more area in which I needed to trust the Lord. Though difficult, I realized I would not find peace if I did not wholly put my faith in God to bring good from this heartbreaking situation. Only He could use this for His purposes and make it all right for me in the end.

As I clung to His promises—that His grace was sufficient for me, that He never slumbered nor slept so He was fully aware of my daughter's location, and that He was always in control—I could slowly let go of my daughter and my failing marriage. And when I did, I discovered that my faith in God became stronger than ever before. That small seed, planted when I was just five and accepted Jesus as my Savior, now blossomed in a different way. My intense pain drew me closer to God, not away from Him. And my confidence in Him to know what was best for me continued to increase.

Did I believe He'd restore my marriage? I believed He could if it meant it would serve His purposes, not mine. Did I believe He'd bring back my daughter? Yes, if that would help her seek Him. Did I believe He'd give me peace during my horrific circumstances? He'd already done that. And as I continued to put my faith in Him, that peace swept over me.

Over the next weeks, I still sobbed quite often. I still knelt and cried out to God. And my heart sank a few more times—when I had to give up my dream house, when my Mustang convertible got stolen, and when the divorce papers were signed. But the Lord always lifted up my fallen heart, and my faith in Him did not waver.

Many months later, my daughter returned. She moved back in

with me and eventually tested for her GED. Soon, she met a great guy she'd later marry and have a child with—my grandson. Today, the relationship with my daughter is truly one of love and acceptance. For that, I am extremely grateful. And remarkable as it sounds, I'm also grateful that, though painful, God used her running away as a time for me to fall into His lap and deepen my faith. Though I'd not like to relive those circumstances, I can honestly say that losing led to gain.

~Georgia Bruton

The Faith of Jake

The human spirit is stronger than anything that can happen to it.
~C.C. Scott

Children aren't supposed to die. In pediatric medicine, we fight to keep that from happening. But children live in the same world as adults, with all its illness and pain. The good thing about kids is that they're resilient. Most will recover from the worst of diseases and thrive even with their scars. The problem is, a few don't. Despite our best efforts, health care providers are human, and modern medicine still has its limitations. One patient in particular—I'll call him Jake—reminded me that I may know a lot about healing children, but there is only one Great Physician, and healing doesn't always mean recovery in this life.

Because children don't have the life experience of adults, they approach illnesses differently. They believe the world is a good place despite the bad. Even though they put up a fight for things, such as shots or nasty medicine, they forgive you because they really do believe you're helping them. They naturally see things from the positive perspective.

Jake was no different. He was in the hospital for his second fight with a neuroblastoma. He'd done well with his first treatment and had been in remission for two years, but we all knew the prognosis for relapse was poor. The neuroblastoma was going to win, but still we tried. He deserved that much.

One evening, I was with Jake on the oncology unit. His parents had gone out for dinner, taking a much-needed break. His aunt was staying with him, but was in the cafeteria. When I went to check on Jake, I found him crying. It was the first time I'd ever seen him without a smile on his face. I sat by him on his bed and asked him what was wrong. I thought he must be hurting or the chemo was making him sick. What he said surprised me.

"My mom doesn't want me to go to heaven."

Now, Jake's family was faithful to God. They prayed, they read Scriptures. Their pastor or other church members were often in attendance, ministering to them. Jake's parents had taught him and his sisters about Jesus. Jake himself had expressed his faith.

"Why do you think that?" I thought maybe he knew how upset she was about what he was going through. We'd had a meeting with the family regarding end-of-life decisions. When parents were deciding for their children, it was always difficult. Jake's mom was taking everything especially hard.

"I heard her tell Dad she didn't want me to be with Jesus." He said it in a whisper as if he thought someone might overhear. "I don't want her to be mad, but I want to go."

"Your mom would never be mad at you. She wants you to be with Him, but she's not ready for you to go yet. Moms always want their little boys with them," I tried to explain.

"But if heaven is where I won't be sick anymore, then why doesn't she want me to go there?"

In his seven years, Jake had suffered more than most do in a lifetime. He'd known his share of pain. But he hadn't seen enough of life to know he could be depressed. It never occurred to him to be angry at us, his parents, or God. With the faith only a child could have, Jake had perfect trust. He knew he was sick. He knew he didn't like the chemo or radiation. He knew that when he died, he was going to be in heaven with Jesus where kids didn't get sick. They got to play and have fun.

To him, it all made sense, and at that moment, I had to agree. Jake didn't want to die, but he was tired of hurting. God offered Jake healing that was complete, not just remission. Why would anybody not want that for him?

"Jake, your mom wants you to get well. She just doesn't want you to have to go away to do it. She wants you here where she can take care of you." I prayed for God to give me the right words to say. How do you explain the loss a parent feels to a child who will never get a chance to see past age eight?

"But Jesus will take care of me until Mom and Dad are in heaven." Jake's mind was made up.

Jake made me promise not to tell his mom he was ready to go to heaven. He didn't want her to be upset or mad at him. Three days later, I was with him when he died from respiratory failure after developing pneumonia. His family was devastated. I was sad, but I couldn't help but think Jake was happy now, pain-free and running like a maniac with all the kids who had gone before him.

The most wonderful privilege God has given me is to be able to help Him take care of his most precious possession: His children. Working in pediatric medicine is the most amazing, joyous, and heartbreaking endeavors a person can take on. Most days, it's worth everything I give it, but sometimes everything isn't enough. When my faith in myself and in what I do starts waning and I get discouraged, God reminds me of Jake. I remember my job isn't to save every child. My job is to laugh and cry with, fight for, and give my best to the families that are given to me—and to trust God to take care of the rest. I'm just the assistant. He's the one who gives the perfect healing.

~Beth Savoie

Chapter 5

Finding Faith
Through a Stranger

Strangers are just friends waiting to happen.

~Rod McKuen, Looking for a Friend

A Stranger's Eyes

People see God every day; they just don't recognize him.
~Pearl Bailey

I was twenty-five. I had a rewarding job and a close circle of friends. I was loved by my family. I had a good education, food on the table, and a roof over my head. I was healthy. It looked like I had everything, but I was just going through the motions. I was lonely.

The night that I became aware that there was something missing from my soul was on a cross-country driving adventure with my sister. As we drove across the flat darkness of Kansas, she described a feeling that someone was always with her, guiding her. She felt as if there was a greater force that comforted her. After a long philosophical conversation, she fell asleep as I drove. I secretly cried that night.

My downward spiral of doubt, pain, and sadness continued until one night, as I lay awake, the phone rang. My sister was calling to let me know that my brother and his wife were on their way to the hospital to deliver their first baby three months early. As my sister-in-law was rushed in for emergency surgery, my brother stood alone and scared in the sterile, pale blue hallway. When I arrived, he met me with a quivering chin, fearful eyes, and a request for prayer. Although prayer had become a thing of the past for me, I was struck with the urgency for some sort of faith.

The next couple of days we waited while my nephew, Taylor, lay in the incubator with tubes attached to his feeble body. The rest of the family came daily to the hospital where we all prayed, cried, and even laughed at times.

On the third day after Taylor's birth, I went grocery shopping and someone caught my eye as I was getting out of my car. She was an ordinary-looking little old woman wrapped in a long wool coat. As she walked slowly past, she looked at me, and in her eyes I saw oceans of kindness and warmth. When she smiled, my fear for my nephew's life disappeared. Her eyes and her gentle smile touched me so deeply that in one second I forgot what it was like to feel alone. After she continued out of sight, I continued to look at the people passing by, only this time they were different. Every person carried with them, whether it was obvious or not, innocence and the ability to heal—God. I cried for two weeks from the overwhelming feeling that He was, and had always been, right there with me.

Taylor will be sixteen this year, and my faith has not wavered since. In all those years, I have gone against everything I was taught as a child about avoiding eye contact with strangers. I listen with my eyes to what they have to say. In their eyes, I see laughter, I see tears, I see loneliness. I see a new engagement, a celebration, an anniversary. I see longing for forgiveness, and I see absolution. I see the child within. I see old age. I see sickness, and I see confusion. I see regrets, hope for a new job, fear and victory. I see culture, and I see family. I see love and faith and hope. I see the future, and I see humanity. But, most importantly, I see God. And I know that I can give to others the gift that was given to me in a stranger's eyes.

~Mary Eileen Oakes

An Unexpected Blessing

The angels minister to God's servants in time of hardship and danger.
~Billy Graham

I met the elderly man by the butcher counter in front of the marked-down meats as we both pawed through the shrink-wrapped soup bones and steaks, now faded to a putty shade of gray. I grabbed deli loaf ends of cheese and turkey, too small to be sliced by the store's machine. After I ran them through my meat grinder at home, they would make good sandwiches for my family. Our food budget was tight, and I got creative with our meals—sometimes very creative, like Hamburger Helper without the hamburger.

"You have beautiful children," commented the old man. I thanked him and turned back to my cart. The baby sat in the seat, the four-year-old leaned back precariously from the end of the cart, and my seven-year-old stood reading the back of a cereal box. Their combination of auburn hair and deep brown eyes often drew comments.

I'd seen many grandfatherly men like this one since moving to Baltimore six months before from the Midwest. We had never lived in a big city, but my husband's education brought us here for a two-year fellowship. I discovered that like many older cities, Baltimore is pieced together from ethnic neighborhoods. Our apartment complex nestled in the heart of the Hasidic community, and I had grown accustomed to seeing clusters of old men gathered on benches at the park and the shopping centers, arguing animatedly about anything. This man appeared to be one of this fraternity of elders.

"Children are such a blessing. How old is the little one?" he asked in his formal-sounding foreign accent.

"Almost a year," I replied. "She'll be one next week."

"And the older ones?"

"Seven and four."

He spoke to the older children. "You help your mama buy the good food, eh? You good help to your baby sister?"

They smiled shyly, and the baby began gnawing on the cart handle. Distracting her with my keys, I wiped the drool from her chin and headed for the dairy case.

The old man followed, clutching his small basket of food. "You live near to the store?"

"Not too far," I answered, rearranging the produce to make room for a gallon of milk.

"I am also living not too far. You could give me a ride home?"

I noted the man's meager groceries: two bananas, some cereal, carrots and a package of chicken thighs from the discount bin. Fraying threads straggled from the cuffs of his suit coat, and the fabric of its elbows was shiny from long wear, though his pants and shirt were neatly ironed. Comb marks furrowed his gray hair.

"I can give you a ride," I told him. "I just have a few more things to get."

"Thank you," he nodded. It was almost a bow.

Inspecting a carton of eggs, I shook my head at my own naiveté, realizing that I'd been conned. Should I have agreed to drive him home? A few compliments on my children appealing to my vanity, and I was ready to open my car to a stranger. What was I thinking? The old man was obviously using me. Undoubtedly, he'd scammed other moms with little children before, approaching them in the store and ingratiating himself. Why did he need a ride, anyway? Did he not drive? Bad eyesight? Or maybe he was just too poor.

I knew how hard it was to afford a car. We'd just bought a small Honda so my husband could commute downtown while I kept the station wagon. Until recently, I'd shopped for groceries and run errands only on weekends, confined to the apartment during my husband's working hours. I missed my family, my friends, and my church back in Minnesota.

"Why did we have to move here?" I'd grumbled to my husband. Maybe now that I had a car, I wouldn't feel so isolated. It had been hard to form new relationships when I couldn't go anywhere during the week.

Thinking of my newfound four-wheeled freedom, it seemed selfish not to give him a ride. It wasn't like picking up a hitchhiker; this man was too elderly to be any threat. And so what if he'd picked me out as an easy mark just to score a ride home? Wheeling my cart into the checkout line, I decided it would be my good deed for the day.

Somehow escaping the sugar gauntlet of expensive gum and candy near the cash register, I unloaded my groceries and wrote a check, then looked around for the old man as the clerk bagged my purchases. Sure enough, he stood near the door with a cart holding two brown bags.

"I'm this way," I smiled, and he followed me to the car, insisting on lifting my bags into the back of the station wagon for me.

I followed his directions through a maze of twisting streets, noting landmarks so I could find my way back to the main road, then home from there. Pulling up before a drab brick apartment building, I turned off the ignition and started to open my door.

"Wait," instructed the man. "I want to give you something."

"No, that's not necessary," I protested, thinking he wanted to pay me for the ride.

"I want to give you something," he repeated. "A blessing for you and your children." The old man turned sideways to face me on the front seat and solemnly bowed his head. He intoned words in Hebrew, words I did not understand. My children sat quietly, listening and curious. He repeated the blessing in English, and this time it had a familiar ring to it. I recognized the benediction from my own Christian upbringing:

"The Eternal bless you and protect you.

"The Eternal deal kindly and graciously with you.

"The Eternal bestow favor upon you and grant you peace."

"Thank you," I whispered. My heart was touched by the old man's unexpected gift, his generosity of spirit. I felt the warm comfort of God's hand through this small gesture.

As we waved goodbye, I knew God's blessing was with us, here in this new place or wherever we would go, and would be with us always. I'd just needed a reminder.

~Betsy McPhee

46

The Angel Wore Cowboy Boots

*I just thank God I can make a living doing something I enjoy
as much as I do playing music.*
~Charlie Daniels

Monday, January 19, 2004, dawned crisp and cool. It was going to be another beautiful day here in the Rio Grande Valley. As I headed upstairs to my home office that morning, I distinctly remember thinking that my daily routine would be back to normal after all the holiday celebrations.

Our oldest son, Jason, had left the day before to return to Texas A&M in College Station. Our middle son, Ryan, was back at high school, and over the weekend our youngest, Jeremy, had enjoyed his eighth birthday with a big pizza party with his friends. For the first time in nearly a month, I would have a quiet house to work in.

That evening, my wife Donna and I returned from a booster club meeting at the high school. We were surprised to see Jeremy still sitting at the kitchen table doing his homework. In a terrifying moment, our "normal" life changed forever. Jeremy could not hold his pencil in his right hand. Something was very wrong.

After three days of numerous doctors and tests, we learned that Jeremy had a tumor the size of a golf ball located deep in his brain just above his brain stem. After the initial eight-hour surgery, we were relieved to hear that the tumor was categorized as a low grade. It was a good tumor to have if you had one, but it was in just about the worst place to have it. Because of the depth and size of the tumor, the neurosurgeon had to operate a second time a couple of days later.

An ICU is never a quiet or dark place. Following his second surgery, Jeremy lay motionless in what seemed like a black hole. Tubes were coming out of everywhere, and it was at that point I hit absolute rock bottom. As I sat in the semi-darkness and cried silently, a little voice asked, "Daddy, what time is it?" I was so shocked that I looked at Jeremy, but his eyes were still closed. Had I imagined it? I reached out and grabbed his hand, calling his name softly. Again, "Daddy, what time is it?"

"5:15," I said.

"A.M. or P.M.?"

"A.M.," I replied.

"Okay," he said without ever opening his eyes. My tears of fear turned to tears of joy.

Jeremy's long rehabilitation began a day or two later. Because of the location of the tumor, his motor functions on his right side took a real hit. It was like he had suffered a stroke. Initially, he could not even move his right arm or leg. The right side of his face was paralyzed and turned a nasty yellow color.

He had to learn to walk again, but within the week he was proudly running laps around the hospital floor. We began intensive work with a speech therapist to rebuild his vocabulary, as he would confuse the names of similar objects, like calling a giraffe a gorilla.

Nearly two weeks later, on a cold and rainy February afternoon, our favorite neurologist, Dr. Mike, surprised us with "Are you ready to go home?" The three-hour drive home seemed like three days. Jeremy slept in the back seat as Donna and I sat mostly silent and exhausted, lost in our thoughts and fears. As we finally exited the freeway a couple of miles from home, Jeremy's voice surprised us from the backseat. "Can we play my favorite song?" A quick push of some buttons, and "The Devil Went Down to Georgia" by The Charlie Daniels Band filled our Suburban. In that moment, as the first few chords broke the silence, the curtain of darkness was lifted!

As usual, we all sang along and changed the name of the boy from Johnny to Jeremy like we always did! Donna and I laughed until we cried tears of joy because we realized for the first time that just maybe the worst was behind us. The song ended exactly when we pulled up to the curb in front of our house. We were home!

Jeremy missed a month of school and then went part-time for another couple of weeks. Along the way, he had to learn to write with his left hand, which was remarkably easy for him. His friends in his second grade class become his protectors, and he bravely went to every doctor's appointment and therapy session without a single word of complaint. Although he was participating in his recovery, he had yet to move from a victim to a survivor.

We knew from research that reaching that milestone of "survivor" was the key to a successful long-term recovery from any type of major injury or illness. As the summer months came and went, Jeremy still had not crossed that mountain. He was going through the motions of therapy three times a week, but he simply was not making the progress we had expected or prayed for. As third grade began that fall, we wondered if that day would ever come.

Fast forward to December of that same year. I'm in the advertising business, and one of my radio reps let me know that one of their stations was changing formats to classic country—and they were bringing The Charlie Daniels Band to town for a concert to kick off the new format! I asked for backstage passes to meet Charlie, but was told that all the passes had already been given out. However, they could seat us right up front at the concert.

I was not to be denied. I located an e-mail address that I hoped would get to Charlie and wrote to him about Jeremy. Later that very day, and much to my surprise, an e-mail arrived that simply said, "I would love to meet Jeremy… Come by our hotel and pick up the passes at the front desk the day of the show." It was signed simply "Charlie."

Concert night came quickly, and we had not told Jeremy what the evening would bring. As we drove up to the La Villa Real, he quickly figured out we were going to see Charlie Daniels in concert,

47

Overcoming Fear

Do the thing you fear, and the death of fear is certain.
~Ralph Waldo Emerson

t was happening again. I couldn't breathe, and my heart slammed against my rib cage. Was I dying? But I was twenty-four years old, and I wanted to live. I tried to suck in enough air to breathe as I stumbled next door and rang the doorbell.

"Please help me," I said, gasping out the words around my fear. This was a new neighborhood, and I didn't know my neighbor, but she got her car keys and purse and drove me to the nearest doctor's office.

When we approached the receptionist, her face reflected the same fear I felt. She jumped up and went through a door, coming back in seconds with the doctor, who led me to a treatment room. In a soothing voice, he asked questions as I wrung my hands and tried to keep fear at bay. But all my senses were focused on the need to breathe, which was harder and harder and drained my energy.

After listening to different areas of my chest and back, the doctor sat on his stool and looked into my eyes. "You're having a severe panic attack. Can you tell me what's wrong?"

What's wrong? I was twenty-four years old and life wasn't working for me. I had a sad, lonely childhood, and now I was married to a serial adulterer. I was the problem, and everyone knew the secret to happiness but me. I didn't want to live and die with nothing good in between.

I walked out of his office on trembling legs with a handbag full of tranquilizers that were supposed to help me cope. They didn't work because they couldn't make my husband faithful; they couldn't make me feel worthy of love; they couldn't convince me that life was full of promise or give me hope for the future. The pills only dulled the fear, but didn't get rid of it.

I soon found a way to diminish the severity of the attacks. I would stay in a safe place and not leave home—for the next ten years. Alcohol helped to relax me more than the tranquilizers, so I ditched the pills and couldn't wait until five o'clock every day, when I deemed it acceptable to have a scotch and water.

At times, I felt strong enough to go to dinner with my husband and children. On rare occasions, I went shopping or attended something at one of the children's schools. But those occurrences were rare, and for ten years I was mostly housebound.

To the outside world, it looked like I lived a privileged life. The maid drove the children to school and did the shopping, a hairdresser came to the house to do my hair, and department stores sent saleswomen to my house, their cars loaded with clothes for me to try on in my bedroom while terror held me prisoner. When the attacks came, it was like living inside a horror movie that wouldn't end.

After years of suffering, I would have talked to a monkey if I thought he could help.

One bitterly cold winter day, I felt desperate. I had to find help or I couldn't go on. The president of my daughter's P.T.A. had the reputation of being "religious." The few times we spoke at school, she seemed to have a sweet, gentle spirit, so I decided to risk it.

I called and asked if I could talk to her about school-related things. We made a date for two o'clock. I had learned to function with the alcohol, so I tossed down two scotch and waters for courage and drove the four long, terror-riddled blocks to her house.

The maid ushered me into a lovely home that smelled of oranges and cinnamon. Marilyn Nislar waited for me in the family room, and we settled onto a comfortable sofa before a roaring fire and drank Russian tea.

Marilyn's family had been chosen Family of the Year by the *Lubbock Avalanche-Journal* recently, and the room was filled with loving touches and photographs. I didn't belong in this house. I wasn't sure I belonged anywhere, but I was sure I wasn't worthy to be there. But where else could I go?

After a few minutes, I took a deep breath and decided to find out just what kind of Christian she was. I had nothing to lose. My life was out of control, and I couldn't fix it. In a torrent of tears, I spilled out my story — the awfulness, the pain, the despair, the hopelessness, and the shameful secrets of my wild-child youth.

When I finished, she did an amazing thing. With tears sliding down her cheeks, she put her arms around me and said, "Oh, Jan, I always knew you were one of God's special kids. I just didn't know how special you were."

I was stunned. She thought I was special. Was it possible God loved me? Wouldn't He count as someone who cared, and did Marilyn, really? This was heady stuff.

I didn't walk out of her house whole, but I walked out with a hope that changed my life. Sitting in her cozy family room, I saw Jesus, just like it was two thousand years ago when He hung on a cross for me.

Ralph Waldo Emerson said, "Do the thing you fear, and the death of fear is certain." I began the process of recovery by leaving my safe place — my house. Hope gave me the courage to try. Sometimes I hyperventilated the whole way, but I went.

I wasn't alone anymore. God cared, or so I had been told. I started taking tiny steps toward freedom.

~Jan Brand

Upon This Rock

There is nothing in the world so much like prayer as music is.
~William P. Merrill

"You've got a beautiful voice. We'd love it if you would sing a special song Sunday."

I enjoyed the obvious warmth in the pastor's words, but the style of music was foreign to me. This was a Presbyterian church with music so different from what I'd known in my Catholic childhood.

Even though I'd only gone back to church to get a free hour of babysitting for my two toddlers each week, I enjoyed the people. If I was going to continue with this church, I should get involved. My brothers had all begun attending Assemblies of God churches, and my youngest brother was even a pastor. Maybe he would have some suggestions.

"Merrill, I need to sing a song at church, and I don't know any of this kind of music. Where do I start?"

Merrill's counsel led me to a small Christian bookstore. I'd never been to a store devoted to Christian books and music, but on a lunch hour from work, I climbed the steps and entered the small store. Every shelf was filled, and an overflow of products made it hard to navigate through the narrow aisles.

The owner, Peter, was obviously busy, but he took the time to help me select songs that might fit my voice. He patiently listened as I mentioned various pop artists and songs I enjoyed. From that list, he was able to send me to a tape player and headset with accompaniment tracks from well-known Christian artists.

For years, I had sat in a hard pew at Holy Name Church, whispering with my siblings, making fun of the rituals, and being bored. I was only there because I had no choice, and as soon as I left home, I left the church. Even though I thought I had retained nothing from my youth, the music made me realize I not only remembered words from the past, but now understood them. What had been like Greek to me, seemingly going in one ear and flowing at lightning speed out the other, had simply been waiting. Like a flickering flame needing only the slightest breeze, the words set to music fanned the embers of belief already in my heart. The songs I listened to that day had portions of scripture in them, just waiting to be remembered. My lunch hour passed all too quickly, and I dashed back to the office.

For the rest of the week, I quietly slipped up the stairs into the overcrowded shop, and grabbed some cassettes and a player. Artist after artist sang of a God I wanted to know. He seemed more real to me after those few days than He ever had growing up.

The Presbyterian church I was attending was filled with pleasant people, but they never had an invitation or explained what it was to be a Christian. I could have gone months, or even years, and never known about a personal relationship with Christ.

On the last day of that fateful week, I listened to Sandi Patty singing a song called "Upon This Rock." My eyes filled with tears, and I knew, without really knowing how, that I had to invite Christ into my heart, to become a follower of His.

God is perfect in His choice of timing and location. With strangers surrounding me, and tears cascading, I gave my life to Him. I also knew I wanted to use my gift of music for Him, since it was music that had opened my heart.

I never told Peter what his shop did in my life. Rhema Bookstore was a struggling business, and there must have been times when Peter wanted to give up the dream of using his abilities to win souls for Christ. I'm sure Peter must sometimes wonder if his work really matters.

Yes, Peter. It does.

~Carmen Leal

Mr. Sunshine

He giveth more grace when the burdens grow greater.
~Annie Johnson Flint

I wake up in a cold sweat and can't stop sobbing. The dream is so real—a child trapped, screaming that will not stop. It is me screaming. I cannot quit shaking while I pull the bedclothes around me. Restless, I can't go back to sleep. In the darkness, I pray, "God, when will these nightmares end?"

There is no answer as I stumble from my bed and into the shower to calm my nerves. It isn't morning yet. I must get away for a while to think. No, I don't want to think. The shadows of my past cling to me. No matter how I try, I can't cast away the burden of me as a child, abandoned, hurting.

I scrawl a note for my oldest daughter of five kids telling her where I've gone. Being a Saturday, they will probably sleep until I return. I am a single mom.

I rush out the door and down the hill. "I can't take anymore," I tell God. He already knows my pain, but I don't seem to reach Him. I feel too desperate, too hopeless.

Recklessly, I half-walk, half-run for what seems like miles. I end up near my favorite lake. In the pre-dawn, I notice an old coupe parked there and groan inwardly. Someone must be here this early when I'd like to be alone.

Light barely filters through the trees when I pass the car and slowly follow the path down to the stream bank.

I see a bald man in ragged jeans and a faded sweatshirt crouching at the water's edge. For a fleeting second, I wonder if he will accost me. Should I leave? Then he turns slightly and notices me. His features aren't striking. He's an ordinary man until he smiles. My fears dissolve as warmth floods through me. The sun isn't up, yet the heat of its rays flow from him. I stand rooted to the spot, transfixed.

"I leave you be and give you your space," he says.

"No," I answer, surprising myself. I thought I wanted my solitude. Now as I sit down on a large boulder not far from him, I add, "I'd like the company."

His serene manner brings tranquility to my troubled mind. His glowing countenance penetrates my aching heart like a healing balm.

He lays down his fishing pole and concentrates on the rocks before him.

"Lookie, here's a pretty one. You can always find a pretty one." He grins at me and doesn't seem to mind me staring.

My eyes focus on the stones by him. "They all look like gray blobs to me in this gray dawn," I reflect. "Kind of like my life."

I realize he seems to be peering through me. His look pierces my soul, but it doesn't frighten me or make me feel uncomfortable. I turn my hot face away to hide my unbidden emotion.

He walks over to me, reaches out his stub of a finger, and gently lifts my chin. I don't flinch or pull away. He wipes at a tear on my cheek.

"There's lots of sadness in the world, and I'm sorry you be carryin' more than your share."

I wonder if there is a hurt in his old heart since he seems to understand me so well. I can't speak through the lump in my throat. I have not received this kind of comfort in a long time. His whole being radiates a peace I had never known.

I have the urge to snuggle up to him, to become a part of that assurance he seems to possess within his entire self. He reminds me of a big, safe teddy bear. Who is he? Someone sent to rescue me from the harshness of my circumstances. I long for his strong arms to steady me the way God tries to do so every day of my life — if I would let Him. How could I have shut Him out?

I sweep my arm across the sky to take it all in. "I want to thank God for all this and embrace this new day with joy, not dread."

"Ya can't heal until ya get rid of the anger and bitterness," my companion acknowledges. Handing me a large stone, he motions for me to throw it into the depths below.

This is silly, I think. To humor him, I hurl the first stone into the river. It hits with a thud. Amazingly, I feel better.

Each time I thrust more rocks farther into the water, I imagine letting go of revenge toward my abusers. The agony of my own deep wounds seems to lift.

"The shame and guilt are gone," I exclaim in awe.

"The relief of getting rid of something pent-up can give ya a solace ya have never known."

"And forgiveness," I whisper.

The exercise leaves me spent. I relax against a nearby tree and close my eyes.

Suddenly, the sun peeps over the top of the hill and glimmers with hope. It shatters the ice that has been in my heart for years.

"Jesus be here with ya," the man states.

It is true. I know this with every fiber of my soul.

"Give that burden ya got to Him. He's strong enough, and He's able to bear it. Ya be a lot lighter feelin' goin' home."

I feel a glow from this man and believe he knows a great deal about Christ's love for me.

I squeeze my eyes shut while I picture God taking sacks filled with my darkness and garbage from me. As the weight and baggage and anguish I had packed around lifts from me, I offer up a prayer of gratitude to God.

I open my eyes, and the man is gone. I blink in disbelief. Did he go through the woods, disappear or what? I will never know, but his presence remains like a candle, giving me faith.

I accept that the Lord has been here with me through this old man. God is not a stranger anymore. He knew I needed Jesus with skin on.

I sense someone touching my auburn hair and speaking to me with perfect harmony. I can hear the old man say, "There be no regrettin'! Every day be a golden one like that sun risin' high in the sky to bless ya."

My heart cries out, "What if sadness comes again?"

I hear his answer. "There will always be sadness. Ya are not alone with it as ya feel those feelings. God be helping ya' through it."

I would never have the same despair again. That day in the mountains, my life was impacted forever by an angel.

~Pam Bostwick

The Second Mile

Angels whisper to a man when he goes for a walk.
~Raymond Inmon

I n October 2010, I was volunteering at the animal shelter in Waynesboro, Pennsylvania, and this particular day it was shutting down early. Being only fifteen, I could not drive, and my father was coaching a team in a soccer tournament about four miles away from the shelter. I had no cell phone, so I tried to call from the shelter's phone, but received no answer.

I left a message: "Hey, Dad! The shelter had to close early, so I'm going to start walking toward the soccer fields. I'll see you soon."

It seems to me that when you are walking a long distance alone, you notice things you wouldn't normally notice, and you think of things you wouldn't normally think about. You hear the birds, the wind, leaves rustling in the trees, and other noises. But your thoughts are what really occupy your attention.

As I was walking down the road I began asking myself questions I had never really asked before. I was questioning my faith, the reality of a one true God, and other related topics. I went to church almost every week. I sang the songs, prayed with the pastor, and listened to the service. But it just didn't make sense to me.

About a mile into my walk, I realized that it isn't the facts themselves I don't comprehend; it's the way they're taught. I didn't like the fact that a man stood in front of me and two hundred other people every Sunday and told us what we should believe. He told us what we should be doing, and if we didn't do it, we would spend eternity in fire.

At my age, I did not like taking orders. It made me feel as if I was living in a dictatorship—God being the all-powerful dictator, the preacher his obedient soldier, and me the helpless civilian. But I gave God one last chance and prayed for what I thought would be the last time. It was a prayer I'm sure many have said before: "God, if you really are there, show me. Send me some kind of sign to prove it." I said it aloud, and then I kept walking.

As I entered downtown Waynesboro, I saw a man walking on the same side of the street in my direction. I had been walking for about two miles, and this was the first person I had seen. It was a relief to finally see another person and know I was not too far from my destination.

When he was a few feet in front of me, we both smiled and nodded. The man asked, "How are we today?" And not wanting to be rude, I replied, "Not too bad, sir. And you?" The man was older, maybe fifty or sixty years of age, and I didn't want to be disrespectful.

"I'm great!" he replied with the biggest smile on his face. Up to this point, our conversation had seemed to be a normal walk-by greeting. But it is what the man said next that changed me.

"And let me tell you why I'm so great, young man," he exclaimed with a smile. "I know something—or someone—that makes my entire life worth living." I had stopped to listen to the man at this point. Something about the way he spoke with such enthusiasm made his words worth listening to.

"I know God!" he said with his hands in the air and his eyes looking to the sky. He explained to me how much his life had changed since he began believing and how he now feels everyone should know the Good News.

Then the man looked at me and asked, "Brother, do you know God? Do you believe?"

I looked down for a second, and many thoughts ran through my mind. I had prayed for God to show me a sign, and I asked Him to prove himself to me. And then this stranger had approached and questioned my faith.

With a smile, I looked up at the old man, still with the happiest expression on his face, and I said, "Yes, sir, I do. And you are the reason I do."

I told the man the story of my walk, my questioning, and my prayer. And the smile on his face grew wider with excitement. Then I shook the man's hand, gave my thanks, and wished him a nice day. I walked the last two miles with a smile on my face—the same smile that had adorned the stranger's face. One man on that second mile changed my life.

~Nik Schanzenbacher, age 17

Without a Word

*And the peace of God, which transcends all understanding, will guard your
hearts and your minds in Christ Jesus.*
~Philippians 4:7

Doughnuts. Krispy Kreme doughnuts. That's what I wanted. Who ever heard of a Southern town without a Krispy Kreme? It was early on a weekday morning, and I had been more than an hour early for an appointment, an odd twist of fate that left me with nothing to do except feel my stomach growl. I was vaguely familiar with the little city nestled into the mountains, but I was hungry, and there wasn't a single doughnut shop around. I settled for a Danish at a local burger place, along with a big cup of black coffee. The girl smiled at me as she handed me the Danish and coffee.

"Are you new in town?" she asked.

"Well, yes and no," I answered. "I have to wait for an appointment, and this is the closest I could come to a doughnut shop."

She laughed as she assured me that the Danish was about as close as I would ever get to a doughnut in her town. I smiled back as I grabbed a newspaper and headed to the back, away from the smoking section.

I barely glanced at the headlines as I bit into the Danish. It was a time of reflection for me. I was miserable. I had always been a spiritual person, but I had found that I could no longer pray. It had been years since I had stepped into a church and, frankly, if there was a God, why was He not answering me? I felt as though I was going out of my mind.

About that time, I noticed a man sitting just inside the non-smoking section, reading a book and busily scribbling notes. I guessed him to be about seventy-something. Quite handsome, he was an African-American gentleman with beautiful white hair. He called out greetings to anyone who spoke to him, and all the young black men treated him with quiet dignity. He seemed to be related to everyone in town.

Between greetings, he went back to his book and his notes, and continued to scribble. Every once in a while, he would read a phrase, and he would smile. It must be a diary, I thought. Perhaps it was the writing of some beloved person in his life. Without a word, he conveyed a sense of gentleness. The expression on his face was like nothing I had ever seen. I longed for that peace. I needed that peace!

I was captivated by this man. He was… well… beautiful, as though angels surrounded him. He continued with his reading, writing, and greetings.

Finally, I got up the nerve to speak to him. "You seem to know everybody," I said. He looked up and smiled at me. His dark eyes behind his round glasses were kind.

"No," he said. "I've never been here before."

"Really? People you don't know say 'hello' to you?"

"Sometimes." He smiled and went back to his reading.

There was something about that book. What was that book? I tried not to stare, but peripherally I never took my eyes off him. He continued to pore over the words in the book and, finally, he moved. He turned to reach for something, and the title of the book became visible: THE HOLY BIBLE!

I sat there for what seemed like forever, captured by a man who exuded holiness from every pore. I was really familiar with phonies, and this man was "for real." You could see it on the faces of everyone who walked within ten feet of him. A kind of hush settled over the little burger joint, and I was enthralled. I realized that this man was totally comfortable with his God. This man was involved in a relationship! I wanted what he had, but I hadn't the slightest idea how to get it.

It was time to go or I would be late for my appointment. I stood and had an incredible impulse to walk over to him, so I did. I thanked him for just sitting there, reading the Bible, as though he were reading letters from a friend. My eyes filled with tears. My voice broke as I tried to convey the power that was released in his simple, unconscious relationship. He took my hand and held it for what seemed like an eternity. One confused white woman, and one kind, elderly black man. I felt an unearthly love for that man, but I just couldn't speak.

I listened as I held his hand, and he told me about his aunt, who was elderly and very ill. He was from Ohio and had just traveled down to check on her. She was being hospitalized, and he was only in the burger place waiting for her to be settled into her room. I could feel his goodness steal through me, and I wanted to do all sorts of things. I wanted to weep, just break out into uncontrollable sobs and tell him all about my life. More than anything, I wanted to know who gave him his incredible peace, but I never asked. He let go of my hand, and we said farewell.

Before I left, however, he gave me some pamphlets and said, "Whenever you are ready to have your questions answered," as though he had read my thoughts, "read these. In the meantime, I'll be praying for you." I wanted to throw my arms around him, but I just said "thank you" and left.

It was a long time before I began my journey to an understanding of God, and I lost those pamphlets somewhere along the way. In the years since that brief encounter, I've come to experience that peace "which transcends all understanding," and the God who gives it. So, thank you, my friend, my angel. You changed my life.

~Jaye Lewis

Finding Faith
Through Signs

"Ask the LORD your God for a sign, whether in the deepest depths or in the highest heights."

~Isaiah 7:11

A Sign from Above

A faith is a necessity to a man.
Woe to him who believes in nothing.
~Victor Hugo

Whoooosh! Whoooosh! My head shot up from my reading. What was that sound? It seemed to be coming from just outside my sliding glass door. I'd lived in my condo for two years and had never heard anything like it. Whatever it was, it was very close. It demanded my attention as I was poring over the help-wanted ads in the Sunday paper. It was the weekend after Labor Day, and I was nearing the end of my third month without work. With each passing day, my anxiety went up a notch, and my faith went down a notch.

I'd moved from my home state of Michigan to Nevada for a job promoting tourism. After nearly five years, I was shocked by the news I was being laid off along with some others in the organization where I was employed. But I figured I wouldn't have much trouble finding another position in my field of public relations with the contacts I'd made through the years.

Yet, I'd only averaged two job interviews a month. I tried to ignore the fact that the state's unemployment office had flagged me as someone who might be hard to place. The designation required that I attend some employment counseling sessions. They don't know me, I thought. I was a hard worker and would make a job out of getting a job. But here it was months later, and I had nothing. I had to pay for my own medical insurance now and had a large house payment. More money was going out than was coming in.

Summer was drawing to a close. The evenings were cooler and the days were shorter, a reminder that time was marching on. My family back home was supportive and called to check in, but living across the country all they could do was pray. My faith was beginning to waver.

At church, I was slowly withdrawing from activities, which was unusual for me. Since joining the congregation, I had rarely missed a Sunday and counted many of the members as close friends. Now, in my worst moments, I had fleeting thoughts that God didn't exist and I was totally on my own.

There was one bright spot. One month prior to Labor Day, the owner of a local ad agency had called me with an offer to work as a publicist to promote an annual hot air balloon race held in the area. I gladly accepted, though the job was temporary.

The balloon races were always a big event. They drew thousands of tourists, who watched dozens of hot air balloons rise at dawn over the course of three mornings. The races were always held the week-end after Labor Day.

The balloons came in all shapes and sizes, with some advertising a product or service. Along with the traditional shapes, there were balloons in the shape of the Energizer Bunny, a cow, Tony the Tiger, a whiskey bottle, the old woman who lived in a shoe, and others. Each race morning, excited spectators gathered in the pre-dawn darkness to witness this amazing sight of glowing gas-fired balloons inflating and then rising up in the morning sky.

As a publicist, I began working a few weeks prior to the race as a receptionist at the agency. On the mornings of the event, it was my duty to assist TV stations broadcasting live from the race. I loved the feeling of getting up and rushing out the door to a job.

But now it was my second-to-last day of work. After working at the races in the early morning, I had returned home. Though the balloons were still in the air, my job assisting TV reporters with their live shots was done. The first thing I did was tear into the Sunday paper. While out of work, each Sunday morning I always opened the newspaper jobs section with a burst of hope, thinking this might be the day I would spot a position with my name on it. But as I got closer and closer to the end of the listings and saw nothing I was qualified for, my heart began to sink.

Though I was almost too anxious in those difficult days to pray, I began to pray anyway. "Dear God, when will this freefall end?" I pleaded. "Don't you know that I'm getting tired?"

Then I heard it—that whooshing sound. I couldn't imagine what it was. I got up and stepped onto the patio. There in the sky was a hot air balloon in the shape of Jesus. In his robe and beard, the image was unmistakable. When I'd seen the balloon ascending hours before at the park, I had thought little of it, just another of the many balloons out there that morning. Now I couldn't believe how close it was to my house.

I stared in disbelief. The sound of the gas burner signaled its presence. The amazing thing was how close it was to my home. I gazed up at the people in the basket.

Eventually, it drifted away. I walked back in the house stunned by what appeared to be a sign from God. Being someone who is wary of so-called signs from above, I had to admit that the close presence of this particular balloon, at the time I'd needed some hope, seemed more than coincidence. I felt a rush of assurance that God was present in my fear of the future.

What were the chances of this happening? It wasn't the cow, liquor bottle or real estate balloon. No, it was the Jesus balloon that needed the right air current to find my house. I went about my day with a new confidence that something would come my way.

Eventually, I moved back to Michigan to be closer to family and I landed a job in my chosen field of public relations. I still treasure that experience with the hot air balloon, which reopened my heart to faith and made me more accepting of a sign from God—especially when it was nearly a hundred feet high and hovering at my door!

~Carol Tanis

Leaves

The fall of a leaf is a whisper to the living.
~Russian Proverb

My neighbor, Ben, took his own life. He was in his late fifties and left behind a wife and two daughters in college.

No one in our modest cul-de-sac of three carefully tended homes suspected anything was amiss. Ben was devoted to his family and doted on his girls. A voracious reader, he was quick with a joke or a wry observation. Recently, he had taken up bicycling to reduce stress and stay fit. Only weeks before his death, the three couples had dinner at an upscale restaurant, and Ben talked about his brood, his job and the future.

Ben was a giving man. My own two daughters, who had lived next to Ben's family since they were barely able to talk, knew where to get bicycle tires fixed, secure a tasty snack or find a sympathetic ear about their youthful tribulations. Ben's asphalt driveway served as a launching pad for the dreamy thoughts of my two girls and their friends.

Ben was a fastidious person. On weekends, when he was not avidly reading, he was tending to his car or home. In the fall, he was the first among the three houses to remove the leaves from his front yard. In the winter, he would plow his driveway even before the snow had stopped falling.

I was very different from Ben. My car was old and scarred, my lawn was the last to be raked, and we were always the last to shovel. More than once, after Ben had carefully purged his front yard of leaves, a vigorous October wind would launch a supply from my own property and bury his fine green lawn. Yet he never complained, offered an unkind remark or otherwise made me feel less of a neighbor. In the time we had together, a cross or disparaging word never crossed our lips, and it was Ben's good nature that made this possible.

When we learned of Ben's death, in fact witnessed its grim aftermath in the flash of police lights and ambulance sirens at the foot of his property, we were devastated. In stunned silence, as his white-draped body was carried out on a stretcher, my wife and I turned from our grief and confronted the dreadful task of informing our two young daughters that Ben was gone from our lives. Looking into their immature eyes—one fourteen, the other only eleven—I struggled for the right words.

In such times, I am told that one's faith should be a source of strength, but I was not particularly religious. My upbringing was a parade of ritualistic and meaningless holidays and events. In my belief system, there was no room for anything other than hard-bitten honesty: Ben was dead.

In the days that followed, we were consumed by sorrow, self-doubt and especially questions. Why had Ben taken his life? Had we missed the signs? Could we have done more? Should I have been a better neighbor and friend? Through it all, there was no room for faith. Ben was gone.

My older daughter took it particularly hard. An imaginative child, her afternoons before Ben's death often would be consumed by drawing figure eights on his driveway. The method was not important. Sometimes, she was on her bike, other times her Rollerblades. Since Ben worked from home, they would talk about everything.

Ben's funeral service was held in a quintessential New England church on a beautiful fall day with the leaves in full splendor. Dressed in my finest navy suit, I thought how Ben might have loved and hated those leaves. Loved them for their beauty; hated them for finding their way to his lawn or, worse, to mine.

My older daughter wrote a moving tribute, but given her age, Ben's wife asked that I deliver her words at the service. With Ben's coffin set in the middle of the church, we spoke of his life and our collective loss. We bade farewell to a husband, father, son, neighbor, friend. It seemed too much to bear.

As the minister's hopeful words sought to heal, I felt nothing. If faith was a teacher, I was not a willing student. If religion had healing powers, I was having none of it. Ben was gone, and I was angry.

Afterwards, Ben's family held a reception in his memory at a Victorian-style inn overlooking the bay. With photographs of my neighbor on display, I wandered in a daze through the crowded rooms, mingling with strangers and fellow neighbors. Engaging in small talk, I tried to bury the burning question: Why?

We reminisced about Ben's life. Each person had a special recollection about our friend. From one neighbor, I learned that Ben had been a Navy officer in Vietnam. Another shared that Ben participated in a weekly pick-up basketball game with friends, while a third recalled that Ben had completed several century rides of 100 miles on his bicycle. In those moments, I felt guilty that I had not done more over the years to get to know Ben better.

Sitting at the bar nursing a drink, I learned something else from a fellow neighbor: Ben would get upset when my leaves blew onto his property. Stunned and embarrassed by this admission, I excused myself and went outside to be alone. Gazing at a majestic blue sky, I apologized to Ben. For not knowing him as I should. For not being a more caring neighbor. For the leaves.

As I turned back inside, I felt something gently pass across my chest. At first, I thought nothing of it. But a moment later, my hand slipped inside my suit jacket, into the breast pocket. There, near the bottom of the pocket was a... leaf.

I would like to believe that the leaf was a message from Ben: All is forgiven.

I will never know, of course, if that leaf came from a divine hand or something more earthly, perhaps a wayward gust of autumn's fury. I suppose it does not matter. For me, the leaf is a reminder that Ben's spirit lives on in the hearts of those he left behind. I know he will live in mine. That, I am sure, is the essence of faith.

~David A. Wollin

Sea Treasures

The cure for anything is salt water—sweat, tears, or the sea.
~Isak Dinesen

I stood at the shore alone, weeping. Gray skies and silvery waves were all I could see on this blustery February day, the coastline as rough and rocky as our lives had become. And there wasn't a thing I could do to fix it.

Months had passed since my husband had lost the job he'd held for more than twenty years. Work he'd done well, and taken pride in. Work we assumed he'd have until he retired in a few years. We shouldn't have assumed.

After lunch the day they let him go, we started on a résumé, compiling information on employers from as far back as a quarter century, despite the fact that many of the businesses were gone, the owners deceased. We drove downtown and bought a newspaper. Snapped the rubber band and scanned the classifieds. Searched the phone book for similar businesses in nearby towns.

Every morning, he'd get out of bed, grab a cup of hot coffee, and apply for jobs at several places. And every afternoon, he'd return, just a little more worn down, a bit more discouraged. The bills were starting to pile up. I was concerned about keeping the house.

We were so naïve. Even at the start of a recession, businesses are cutting back. Hiring slows to a stop. And with David being so close to retirement, his age had become a liability. His job skills were too specific, and he'd performed them for so many years, they'd become obsolete.

We were determined to not only survive this setback, but to find an even better job for him. A better life for us. Something we could count on.

And then we got the news. A tumor. Centered near David's carotid artery, his pituitary gland and his optic nerve, we listened as one doctor called it a pituitary tumor, the surgeon choosing the term brain tumor. We were stunned. The doctors wanted to perform the surgery as soon as possible.

We set the date for the operation. In a couple of weeks, our lives would be irrevocably altered, for better or worse. We could only hope. Heading home from the hospital, we sat like two automatons side by side, silent in our thoughts. The unspeakable had intruded on our lives. There were no words left.

We decided to rent a cabin for a couple of days on the rugged coast near our town in Oregon. We set up camp, cozy in the small space. The drive, the stress, the warmth of the cabin had all caught up with David.

"I'm going to take a nap. Aren't you tired, Heidi?"

Tired, yes, but so restless that sleep was out of the question.

"You go ahead and sleep. I'm going to take a short walk. I'll be right back."

David had been changing over the past months, so gradually that I'd scarcely noticed. Once full of energy, he now loved to nap. His face and body had rounded. His stomach was always upset. He forgot things, became confused easily. I had attributed all these things to just getting older. Now that I knew the truth, I was terrified.

Quietly, I shut the door. Outside, the craggy mountains tumbled down to the shore. Tall pines swayed as the wind cried and moaned, sea foam whipping up and spraying me. There were no boats out to sea that day as far as I could tell—just endless churning water. Gray and empty.

It matched my emotions exactly. Helpless. Hopeless.

Walking the strand, I listened. A gust of cold air covered my sighs. I felt the mist gently wet my face, as though offering to hide my tears. At last, I could let go, my sobs mixing with the sounds of nature's discontent. I stared up at the stormy sky.

Through the years, my faith had ebbed and flowed like the waves of the sea. I considered it deep and strong, but then I'd never ridden a storm so big.

"What have we done to make you so angry?" I cried. "Why are you breaking us bit by bit?"

No answer, just silence.

I took a couple of steps farther. Looking down the rocky beach, it was covered with mature sand dollars, shattered by the current. Not a single one whole. Just like our lives together — broken, useless.

"Is this how we'll end up, God? Is that what you want?"

Still no sound, no clear answer. But as I let my eyes wander, an inexplicable sense of peace came over me.

"What is it, God? What are you saying?" I whispered.

I glanced down. And there, set apart from all the other shells, was one tiny, pristine sand dollar. Safe, sound, unbroken. I heard Him speak, silently, wordlessly, a vibration in my heart.

"Am I like this shell? Are things going to be all right?"

My nerves calmed as I felt and accepted His promise.

"But what about David? The surgery? His job?"

I knew it would be there even before I saw it. Just a short distance away was another baby sand dollar, in perfect condition despite the storms that blew all around. I scooped it up in my hand, rejoicing. Wind and waves that had crushed shells far larger had been unable to even crack these little ones. And though I searched, there were no more of them to be found.

I still have those sand dollars, framed on my wall in my office where I can see them every day. About a half-inch in size, they remind me of that time when my faith hung in the balance.

Since then, we've been so blessed. Or maybe I'm just finally noticing the blessings. I can't say for sure. But I do know that my husband's surgery was a success. He's healthy and happy, working at a job that enables him to be near preschool special needs children.

Every so often, we still visit that lonely beach where I learned about faith once and for all. I am not strong, I am not powerful, nor am I rich, by any means. But that day on the beach, I heard God's voice tell me that I am His child. I am loved. I am protected. And I will not be forgotten.

~Heidi Gaul

The Path Chosen

Jesus answered, "I tell you, Peter, before the rooster crows today,
you will deny three times that you know me."
~Luke 22:34

By my mid-fifties, I had not lost my faith so much as lost use of it through infrequent practice. I often attended my wife's church. The possessive is well applied and says much. It was my "wife's" church—I was more an observer than an involved member. I listened to Sunday sermons while not forgetting that, in my time zone, church ended just before Sunday NFL games started on TV. At this time, career goals and accomplishments, fears and failures, friends and enemies, debts and investments consumed my life. I believed in Jesus, of course. I was certain I'd met a couple of angels in my life. But I was now a shaky pillar in God's House, a weak flickering light of faith that required the tiniest of baskets to hide.

My journey back to faith began in a mall parking lot on a late summer day as I was going to a restaurant for lunch. A disheveled and desperate-looking man approached me and asked for money. I was nervous, even a bit afraid. I gave him what small change I could grab quickly from my pocket, ignoring the bills that were there. I told him, "I will look for you when I return. I will have some dollars then." It was a lie. I wanted to get away from him. When I came back to my car, I did observe this man—being pushed into the back seat of a patrol car. I was relieved.

Some weeks later, I was on a lunch run to the local deli. A

different, but equally disreputable-looking man approached me outside the deli. He told me that he was starving and asked for a couple of dollars for a sandwich. "Sure," I said, as I quickly walked around him. "When I come out, I will have some change. I will give you some money then." Exiting the deli with a bag of sandwiches, I saw him sitting in the back seat of a patrol car. This time, we made eye contact. He gave me a long, sad look—not accusing, not judgmental, but weary and sad.

Just a few weeks after this, I was happily pushing my daughter's wheelchair into the huge Halloween pumpkin lot in our town. She looked forward every year to buying the perfect pumpkin for Dad to carve. A shabby-looking young man with bleary eyes confronted us and begged me for some money. He told me he had not eaten in days and admitted that he sure would like a beer. He looked like he needed a beer, maybe two beers. "Absolutely," I said. "After my daughter and I buy our pumpkin, I will look for you in the parking lot and give you some cash." I still had not picked up on the developing trend. But as we headed back to our car, my daughter said, "Dad, there is that man—he's being arrested." She was correct. He was sitting in the back seat of a patrol car. His eyes met mine. No beer today. I heard other customers saying, "Serves him right for begging."

Three strikingly similar situations where I was asked to help a hungry person. Three times, within less than three months, I denied the request. Three times the person was hauled off to jail before my eyes. I might appear somewhat slow, but this time I felt the giant whack upside my head. Although I did not fall to the ground, I have never been the same since.

Who did I deny three times? That question burned in my mind as I pushed my daughter slowly toward our car. The answer flooded my soul and filled me with peace. We can find Jesus in the eyes of the poor. My Sunday school teachers had taught me that. My journey back to faith had begun.

What a trip. Not a straight path, no quick and easy shortcuts, it has been a tough, demanding road, with twists and unexpected hairpin turns. When mountains of doubt jumped up, valleys of resolution made the climb rewarding. What kept me going? A kindly priest, who had never noticed me before—an anonymous and faceless periodic Sunday attendee—suddenly began finding me, talking to me and encouraging me. My wife and I were asked to join a prayer group. We said yes, and I began listening and learning from the journeys of faith shared by the members.

After retirement and a life-changing move across the country, I formally joined our new church and became an active participant. New friends kept showing up and pointing the way as if on cue. Opportunities arose to join service and charity groups within my church, and I met inspiring spiritual role models. Doorways I had not seen opened. I continued exploring a book with self-turning pages, reading each page and anticipating the next.

I work with a charity organization. My calling to help the needy comes from my heart, but I also know I must not forget how easily the false promise of worldly demands can blind us to the poor who walk among us. Each time I am gifted with the opportunity to look into the eyes of someone who needs food or help paying the rent or just hope, I remember who I may be looking at. Those reminders help keep my journey on track. I am making my own signposts.

The number 3 is used in the Bible to send the most powerful messages. Three failed opportunities with poor beggars delivered an overpowering message. Yet I thank God for allowing me the time to finally hear a message that likely had been sent many times. What if I had passed away younger, say in my raw twenties, or striving thirties or forties? I know God is a forgiving God, but I suspect that my soul at that time would have increased His workload considerably. My journey continues, and I thank Him for getting me started. I will keep following the path as it opens.

~William Halderson

56

The Ice Cream Cone

"For I know the plans I have for you," declares the Lord, "plans to prosper you and not to harm you, plans to give you hope and a future."
~Jeremiah 29:11

Climbing into my car after a hard day at work, I sat there gripping the steering wheel and trying not to cry. I still needed to pick up my boys from daycare, so I made myself stay strong. Pulling out of the parking lot, I noticed the dark Portland sky threatening rain, which didn't help the melancholy mood that I was already in.

As I drove down the highway, I was bombarded with thoughts of failure and an overwhelming sense of shame. My life was far from what I had imagined it would be. I was only twenty-seven years old and a single mom of three boys. What had happened to the house with the white picket fence? To happily ever after?

Recently, I had started attending church with a friend, but there was still so much I didn't know about God. I heard sermons about His love for us, but I always felt that I had messed things up too much for Him to even know me. I seemed to be on the outside always looking in. Sometimes, I even questioned if He was there at all, the thoughts adding to my despair.

As I continued driving, I decided to stop at a grocery store along the way to surprise my boys with ice cream. Once inside the store, I headed down the aisles in search of cones. Scanning the shelves, one lone box with a clown's face caught my eye. They were the same cones my grandmother, who had raised me, would buy occasionally. They were such a treat because the cones were far different from others — each one was embossed with a boy's or a girl's name. My childhood friends and I would search the cones, trying to find our names, or we would choose the most beautiful sounding one from the stack. I grabbed the lone box from the shelf and headed to the checkout, feeling that somehow the box had been placed there just for me.

After dinner, I let my boys choose the cones they wanted. It warmed my heart to hear them laugh and giggle as they read the names on each one. When they were finally tucked into bed, I headed back to the kitchen to clean up. As I rinsed off the dishes, the tears that I had held back all day began to flow down my cheeks. Silently, I cried, feeling so lost and alone.

After I had wiped my face and finished my chores, I decided to make myself a cone, as well. I reached into the box and pulled one out. As I read the name on the cone, I couldn't believe my eyes. In capital letters, the cone was embossed with the name JESUS.

As I stood there blinking, not sure if it was real, I felt the loving arms of God wrap all around me. I began to cry once again, but this time it was from pure joy. In that moment, I realized that the Creator of the universe knew me. He knew me so intimately that He would use an ice cream cone from the memories of my childhood to show His love for me and that I was not alone.

Many times after that day, when talking to someone who was depressed and hurting, I would show them the cone and share my story. It was wonderful to see their faces transformed with a renewed sense of hope, as God revealed His love to them through an ice cream cone.

~Rose Lee Brady

57

The Lonely White Goose

Get lost in the clouds every now and then
so you never lose sight of God's wonder.
~Paul Vitale

One afternoon, I left work early. I was feeling so lonely and discouraged that I was of no use anyway, and on this particular day the weight of the world was on my shoulders. Finances, strained relationships, my mother's dementia—just to name a few—consumed my thoughts. Adding to all this was the absence of my younger daughter, who had recently left for college. I never knew I could feel so empty and alone.

I often stroll along the paths by the Mississippi River when I need to think. On this particular day, I meandered for quite some time until I got tired. I found a bench and lay down. I closed my eyes and opened my heart to God, silently bringing Him all my issues. When I finished, with tears streaming down my face, I listened to the sounds of creation around me. What caught my attention was a flock of geese pecking around in the grass. Eyes closed, I listened to their lazy honks, wishing in that moment I were a lesser animal in God's creation with fewer worries to go along with it.

When I finally decided to head home, I opened my eyes and beheld the geese. There must have been fifty of them. Scanning the flock, my eyes could not help but settle on a lone white goose. How completely out of place she looked in the midst of all the gray Canada geese around her. With her beautiful snowy down, she preened and flapped her wings. And as I watched her antics, I observed not only that she was different in color from the others, but she also stood detached from most of the rest. Were they discriminating against her?

As I continued to observe her, I noticed, though set apart from the flock, two others remained close. The three of them seemed to take pleasure in the pecking and honking in their own little circle. And as I sat with my eyes glued to the threesome, I received my sign. A voice in my heart said to me, "Just like her, I made you different from the rest. It is why you feel alone. But you never are. I am here, and you also have others to share life with you."

How true, for I immediately recalled a handful of women with whom I share the ups and downs in life's journey. My little circle never judges me, but they listen and support me through good and bad times.

As I left the park bench, instead of wishing I were something or someone else, I felt encouraged to live out the best "me" I could. I was reminded that afternoon that God made me the way I am, and although I can always improve, He was purposeful in my uniqueness. He also reminded me that He is always with me, and has provided my own circle of companions.

Since then, I have often gone down to the same area, hoping to spot the white goose again. I never did, at least not until the other day...

I found myself experiencing another type of empty nest. My son-in-law accepted a new job over 900 miles away, which meant saying goodbye to my older daughter who had lived near me for twenty-six years. I delighted in the relationship we had—meeting regularly for lunch or coffee, baking together and making our annual savory salsa batches every summer. What made it even more difficult was that she had recently given me my first grandchild. Jacob Eric was six weeks old when I traveled with this young family to help them get settled in their new home. I realized that I had let myself hope that I could be the type of grandma who would see her grandchild often—popping in here and there, not missing out on the big and the small events.

I mourned the loss of that hope on the airplane ride home, crying silently half the way back.

A couple of days later, sad and lonely, I found myself along the familiar path by the river. As always, I searched for my white goose, but although many gray ones were poking around, the white goose remained elusive.

"I guess she was the encouragement for just that day, huh, Lord?" I asked, looking heavenward. But as I did, I received a message in the sky that reminded me once again that God hears my cries, and I am never alone. The only cloud in the expansive blue sky was shaped in the unmistakable form of a perfect white goose.

~Sheri Bull

The Cross

"... The eye is the lamp of the body. If your eyes are healthy, your whole body will be full of light. But if your eyes are unhealthy, your whole body will be full of darkness."
~Matthew 6:22-23

My friend Susan and I had just passed through Amarillo on our way to Oklahoma City when we noticed something large and white rising high above the flatlands bordering Interstate 40. At first, we thought it was some type of silo or maybe even a gigantic oil rigging. After all, we were in Texas. But upon nearing the structure, we realized it was a cross.

Even though she hadn't been to church in several years, Susan suggested stopping. "We've been driving for hours, and it'll do us good to get out and stretch our legs. Besides, maybe they have a gift shop... you know how I love to browse."

We pulled off the interstate at the Groom exit and drove the short distance to the cross. Casting a shadow almost twice its height, the nineteen-story white cross was surrounded by paved walkways, life-sized bronze sculptures of the Stations of the Cross and the three crosses of Calvary. Fully expecting Susan to make a beeline for the gift shop, I was somewhat surprised when she walked toward the crucifixion scene.

It was late afternoon, and most of the cars on the highway were headed toward home or a place to call home for the night. Possibly noticing we were two of the last visitors remaining at the site, Susan knelt beneath the center cross and bowed her head. Fearing she might be injured, I rushed to her side and asked if she was okay.

"Yes," she whispered. "It's just that I've been so wrong. Ever since college, I've been afraid to show my faith because I thought it would make me look weak and people would ridicule me. I quit going to church, and whenever someone asked me what religion I was, I said I didn't believe in religion. I turned my back on the Lord, but look—He placed this huge cross in my path just to tell me He's still here." She hung her head and sobbed.

As difficult as it was to watch, I understood what Susan was going through because I had experienced something similar after my dad died. Hoping it might encourage her, I knelt down and told her my story.

"My dad had always been a take-charge sort of person. Virtually self-educated, he married Mom when they were both eighteen. Like many other men his age, he made an adequate living by working on an assembly line. Following a couple of years of service during World War II, he took a second job, scraped his pennies together and moved our family to a small house in the suburbs. As our family's needs grew larger, Dad's work hours grew longer. Eventually, he started his own business, but he never seemed happy. He spent a lot of time away from home, neglected his health, and drank and smoked too much. When he reached retirement age, a time when he could finally relax and enjoy life, he was diagnosed with lung cancer."

Even though it was difficult to talk about my father, I continued. "When Dad told us about his cancer, he said, 'I'm gonna fight this.' And he did. He gave up drinking, but not smoking, changed his diet, underwent chemo, radiation and surgery, and tried every herbal, holistic, and radical treatment he could find, but nothing worked. Four months after the initial diagnosis, Dad lost his battle."

Susan stopped crying and gazed at me attentively. "As often happens when one spouse dies, Mom died a couple of years later. Feeling I was totally alone, I blamed God. After all, I had been brought up to believe that God was compassionate and that He answered prayers.

Where was the compassion in taking both my parents? Why hadn't He answered my prayers? How could I go on believing in a god that had turned His back on me? I couldn't... so I turned my back on Him."

Taking a deep breath, I raised my eyes to the cross. "Believing that the riches of the world were more valuable than those of the Father, I turned my attention to the pursuit of worldly treasures. Like my dad, wealth became my god. I bought a house, a new car, and more clothes than I could ever wear. I went on cruises and expensive vacations. I even married a man whose quest for wealth was stronger than my own. Together, we accumulated more 'things' than any of our hanger-on friends owned.

"One day, I looked in the mirror and didn't like what I saw. I had become the feminine equivalent of my father. My hair was perfectly coiffed, my make-up was flawless, the diamonds on my ears sparkled brilliantly, but my eyes were empty and cold. In Matthew 6:22-23, it says, 'The eye is the lamp of the body. If your eyes are healthy, your whole body will be full of light. But if your eyes are unhealthy, your whole body will be full of darkness.' My life was in darkness, and I knew I had to find the light."

The sun was beginning to set, but neither Susan nor I hurried to leave that place. There was peace and serenity there—a feeling of acceptance and safety.

Susan reached for my hand. "So what did you do?"

"I found a church and started going to services again," I replied. "Then I bought a Bible and started reading it every night. It didn't take long before my husband noticed a change in me. He didn't like it and insisted I make a choice between him and God. I chose God."

Susan turned her tear-stained face toward me. "What would you have done if God hadn't accepted you back?"

Knowing that even though I had walked away, God had always been with me, I told her, "The second book of Timothy tells us that 'if we are faithless, he remains faithful, for he cannot disown himself.'"

Susan stared across the horizon. The setting sun cast an amber glow on the cross. "God works in mysterious ways, doesn't He?" she said. "He knew there would be thousands of people passing this spot every day and that many of them needed His help, so He had someone build this cross just to remind them that He is the Way, the Truth, and the Life. He always has and always will be here... all we have to do is look for Him."

Rising from her knees, Susan smiled. "I'm glad we stopped here. This was exactly what I needed. Now I'm ready for the rest of the journey."

And so was I.

~Margaret Nava

A Ray of Light

*Hope is some extraordinary spiritual grace that God gives us
to control our fears, not to oust them.*
~Vincent McNabb

I stood still as a statue, holding a rusty, iron horseshoe in my right hand while dressed in a stylish black tuxedo with matching tie and polished shoes. It was my wedding day, and I was nervous. When I said "I do" an hour later, I would be gaining not only a wife for life, but also three teenaged stepchildren very much set in their ways. I was just twenty-seven and had no parenting background. And now I was having second thoughts.

"God, if this is your will, let me throw a ringer, and that'll be a sign to me that you're on board with this marriage," I prayed anxiously. The great Creator of the universe probably receives thousands of requests on a daily basis from around the globe, but I doubt He ever got that one.

Love at first sight? It happens; I can testify to it. When I first saw Bev, I whispered confidently to myself, "There's my wife, the special woman I've been awaiting." I chased her for three months before she finally agreed to a simple, short date. She didn't share my initial interest, but I eventually wore her down like a stray puppy does with his new master.

To truly test God, I closed my eyes as if blindfolded. Without hesitation, I swung my arm instinctively back, then forward in a smooth rhythm and released the horseshoe. I kept my eyes sealed and listened. I was never a great horseshoe pitcher and seldom threw ringers, but I had found the game to be a peaceful, relaxing experience and a place to be alone with your thoughts.

The shoe clanged strangely against the iron stake forty feet away. Normally, I slid a shoe into the sandy pit, but this struck the target dead on. Curious, I opened my eyes just in time to witness my shoe hugging the stake tightly, circulating it like an orbiting planet until it rested flatly on the ground… ringer! Not just a ringer, but perhaps the most awesome, perfect ringer I'd ever tossed. God, I believed, had answered my prayer.

But four years into our marriage, we began to argue with great frequency. Our disagreements centered on two repetitive topics: finances and disciplining children. For the record, our discussions seldom included harsh words and never involved abuse, but it was enough to alter the heart of my spouse.

The news came six months before our fifth wedding anniversary, during a World Series baseball game involving the Yankees. I've hated the Yankees ever since.

"I don't think I love you anymore," she flatly said. "Let's give things until Christmas, and if I don't feel differently by then I'm going to ask for a divorce." I was shocked. I still loved her very much. How could this be happening?

For more than two nightmarish months, I begged for us to see a professional counselor or our parish priest. I believed this relationship could be repaired. She replied that I was the one with the problem, not her. I stubbornly would not go without her, but I prayed our marriage would somehow be healed. It wasn't.

She filed for divorce after the New Year, and I was served papers as I sat down to dinner one evening. I never touched my food. Instead, I quietly went into the bathroom and vomited between violent sobs. I was heartbroken.

Bev moved to Tennessee after the divorce was finalized, but I was able to keep the house. Suddenly, it was just me and Brandy, our Golden Retriever. Many lonely, painful nights, I would visit Brandy's pen in the backyard and wrap my arms around that dog. She would return loyal love through affectionate licks and the swish-swish-swish of her muscular tail. But down deep I was a hurting man.

Months later, after church, I decided to escape the house and all its memories to take a walk in the forestland behind the house. The sun was shining brightly, a picture-perfect autumn day in late September, but inside the thick woodlands it was shadowy and shaded.

I had never before entertained thoughts of suicide, but that day I did. I had hit rock bottom.

I fell to the ground under a canopy of pines, oaks and maples and hugged the dirt in tears. Crying and shaking, I begged God Almighty for His peace and comfort, but mostly for the pain to end. I didn't really want to kill myself and it would have devastated my parents, sisters and brother.

Then I sensed a bright, brilliant white light just above me, and it startled me to the point that I stopped crying at once. I tried to open my eyes, but the light was blinding. Then I felt a hand touch my right shoulder. The touch, human-like but not of human origin, delivered reassurance and peace in the woods, and something more: hope. Moments later, the light faded, and I stood alone—refreshed and jubilant in the darkened shadows of the leafy trees and thick branches. Somehow, I was healed. I never shed another tear over my failed marriage.

In time, I began dating, but I never thought I'd find another woman who could sweep me off my feet like Bev. I was wrong.

One hot July day, I was at work delivering copies of investigative reports when I felt that I had to look up. And there was Geralynn, looking like an angel with her long locks of blond hair embracing her lovely face, and dressed in professional and attractive business attire. She was stunning. By the following summer, we were engaged. Not long afterward, we were married during a tearful, precious ceremony at the altar of the One who grants second chances and restores broken souls.

Fifteen years have passed, and we are still happily together, crazy in love, only now we've been joined by two rambunctious children, a son and a daughter, and our second Golden Retriever, a rescued dog named Buddy Bear. Brandy died at the age of thirteen in 2003, but will never be forgotten.

Over the past decade, my scalp has become follicle-challenged and we've both gained a few pounds, but I still feel like an excitable teenager when I'm around my love, Geri, my gift from God and partner for life.

Sometimes, I remember that day in the woods, and it quiets my spirit. Hopeless and dismally lost, streams of purified light from above delivered a message of hope that if I would simply trust in Him, better days would surely come. And they did.

~David Michael Smith

Wait for Juliana

Faith and doubt both are needed — not as antagonists, but working side by side to take us around the unknown curve.

~Lillian Smith

My parents raised me to be a devout Catholic. I went to church every Sunday, performed community service projects, and tried to live honorably. Over the years, I prayed in thanksgiving for all of the magnificent gifts that God had given. I also prayed for help through trying times. There were many rough patches, but they all seemed to make me stronger and deepen my faith.

My first difficulty occurred when I needed surgery as a teenager. With prayer, God carried me through, and I was fine after a brief recuperation. During that vulnerable time, I became a pen pal to a Marine who was stationed in Cambodia during the Vietnam War. He wrote about his volunteer work with nuns who rescued and nurtured orphans. I was touched by his devotion and vowed to someday help orphans, too. Every night, I prayed for this Marine, that God would keep him safe and help him with his worthy cause.

Once I entered college, his letters became less frequent, and we both moved on to do different things with our lives. All throughout school, I constantly struggled with my goals and desire to work with orphans. It didn't seem likely that I ever would, especially since I also wanted to get married and have a family of my own after graduation.

I felt guilt-ridden when I later married and planned to build a life with my new husband, Patrick.

However, when no children came to us, I turned to prayer. God had never let me down before, so I figured it would be a matter of time before God blessed me. I put all of my faith in Him. Patrick and I learned that there were thousands of abandoned orphans in Romania, and we wanted to adopt one. I couldn't stop thinking about my pledge to help orphans.

When Patrick and I walked through the orphanages in Romania, we were shocked by what we saw. There were countless rows of dilapidated cribs. Each bed cradled a child wearing tattered clothes. They lay on soiled and putrid mattresses with no sheets or blankets. The children were covered with sores or bugs, and a variety of animals wandered freely down the halls. Formula was rare, and most of the children got cold chamomile tea. There were no toys, and the children rocked silently in their cribs because there was no one to love or comfort them.

There was a mountain of paperwork before any child could be adopted. Pat and I worked anxiously on the stack of forms. Completing the documentation was overwhelming because each set had to be copied, translated, notarized and certified, which required many trips to different places. It wasn't long before we doubted ourselves. For every two steps we took forward, we took one step back.

During quiet moments in Romania, I recalled stories and prayers from my youth that provided the answers I needed to continue with the adoption. Was it a coincidence when I remembered those prayers and Biblical stories from the past, or did God whisper them in my ears? When I asked for more, God allowed me to witness a miracle.

On May 20th, on the outskirts of Buzau, Pat and I had spent the entire day scouring the countryside for a child who was available for adoption.

"Aren't you discouraged?" I cried to Patrick.

"Who would have thought that so many of the orphans are unadoptable?" He looked at me with tear-filled eyes.

"The biological parents must truly believe that they will take their children home someday," I said. "Sadly, they never will."

"The government's moratorium on adoption will soon make matters worse for us." Pat sighed deeply. "We only have a few days to pull a plan together."

We prayed as we trudged along. Suddenly, a vision of the Virgin Mary appeared on a miniscule transparent movie screen over my eyes. I tried to blink it away, thinking my mind was playing a trick on me. But no matter how hard I rubbed my eyes, the image of Mary would not disappear. I could not absorb the magnitude of it. Our road trip was winding down and we had no prospects of a child to adopt, and yet we were in a country with thousands of orphans. Nothing was making sense. The only thing we could do was trust in God.

In retrospect, the entire ordeal was a miracle, but I didn't see it that way twenty years ago. Back then, I wondered how we would be able to overcome the language barrier with little money in our pockets, oodles of bureaucratic red tape to cut through and numerous roadblocks to overcome. We were engulfed in a chaotic foreign adoption that we had to endure and battle our way through.

Then, late at night, we got a phone call from a lawyer who had a baby for us. We hailed a taxi in a torrential rainstorm with a driver who did not know a word of English. We were chilled to the bone and soaking wet. Even though I could no longer see the Virgin Mary, I could feel her love burning like a blazing fire in my heart, warming me from head to toe. I thought about how she must have felt when she held Jesus for the first time in Bethlehem. And when I gazed down at Juliana cradled lovingly in my arms, I knew that she was a gift from God. She was born on May 20th in Buzau, where Mary had appeared to me. How could I ever have doubted God?

On the long flight home, God reminded me that Jesus was born in an earthen manger surrounded by animals. When the Virgin Mary needed help, no one from the town gave it. Yet, she remained faithful to God that He would provide. And He did.

I consider myself blessed that God chose me to wrestle with the desire to help orphans when I was a teenager because it led me on an incredible journey that deepened my faith on a level I didn't think existed. My convictions empowered me to trust completely in God's plan. They enabled me to understand why I could never have children before. God wanted me to trust in Him, embrace my faith absolutely—and wait for Juliana.

~Barbara S. Canale

Chapter 7

Finding Faith Through Nature

*If you don't know what's meant by God,
watch a forsythia branch or a lettuce leaf sprout.*

~Martin H. Fischer

Finding My Church

Not all religion is to be found in the church,
any more than all knowledge is found in the classroom.
~Author Unknown

Growing up as the child of two florists, I found myself in church nearly every weekend. I also spent time in temples, synagogues and mosques. You could say that I was overexposed to religion, setting up weddings, funerals and other family milestones in every conceivable holy place.

As a result of my experiences, I never associated any particular place with God because I had seen so many different places where He was said to reside. Everyone seemed to believe their brand of religion and worship was the correct one, but to someone who had seen such variety, I knew it could never ring true for me that any of these places was the "true" or "right" House of God.

I spent my childhood dabbling in all religions, which was made possible since we were frequently asked to attend the events we decorated. Over the years, no single experience struck me as being the moving experience I was looking for in my faith. I never felt like I belonged in any specific place. And though the people were all very friendly and helpful when explaining their beliefs, I always felt like an outsider.

My desire to find a place where I could worship, where I would feel welcome and loved, was strong. But as a teenager, I still had yet to find it, and I didn't really know where else to look since I had tried most of the usual places.

As with most things, when you stop looking for something, it usually finds you. Little did I know when I agreed to travel with school during my fifteenth year that I was on the brink of discovering my own church of God in a most unusual place.

The summer before my sophomore year in high school, I took a field trip to study geology in the states west of the Mississippi. As someone who had lived in Pennsylvania all her life, I longed to see the mountains and endless sky of the West. I'd always loved being outdoors, hiking or just sitting and enjoying the beauty around me, and I couldn't pass up the chance to go to a part of our country where there was so much to see.

On a late June afternoon just around sunset, I found myself alone in the immense landscape of Badlands National Park in South Dakota. Atop a butte, surrounded only by eroded red and tan rock, I sat for a moment of quiet before rejoining my group.

The back of my neck was chilled in the shade, and I could almost feel the cold creeping toward me as the sun set. Before me, the land was still molten with golden light from the sun. My face was bathed in warmth from the light, and I closed my eyes to let it sink into my skin before the coming night.

Just then, a light breeze came up from the slope in front of me. Warm from the sun, the breath of air wrapped around me as soft and comforting as a favorite sweater, and the back of my neck lost its chill. The whole of me felt calm and comfortable in the glow of the setting sun.

It was as if I heard a voice in my head, or maybe it was my heart, saying, "This is it. Here is your church, your altar, your pew. And before you is your God."

And I knew deep inside this was my truth. My faith belonged in the open air. No velvet-clad room or stone building welcomed me in a way that the sun and the earth and the air did. My faith felt real and accepted in this place with no books, buildings or people. It felt simple and important. And I felt loved.

From that day forward, for me, the natural world has been the home of God, the one true church. If I ever find my faith lagging, all I have to do is go outside and rejoice in the sunlight, or the moonlight, or a soft breath of air that passes by me. The birds sing my hymns. The passing breeze plays my music. The drops of rain deliver my sermon.

My church is everywhere.

~Shawn Marie Mann

Love Notes
in the Garden

"... Truly I tell you, if you have faith as small as a mustard seed, you can say
to this mountain, 'Move from here to there,' and it will move.
Nothing will be impossible for you."
~Matthew 17:20

My family tree boasts many members with green thumbs who like to dig, plant and play in the dirt. I'm one of them. For us, gardening is fun, not work.

When I was a child, my great-grandfather told me fairy tales, folklore and legends about flowers. My grandmother and mother taught me the secrets of soil and seeds. Many happy childhood hours spent in the garden with them led to my life-long love affair with all green, growing things.

I can always find something to do in the garden: planting seeds, pulling weeds, watering, trimming, fertilizing, and finally harvesting and enjoying the flowers and fruits of my time in the garden. With such a long history of gardening—even taking courses to become a Master Gardener—I have become an observant gardener, aware of all the details and subtle changes in my garden. I check daily and sometimes hourly for seedlings to pop through the soil. I'm vigilant about pests and reluctant to share my vegetable garden with caterpillars and beetles. I even diligently cover my vegetable bed as autumn temperatures arrive so I can savor fresh-picked vegetables a little longer. And, of course, I take pictures and write about my garden.

For my ninth birthday, my grandmother gave me a necklace with a mustard seed in a clear, glass ball. The small, round glass magnified the tiny mustard seed so that it appeared bigger than just a speck. A card with the necklace came with this scripture from Matthew 17:20: "... Truly I tell you, if you have faith as small as a mustard seed, you can say to this mountain, 'Move from here to there,' and it will move. Nothing will be impossible for you."

I didn't really understand the message of the scripture or the mustard seed at that time, but I learned the tiny mustard seed can produce a hardy plant that will grow up to fifteen feet tall. I wondered how anything could grow from a seed so small that it had to be magnified to be seen. Even today, whenever I plant a tiny seed and ponder its potential, I still experience that same wonder and awe.

As I grew up and got busy raising a family and creating a career, I didn't pay much attention to my faith. I didn't spend much time or effort in growing and nurturing it, so it stayed the size of a mustard seed. I took it for granted.

One day, while on my knees in the garden (gardening will keep you humble), I experienced a "wow moment": I noticed that many leaves and flower petals in my garden were shaped like hearts! From morning glories to moon flowers, my garden was filled with heart-shaped leaves and flowers: roses, caladiums, hostas, impatiens, violets, geraniums, and ivy—that's just the short list. The more I paid attention as I walked through the garden, the more examples I saw—plants with scalloped leaves and petals like fancy lace, frilly ones in a rainbow of colors with striped or variegated colors, and ones with velvety and satiny textures. I interpreted each heart-shaped petal or leaf as a personal "I love you" note from God, assurance of His eternal presence in my life.

Oblivious to the obvious, I had rushed through life, ignoring the simple truths that were often right in front of me. I was living the old adage about not being able to see the forest for the trees, and I had missed the natural beauty that surrounded me. In the peace and beauty of my garden, I found messages and lessons from God that my busyness and worries camouflaged.

It took time in the garden on my knees for me to understand the message of the mustard seed and God's love notes to me. Like the seeds I plant in the soil, the seeds God has planted in me require attention and care to develop roots, grow and flourish. God doesn't show me the future, but He knows my potential. It's up to me to nurture and care for that potential like I do the seeds and plants in my garden. But I'm not alone. God's love notes remind me of His constant presence and care. He is always in the details—and sometimes in the most unexpected ways!

~Linda E. Allen

63

Finding Faith in a Spider

Never think that God's delays are God's denials.
Hold on; hold fast; hold out. Patience is genius.
~Georges-Louis Leclerc

Everyone endures trials and tribulations, and people handle them in a variety of ways. For me, growing up as an Italian Catholic, the idea of being angry at God was not tolerated; however, that's exactly what I did. I got angry at God and chose to ignore Him in my life.

Abuse of any kind is traumatic. The abuse I experienced was followed by abandonment by a loved one in my life, leaving me feeling cast-off and alone. I spent many years thereafter living in fear, hiding my insecurities, and never allowing anyone to really know me.

Through the grace of this God that I did not believe in, I had a daughter when I was thirty-nine years old, and she provided me with the motivation to get counseling to start my journey of healing. Six years later, because of the counseling and the joyful exchange of love between my daughter and me, I felt stronger and more confident, and was willing to risk allowing a person to get to know me.

I found that man and we shared many wonderful years. Then as my daughter was on her way to college, he decided that he wanted to move on in his life without me. Devastated by both him and my daughter leaving, I worried that I would react to this "abandonment" by reverting to the fearful, insecure person I had been in my early adult years.

One night, while sitting out on the back deck, feeling sad and despondent, I felt a light, feathery touch on my back. Instead of whisking it away with my hand as you would a fly or mosquito, I turned around. A small spider was building a web directly behind my head.

I can't believe I didn't scream and run away, but for whatever reason, I got up slowly and moved to the other side of the deck to watch how that spider built the web. It was amazing to me. I had seen a documentary on a spider building a web, but that night, with a warm summer breeze and a pale moon as the backdrop, I got to watch a performance that I had never seen in person.

I saw this tiny spider, struggling to find her footing, as she continued to weave. I saw her overcome obstacles when part of the web got damaged. I saw her pause and rest, and then persevere until the web was complete. Then I saw her wait patiently, ready to reap the rewards of her efforts.

I was so awed by this experience that I blurted out, "If I never believed in God before, I have to believe in Him now. Just look at the tools and support that He has given this tiny spider so that she can take care of herself. Just look." And that is what I did.

In that moment, I realized that God was letting me know that He has given me everything I need to take care of myself. He gave me my daughter to help me get my footing and continue to weave the web of my life. He helped me overcome the obstacle of losing the man who was so important to me. He has allowed me to pause and rest in His love and support. While I may not have waited patiently to reap the rewards of my efforts, He gave me an awareness of how I can build my web of truth, love, happiness and grace. God gave all of that to me through a spider to help me understand that while I may have left God for a while, He never left me. I now know that should my web become damaged in the future, God will always give me the strength to continue to weave.

~Judith Fitzsimmons

64

Thin Places

I love to think of nature as an unlimited broadcasting station, through which
God speaks to us every hour, if we will only tune in.
~George Washington Carver

Celtic Christians called them "thin places," locations where the membrane between heaven and earth was thinner than other places. I found mine speeding across the Caribbean Sea, looking at waves reflecting the most amazing blue, against alternating sandy and rocky shores edged with protected, lush green forest. Suddenly, a combination of joy and peace touched the top of my head, filled me up, and then, with a whoosh, pushed out through my sandy toes. It was as if the Great Spirit, the Breath of Life, had just passed through me. Or I had passed through it. The thought paired with this joy was "I need to live here."

As a forty-four-year-old single woman with fibromyalgia and chronic fatigue, the task felt overwhelming. I spent the next six months praying for God to guide me and give me a sign, until it dawned on me that I had already received my sign. A much less dramatic, but just as clear inclination led me to move to the capital city of the Dominican Republic, where I had one friend. I saw him on the third day of my arrival, then not again for five months, as he was driving teams of aid workers across the border into Haiti after the earthquake.

Within two weeks, I had found a place to live, moved in, organized my space, and discovered that I spoke Mexican Spanish, not

Dominican Spanish (enough different to make life difficult), in a city with three million people, yet no geographical concentration of expats. I found myself very lonely and far away from that "thin place" and God.

I struggled with loneliness and depression, questioning my decision to move. Did I sell my belongings and disrupt my life to lie on a bed, exhausted, staring up at the ceiling fan and wishing I could have afforded a room with air conditioning? With communication problems (interpersonal and technological), transportation constraints, monetary limits, college students striking nearby (resulting in tear gas wafting into my room), the dangers of traveling alone as a woman, lack of friends, and getting sick whenever I ate out, I felt, to put it bluntly, imprisoned.

From the rooftop of my building, I could see the ocean, too far away for me to walk to until I built up a tolerance for the heat. I could also see groupings of trees here and there. But at ground level, nature disappeared behind buildings and concrete. I saw only locked gates, high walls, roads full of potholes, vehicles pressing into all available space, and visible pollution spouting from tailpipes. I felt crowded in and conspicuous, with my tall, blond head a walking target for deception and men seeking visas to the United States. My view was closed-in, fearful and limited—"tunnel vision of the heart" is how I can best describe it. Other than gasping sobs of loneliness cried into my pillow, even my breathing became timid and shallow. I had become a different person. The confident, friendly artist who arrived here was locked behind my own newly constructed walls.

Finally, with a visit to the Jardín Botánico Nacional de Santo Domingo, I stepped into another world—a surprising paradise of open space, pretty, brick-patterned sidewalks, and sprawling ponds full of blooming water lilies. I unfolded the map more and more, revealing paths to many different botanical worlds waiting to be discovered. I noticed my constricted lungs releasing all my pent-up sadness and anxiety. I was safe in a world I understood: flowers and landscapes, color and photographic opportunities. I breathed deeply for the first time in months. It was not a surprise to see printed on the map that I was standing literally in "the lung of the city," a large protected area helping to clean the polluted air and provide oxygen to the crowded city.

Later, looking at the photographs I took, I saw my instant transformation in the petals of the water lilies. From being closed up and alone, to feeling the breeze, being caught up in its motion, accepting whatever life has to offer. I saw beauty had always been there, even when my eyes were closed. In the garden, and in the images, I learned it was safe to open up and breathe.

A few days after my virtual lung transplant, I sat on an urban park bench a block from my rented room that I had sat on a week before. The park was actually a large, bricked median in the middle of a busy street. Above my head, large maroon and yellow flowers bloomed in columns from hanging vines that previously, I was sure, had been long, dried sticks hanging from a dark sky. I looked up at the immense green canopy above me, spreading from a giant tree, majestic and lush.

How could I have not seen the tree before? I confess I had seen its sprawling roots, but all those green leaves? Never. For the first time since living there, I had truly looked up. I visited that bench often in the months that ensued, as well as walked side streets where I found balconies with bougainvilleas spilling over their railings, and plumeria trees peeking out of walled-in yards. But the shift of my mindset now placed me inside with the flowers, instead of alone and locked out.

Faith is a strange thing, needing a place in which to rest. I learned I had to take my faith about the decision to move to the Dominican Republic out of a fleeting feeling on a speedboat and into the hands of the God of all creation—otherwise I would not emotionally survive the many trials I faced. I could again recall the rush of Spirit running through me, from head to foot, and remember to breathe—but this time I promised to find, and hopefully create for others, "thin places" wherever I went.

~Heather J. Kirk

Fired Up

*The fire is the main comfort of the camp, whether in summer or winter,
and is about as ample at one season as at another.
It is as well for cheerfulness as for warmth and dryness.*
~Henry David Thoreau

"We need to take a break," my boyfriend of
nine months uttered between sobs. I stared
with vacant eyes at the campfire before us.

"A break?" My heart shattered. "I thought you were feeling better
and figuring things out."

"It's not working. I'm sorry."

I felt him facing me, but I didn't have the energy or desire to
meet his eyes. This was so backward. Why was he crying—and why
was I feeling sorry for him? He was the one who was hurting me!

"Just give me a month," he continued. "I'll work through this."

"What about the past few months? I've given you space to do
that."

"I know. I'm just so tired," he said, the tears continuing to flow.
"Tired of having to work through my past to be present with you."

Our camping trip ended the next morning, and we drove our
separate ways. I knew I couldn't get through the next month without
some hardcore help from God.

When I woke the next morning, I knew what needed to be done.
I had to work on my relationship with God every day. Formulating
my plan, I walked down the stairs to the kitchen to make coffee. With

each purposeful scoop of grounds, I detailed what I was going to do. I would read the Bible every morning. Scoop. I would pray after my reading. Scoop. I would have extended time with God every few weeks, just Him and me, even though that intimidated me. Scoop. I would make a point of talking with God throughout each day. Scoop. I poured the water into the coffee maker, closed the top, flipped the power switch, and strode to the balcony to start my new life, grabbing my Bible en route.

For the next month, I was an astute student. I learned more about the Bible and gospels than I had in the prior ten years. I was also a model patient of God, my counselor. Sharing the sorrow and loneliness of the past few months with my Lord allowed Him to heal and console me.

My boyfriend called at the end of our time apart. "Hi. Can we meet at a park to talk?" he asked.

"A park? Not your house?"

"No. The park by my place."

I realized what that meant. Less than ten minutes after arriving at the park, I retraced my steps, single and devastated.

Soon thereafter, I went on a ten-day camping road trip by myself. I roamed from beach to redwood forest, from mountain to valley, as I worked my way from Southern California to the Oregon border. Each night, I settled in my chair before the campfire. I stared transfixed at the flames.

Those peaceful, quiet nights before the campfires were great times of healing and restoration. God appeared in the sounds of the forest, the burning of the coals, and the cool air that settled around me. He was everything I needed Him to be in each moment: my Father, my Companion, my Savior, my Counselor. My heart had not yet been sewn back together when I returned from my road trip, but the salve of God's love was hard at work within me.

Since then, I have twice repeated a camping road trip by myself through California to connect with my Lord on a deeper level. Over the course of those trips and my continued faith walk, I came to realize that the separation from my boyfriend and the end of our association were the motivations I needed to consistently pursue a relationship with God. Since then, our relationship has been strong and constant; the bedrock of my life. I am so thankful for the impact that my former boyfriend had on me that I e-mailed him a few years after our breakup. I thanked him for helping me find my faith.

~Heather Zuber-Harshman

Discovering God's Message in the Sand

Who rises from prayer a better man, his prayer is answered.
~George Meredith

"Y ou must come to God with the faith of a little child," my mother used to say. "You won't always get answers, but you must always have faith."

Wear your Sunday best; polish your church shoes; sit quietly and listen; you're in God's house. Those were the messages hammered home on Sunday mornings. Three words the pastor spoke that I could relate to were Father, Son and Holy Ghost, but I completely misconstrued the trinity. "Father" conjured images of Dad drinking coffee. "Son" was my little brother, who always got me in trouble. And ghosts, holy or not, were the topic of Dad's spellbinding night-time storytelling.

After the service, the pastor would greet the congregation at the church entrance. I felt sorry for him. Most people I knew had regular names, but everyone called him Reverend. I was much older before I learned that his name was Paul. His wife, who was my first Sunday school teacher, provided nourishment for the body and soul. She baked bread and shared it with others. She also taught me about faith.

We moved away from the old neighborhood and my childhood church. My parents did not join another congregation, but they bellied up to the radio or television and listened to the sermons of their favorite evangelists. The denomination was not important. The messages were.

I was a preteen when my parents separated. My dad frequented inner-city storefront churches. I sat on hard folding chairs and listened to "fire and brimstone preachers" who scared me out of my wits with sermons intended to save my soul. Mom diligently followed a local, charismatic radio preacher who mentioned the names of his wife and children in his sermons.

My mother had little in the way of material possessions, but she had a deep, abiding faith that the Lord would provide. She fed my children goodies and told them Bible stories. She would also provide heaping helpings of scripture to me every opportunity she had. I would tell her, "I'm a believer. A spoonful is fine, but you want to force-feed me with a shovel."

Mom would hold Sunday school services in her living room for her young grandchildren when they spent the night. Her messages continue to have an impact on them now as adults.

Now that I am of a certain age, I have come to realize that not all places of worship have wooden pews or are adorned with stained-glass windows and tall steeples. Likewise, not all pastors have divinity degrees, don robes, or preach with authority from a pulpit.

My most recent church had a ceiling of predawn sky, and the pastor (one who ministers to the spiritual needs of others) was most unconventional. I did not dress up to attend the sunrise service; in fact, I wore a swimsuit. My "church" resonated with the sounds of lapping waves and the tune of "Amazing Grace" as I scuffed my bare feet across the sugar-fine white sand, singing to myself. My heart was heavily burdened, my faith faltering.

My daughter-in-law, mother of two young children, had been blind in one eye since birth. She had recently developed a viral infection in her sighted eye and lost most of her vision. Her condition continued to deteriorate and her prognosis was uncertain.

Perspiration rolled down my face as I trudged along the beach questioning why modern medicine wasn't working. I beseeched God and my late mother. I asked angels to surround my daughter-in-law and lift her spirits. I prayed for healing and understanding. The sun rose over the horizon and spotlighted a lone woman in her mid-thirties, sitting in a beach chair and writing in a notebook. She sifted sand with her feet; her toenail polish matched her bright pink cap. Normally, I'd nod and go about my business, but I felt compelled to stop. I asked if she was writing about the beauty of the ocean.

"No, I'm writing in my prayer journal." She smiled, removed her sunglasses and made eye contact.

"Please add my daughter-in-law to your list." I gave her a brief synopsis. I didn't want to burden this nice lady with my problems while she was on vacation. She wrote down my daughter-in-law's name. I walked on about twenty paces when I heard her call out. I turned to see her running toward me.

"Ma'am, would you like me to pray with you?"

I stood on the desolate beach at dawn and bowed my head. I listened to the seagulls screech, the rhythmic waves pound the shore, and the heartfelt prayer of a stranger. She was small in stature, like my late mother, but also like Mom, she was big on God's message. Tears ran down my cheeks; my burden lifted as she spoke the words I already knew.

"Father, you are a healer, but as Christians we know it is your will be done, not ours; in your time, not our time. We ask that you…" She recited the exact words that would have poured from my mother's mouth. She prayed on and on. I dug my feet in the sand and waited for her to finish. I almost giggled when I realized she was feeding me a "shovelful" just like Mom would have. I echoed her "Amen."

After that prayer in the sand, a calm reassurance came over me. I knew that whatever happened, our family would be okay. The next six months were rough as we dealt with hospitalizations and medical issues, but my daughter-in-law slowly regained her vision.

I believe that God allowed my mother to commune with me via a stranger, as I rediscovered trust and renewed my faith that morning on the beach. I also believe that church can be wherever you are, for the Bible says in Matthew 18:20, "'For where two or three gather in my name, there am I with them.'"

~Linda O'Connell

An Interweaving
of Faiths

The day the Lord created hope was probably the same day he created Spring.
~Bern Williams

Snow pelted the windows of our small farmhouse. My husband Ryan and I finished dinner and sat quietly, bracing against winter's subzero gale. "We should do something special," I said. "Something unique to our new country life."

"You're thinking about Easter?" He stroked his dark beard.

"More than that," I exclaimed. "Let's celebrate spring on our land!"

When we moved to Vermont, we were glad to cast off city stress, but sad to leave our families and community behind. And we missed friends with whom to pray, worship, break bread, talk and laugh. We'd visited area churches in search of a spiritual community to replace our combined sixty years of Catholicism.

After planting and harvesting last year's garden, we'd hoped to find a fellowship that honored the seasons. One Sunday, we'd driven forty miles to Rutland to attend a Quaker meeting. Another Sunday, we attended a Unitarian fellowship in Burlington, thirty miles north.

This night, after dinner, I grabbed the encyclopedia, and read aloud. "Easter comes from the Norse word '*Eostre*' meaning spring season. Towns lit bonfires on hilltops."

"Our parish had a huge Easter candle symbolizing Christ, the light of world." Ryan reached for a pad of paper and penned "Easter" at the top, and then drew a line down the center of the page, creating two columns. One column he labeled "Ceremony"; the other "Menu."

"Candles," he said, writing the word, "and a fire in our new fireplace."

I continued to read encyclopedia pages. "In the Upanishads, the first act of creation was an egg breaking in two. And before Christianity, eggs symbolized fertility, life and creation. Now Easter eggs are symbolic of the resurrection."

"I'm putting 'eggs' under the menu column. And 'bitter herbs,'" Ryan said. "At Passover, Hebrews ate bitter greens as a reminder of the harsh life their ancestors led."

"Dandelion greens, and we have to have grape wine in honor of Passover."

"Steamed greens, kosher wine, and how about a leg of lamb?" Ryan continued his list of menu items: eggs, bitter greens, matzo, leg of lamb, grape wine, as well as the list of ceremonial items: candles, fire, parade, readings, toasting the first fruit, singing, thanks for light and freedom.

"This is sounding like a real celebration."

I cleared the table as Ryan began a new page, crossing out some items and revising others.

"Shinan, what do you think of blending agrarian festivals with our Judeo-Christian heritage?" Then he read a line from his page: "A simple supper to celebrate the passover of winter to spring."

"It's perfect!" I hugged him. "You're so creative."

Ryan had spent ten years in a Catholic monastery, while I had been a missionary teacher in Alaska. Although we'd both committed to serving the faith of our birth, we'd each become disillusioned, deciding to find our connection with God through a back-to-the-land lifestyle.

On another page of his tablet, Ryan wrote "Friends." We hadn't talked about including others, but with Ryan's years as a monk and with my large family, a shared community was a prerequisite for a spiritual celebration. We quickly compiled a list of friends to invite.

Ryan washed the dinner dishes. I dashed upstairs to my desk to gather colored paper, paints, markers, scissors and envelopes. I cut bright green construction paper to fit the envelopes. Then Ryan hand-lettered the inside of each card: "A Simple Supper to Celebrate the Passover of Winter to Spring." I painted a yellow candelabra on each invitation. We addressed the stack of cards and mailed them the next day.

On Friday night, a week before traditional Easter Sunday, twelve friends arrived at our farmhouse bringing the requested "poem, song, reading and/or treat." For folks who didn't know what to do, Ryan had suggested readings from the Old Testament or the Gospel of Mark.

As he had done in his former role as a monk, Ryan wrote and photocopied a program with the order of events: lighting of the fire, readings, music, candlelight parade, sharing of new beginnings, feast, and farewell.

Gathered in our small, still-to-be-refurbished living room, Ryan introduced folks, while I filled their glasses with kosher grape wine. My new friend Nancy played a passage from Mozart's "Spring Song" on her flute, calming the "what's expected?" group. Ruben, a teacher-friend of Ryan's, paraphrased Exodus 6:6. "Like our ancestors of old, we have come out of Egypt, crossed the Red Sea and now search for the Promised Land."

"As ancient ancestors built bonfires on hills," Ryan exclaimed as I turned off the lights, "we welcome spring and light the fire." Ryan had arranged the fireplace with kerosene-soaked kindling and logs. Now, in the dark, I set a lit match to the fuel. In that blaze of light, people sighed with audible surprise as firelight reflected on everyone. Bianca played "Amazing Grace" on her guitar, and Felix read an Algonquian prayer. I passed a plate of matzo crackers, the Hebrew symbol for unleavened bread, and offered each guest another glass of wine. Our neighbors, Nadine and her husband Osgood, sang "All God's Chillun Got Wings." George read an excerpt from a Hindu Vedic text: "God is in everything and worthy of praise...." I handed out candles, lit mine from the fire, and then lit Ryan's. Each person in turn lighted the candle of the next person. We sang "It's a Small World After All" and paraded around the coffee table.

I poured more wine as Aaron read Passover prayers and then said, "Seder suppers have four ritual glasses of wine, which represent the four promises to Moses." Our guests complied with each traditional toast and stood with a lit candle in one hand and a ten-ounce glass of wine in the other. After Helen read from the Gospel of Mark, we blew out the candles and entered our kitchen for dinner.

Several friends literally fell into our dilapidated chairs. For this celebration supper, Ryan and I had lengthened our old table with a sheet of quarter-inch paneling we'd ordered for the living room, placing one end of the paneling on top of the table and the other atop a wooden sawhorse. Both the table and the paneling were hidden under a large white tablecloth. Twelve friends, plus Ryan and I, squeezed around the makeshift table. We juggled salad bowls, serving platters and decanters of wine.

Halfway through the meal, the thin paneling suddenly buckled and caved in. Bowls, platters and decanters tumbled. Ceremonial dishes toppled into a cavern of twisted tablecloth, and the platter of leftover lamb landed in Nancy's lap. The clink, clank and splatter were followed by the forward somersault of several guests. Everything seemed to be tumbling toward spring. I served hot coffee as everyone helped clean up. Our good-humored guests shared our humanness and later caravanned home.

Heartfelt, soul-nourishing, kindred spirits were virtues that comprised our promising spiritual community. In the following years, as Ryan and I continued to gather with friends, we deepened our faith through the interweaving of spiritual beliefs.

~Shinan Barclay

Chapter
8

finding
my faith

Finding Faith Through Fire

*God brings men into deep waters, not to drown them,
but to cleanse them.*

~John Aughey

Being in the Arms of God

God loves each of us as if there were only one of us.
~St. Augustine

I had my palm read when I was in fifth grade. It was at a Camp Fire Girls meeting at the home of our leader, Jane. When it was my turn, the reader looked at my palm and then gazed into my eyes with such alarm that I thought maybe I was going to die soon. Instead, she said I would have a long life. Unfortunately, it would be filled with hardships that would bring much sadness.

Jane immediately spoke up. "Kay will get through whatever comes her way. She is very strong."

What neither of the women knew is that several years earlier, God had come into my life in such a miraculous way that I was not afraid.

But the palm reader was not wrong. My life had been a bit of a struggle since birth. My mother was a singer on the Chicago circuit. She met my dad while performing at a casino he was running. They married. She became a heavy drinker. And by the time I was born, she was an alcoholic.

My parents divorced when I was three. The courts awarded me to my dad, but my mother begged him to let her keep me. Dad agreed, as long as she stayed sober. She remarried when I was four and shortly thereafter started drinking again.

I remember her husband being very angry when he would come home after work to find my mother gone. Each night he would tell me to get into the back seat of the car so he could go from bar to bar looking for her. He would help me into the car with a hefty swat on my rear, and I would end up sprawled on the floor of the back seat.

When I was five, I heard my mother talking to my dad on the phone. "Come and get her," she said. "I don't want her anymore."

So back I went to live with my dad and grandma. There were times when Dad was gone, and my mother would come, drunk, pounding on the door to get me back. Grandma would be very frightened and tell me to hide under the bed.

Dad remarried when I was six, and Grandma went to live with Dad's sister. My stepmother tolerated me, but it was pretty clear she was not especially happy to be saddled with me.

This was a woman who wanted total control, and she did not want any competition for my dad's affection. "Don't you think you're a little too old to be kissing your father good night?" she asked, shortly after moving in. Dad said nothing and, as always, bowed to her demands. I went to bed very sad that night.

I don't know how long it was after that episode that I had my encounter with God. But I do know that He spoke to me.

My grandma had taught me about God. She taught me prayers to say before we ate and at bedtime. I knew that God loved me. I knew that "if I should die before I wake..." He would take me to be with Him in heaven. But I was just a kid. And I don't remember thinking too much about those things until a very strange and wondrous happening occurred.

I was seven years old, skipping on the blacktop road next to our home. It was a very sunny day, and I was happy. I looked up at the sky and thought how beautiful it was. I stopped skipping and stood gazing up. I remember thinking how huge the sun looked. It seemed to mesmerize me, and I couldn't take my eyes off of it.

Then I felt the heat of the sun spreading over my body. But it also seemed to penetrate through my body and into the very core of my being. I felt completely immersed in this comforting warmth.

I didn't hear the words, "I love you," but I felt love. I felt an overwhelming power of love. Then in my mind, I heard a voice say, "You are my child." And in that instant, I knew it was God. I felt totally engulfed in His warm, loving arms.

Wow. Nothing in my life has ever compared to those few moments. And nothing in my life has ever gotten the best of me because of those few moments.

Knowing with a certainty that there is a God is amazing in itself. But knowing, with a certainty, that He loves me because I am His child is a faith-filled fact that empowers me with strength and joy every day.

As the palm reader said, I have had a difficult life with much sadness. My early years were only the beginning. My heart has been broken many times. But, just as He promised, my Heavenly Father is always with me, bringing me joy through my sorrow.

Sometimes, I close my eyes and try to imagine that I am once again that little girl skipping down the road. I never, ever want to forget how it felt being in the arms of God.

~Kay Conner Pliszka

God in the Thick of It

Clouds come floating into my life, no longer to carry rain or usher storm,
but to add color to my sunset sky.
~Rabindranath Tagore

Abuse was parceled out in generous portions at my house any day of the week, but rain brought out the demons, and often I had to run to survive. I always ended up in the same place, in the back pew of my church, the same church where I attended Mass each morning before going to class in my Catholic school. Cold and wet, I would stare hard at the crucifix on the wall, the image of Christ hanging.

By the time I was a senior in high school, I was furious at God. I knew God existed — daily religion classes and Mass six times a week kept me from doubting — but I was not at all convinced God was good, and this was especially true when I was seventeen. One day, the terror began, and I ran as I always did, ending up in one of the darkened pews at the back of the church.

Despite my anger, I couldn't take my eyes off the crucifix. It had been hanging there for my entire young life, but only now did it occur to me that I might be wasting my time talking to some guy nailed to a cross. I felt tears well up for probably the third time in an hour.

"If you care about me at all," I shouted in my head to the God on the cross, "you have to show me now! Today! Because I can't live anymore unless I know you are out there somewhere!" I started to sob.

Just then I felt a hand rest warmly but firmly on my shoulder. "Marla, honey, you're soaked through," Sister Margaret said from behind me.

"Yes, Sister," I agreed without turning around.

Sister Margaret, my school principal, had found me here before on many occasions. She walked around to stand in front of me. I quickly looked downward to avoid her gaze.

"You poor child," Sister Margaret said. "You're going to catch pneumonia one of these days, you know." She gently took my chin in her hands and turned my face toward her. Her dark eyes were kind beneath her nun glasses, framed by her boxy, brunette nun haircut. She studied my eyes, but made no mention of the swollen, purple mess she saw there.

"Let's go back to the convent and see if Molly has something that might warm you up a bit."

It was what I had been hoping for. "Yes, Sister."

In the vestibule, Sister Margaret leaned over and picked up an umbrella from the corner. "See this?" she teased. "This is called an umbrella. Handy little invention. We'll have to get one for you."

With that, she popped open the umbrella, held it over us, and walked me the few short yards from the cold, dark church to the warmth and light of the convent.

Despite the close proximity of the church, the school, and the convent, few students had ever seen the inside of this house where the teaching nuns lived, and they imagined it to be a scary, funereal place. I knew the convent as a place of love and safety, though. As soon as we crossed the threshold, I felt better.

Sister Margaret got me a towel, and I dried myself off as best I could. Sister John, my art teacher, waved hello and smiled hugely as she passed through the kitchen. Any apprehension I might have felt evaporated. The nuns loved me, even if my parents did not. Sister Margaret took my damp towel and draped a blanket around me. She pulled out a chair from the kitchen table, indicating that I should sit. Molly, the convent maid, had already placed a steaming bowl of vegetable soup on the table.

Suddenly, I started to cry, with great hiccupping sobs that shook me to the core. Sister Margaret sat next to me at the table and patted my back. She allowed me to cry, but only briefly. After a minute, she said, "Eat your soup."

The soup helped. Molly gave me one of her amazing hot rolls, too, and that helped even more. Nuns came and went from all corners of the house; most just calling out greetings, but others stopped to chat for a minute or two before heading off to other things. None of them asked about my face, but I saw compassion in their eyes.

When I finished eating and had regained my composure, Sister Margaret asked, "Do you want to tell me anything this time?"

Her phrasing was purposeful and deliberate. In all the times we had made the walk from the church to the convent, Sister Margaret had asked but never pressed me about my home life, and I had told her little. She wasn't blind, of course. She saw my black eyes. She had witnessed my anguish for years.

This time, when I didn't answer, Sister Margaret said, "Tell me who did this to you."

I looked at the table. "My mother," I said. "It's almost always my mother."

Just those few words opened up a dam. While nuns laughed at *Gomer Pyle* in the next room, I talked to Sister Margaret about the horror that was my life. When I finally stopped talking, I was unburdened for the first time.

After a brief silence, Sister Margaret said, "I think you'll stay at your grandmother's house tonight. She'll be happy to see you."

A trill of anxiety coursed through me then, but Sister Margaret saw it and comforted me. "I've known your grandmother many years, Marla," my principal said. "You have no need to worry about her. She will want to help even more than I do."

Sister Margaret was right, of course. Several hours later, I was at my grandparents' house, snug and warm and exhausted in the soft guest room bed. My grandmother and grandfather had accepted my story unquestioningly and offered me respite.

I reviewed the night in my mind. Sister Margaret had rescued me and taken me to safety. Sister John and the other nuns had welcomed me and even made me laugh. I had finally felt safe enough to tell someone about the bad things happening at my house—and they had reacted properly. I wasn't to stay just a night at my grandparents' house, but as long as I needed. (I ended up staying through my first year in college!) I no longer had to run away every time it rained.

Before I slept, I spoke to God. "I saw you tonight. Thank you!"

I had, indeed, seen God. Sister Margaret, the other nuns, and my grandparents had rescued me and cared about me. It was the first time in my life I recognized that God shows up so very often, not in a cloud or in a burning bush, but in other people. Recognizing God in those wonderful people renewed my faith. God was real to me again. It was all I had asked for!

~Marla H. Thurman

Falling for God

We are all dependent on one another, every soul of us on earth.
~George Bernard Shaw, Pygmalion

April 20, 1998 was not a typical spring day in Minnesota, nor was it the day I expected would shape my faith forever. Because of an unusually warm winter, there was no snow on the ground, and there were already signs of spring.

My friend Gretchen and I decided to go hiking at Banning State Park. Our hike began with a leisurely trek along winding trails of spring blossoms and animal wildlife and continued toward Hell's Gate, a rugged trail running parallel to the Kettle River. Hiking over rocks and tree roots, with Gretchen in the lead, I followed close behind, admiring the sheer banks that dropped some thirty feet to the river below.

We continued our trek until we came to a clearing. I guessed by Gretchen's abrupt halt that it was the spot overlooking Hell's Gate. The view was spectacular! The raging rapids beating against the rock ledges, silhouetted against the surrounding forest scene and streaming sunlight, made for a Kodak moment. It was breathtaking, but in an instant it all changed.

Approaching the spot where Gretchen had stopped, I lost my footing. Falling, I reached for a branch extending from the cliff. It snapped. I fell straight down thirty feet to the bedrock below. I do not remember hitting the ground, nor did I feel the impact when I landed. I have no recollection of how long it took me to process what had happened. I only remember opening my eyes to find myself face-down in a puddle of water and hearing Gretchen yell my name.

Breathing was very difficult and painful. I attempted to roll over on my back, but tremendous pain shot through my arms as I tried to pull them out from under me. I could not move either wrist. Using my legs and right shoulder, I rolled over on my back. Gretchen yelled down to me that she was going back to the park headquarters to get help. Hell's Gate was three miles from the park headquarters, so I knew it would be a long wait before help arrived. I was cold and shaking uncontrollably.

Thankfully, the rescue team arrived within an hour. It was a heroic ninety-minute effort to stabilize me and get me to the top of the cliff. They covered me with blankets, administered oxygen, put my head in a C-collar, splinted my left wrist and strapped me to a backboard. I had fallen in one of the most remote and inaccessible areas of the park, so getting me out and to a hospital was extremely difficult. They debated how to get me out of the area. There was no place for a helicopter to land, and a boat couldn't navigate the rapids below where I lay. Lifting me up using ropes wasn't an option, so they finally decided to carry me up the cliff. In a complex effort that took a great deal of physical strength, teamwork and communication, a group of ten rescuers carried me up the rocky bank. It was a hand-over-hand job of lifting and passing me up a series of rock ledges to get me to the top. Rescuers had to find good footing and handholds while lifting and passing me to fellow workers. Anyone could have slipped and fallen.

After reaching the top, I was carried three-fourths of a mile to the campground where a four-wheel-drive truck was waiting. It took me to a picnic area where an ambulance was waiting. I was taken to a nearby hospital and then airlifted to a hospital in Minneapolis. X-rays determined that I had broken both wrists. A CAT scan revealed bruised ribs, but no internal bleeding or injuries. I had a deep cut on my right forearm and several bumps, bruises and scratches. I spent three days in the hospital and returned a week later for surgery on my left wrist. Six weeks after the accident, my right cast was removed.

Two weeks later, the cast on my left arm was removed, and I began an eight-month program of physical therapy.

After my hospital stay and surgery, I spent six weeks living with a friend. With both arms in casts, I was unable to care for myself. Having my independence stripped from me was extremely difficult, but through it I learned to do what I was never good at: ask for help. I have an independent spirit by nature, and always found it easier to help others than to let others care for me.

Before my accident, I had fallen into a deep depression. There were nights when I would cry myself to sleep, praying to God and pleading with Him, "God, please take me home! I don't want to deal with life anymore. I don't care how you do it—disease, car accident, anything—just take me home!" Ironically, when I was falling over the cliff and believed I was going to die, I cried out, "Jesus save me!" Overwhelmed with life, I had begged God to take my life away. But when confronted with the reality of death, I had asked that my life be spared. God heard both pleas, and in His sovereign will and purpose for me, He spared my life.

In the months following my accident, when I struggled to make sense of why it happened, I came to realize that in my finite human understanding, I can never comprehend the ways of God. His ways are beyond human comprehension, yet His love and concern for humanity are realized even in the midst of tragedy. Stripped of my pride and independence, I was forced to rely on the love of God and others. And I found my faith strengthened and renewed. Even now, years later, my physical scars, which are a daily reminder of a horrifying day and the frailty of life, serve the greater purpose of reminding me that life is never without hope.

Since that April day in 1998, I have encountered further suffering and tests of my faith. But because my faith rests in God, who deeply loves me and cares about me, I know for certain that nothing this life brings—disease, pain, hardship, or even death—can separate me from His love.

~Peggy Molitor

Too Many Hats

I will say of the LORD,
"He is my refuge and my fortress,
my God, in whom I trust."
~Psalm 91:2

"I don't think I love you anymore," he said. And then he left our home. Our marriage had been struggling for many years, and my husband's words shouldn't have been a surprise. And yet, they were still devastating. Ours was a marriage plagued with pain and unmet expectations. Jeff and I had married young and started a family soon afterward. Like many couples, we brought a lot of hurt from our childhoods into our marriage. We each had our own ways of dealing with the pain—Jeff turned to alcohol, and I turned to control.

For many years in my marriage, I wore too many hats and struggled to control them all. There was my wife hat, all lacy and pretty, because that's what wives are supposed to be like. My mother hat was a very useful piece of headgear that converted into a taxi cap, counselor's cap or nurse's cap depending on the situation. The banker's visor and domestic engineer hat were not my favorites, but necessary when paying the bills and cleaning the house. I had a college cap because higher education is important, after all. And, of course, I had a work hat because it is expensive to live in Southern California.

Oh, yes, I liked my hats. They made me feel valuable, and I especially liked them all to look good whenever I walked out the door. The actress Julia Roberts is quoted as saying, "I enjoy hats. And when one has filthy hair, that is a good accessory." Julia Roberts may have been using her hats to cover her hair, but I was using mine to cover a messy life. Just like in Hollywood, things are not always what they seem. And now my wife hat had bitten the dust, and I was devastated.

I heard a pastor once say that you don't know God is all you need until God is all you have. I knew God and I put my faith in Jesus for my salvation, but I didn't think He was all I needed. If I got myself into a mess, then I would have to get myself out. I felt I was the one who needed to be in control. God had more important things to do. But for the first time in my adult life, I wasn't in control—not of my emotions, not of my finances, not of the painful choices my husband was making, not of my future or the future of our children. Little did I know, I was getting on an emotional roller coaster called separation that would last for more than two years. It was during this time that I truly learned what the pastor's words meant: Faith in God was all I had to get me through.

Have you ever tried to wear a hat on a roller coaster ride? They don't stay on very well! When I was at the top of the ride, I was feeling optimistic. I would put on my banker's hat and think, "We'll be okay. The kids and I can manage." Then down the coaster I would go! "What happens if Jeff doesn't help out financially? We will never make it!" I would cry. Then I would spend quiet time with God, reading His words to us in the Bible, and it was as if He were speaking directly to me. "Lynne, give me your banker's hat. Trust me to be your provider. I will supply all your needs according to my riches in heaven."

At the top of the roller coaster, I would put on my mother's hat. On a good day, I would think, "The kids are going to be okay. We probably didn't mess them up too badly." And then down the emotional roller coaster I would go. "Oh, no, what if we did mess them up? What if they wind up on *The Jerry Springer Show*? That is every mother's nightmare!" Then I would meditate on God and read another verse in the Bible, and it was as if God would say to me,

"Lynne, trust me with your mother's hat. I love your children more than you do. I knit them together in your womb."

Then I would put on my fortuneteller's hat. You know the one I am talking about, the one you wear when you like to think you have it all figured out—a one-year, five-year, ten-year plan. At the top, I thought I could see clear skies ahead. But then I would plummet down and realized my plans had gone awry. I had planned to be married, and that wasn't looking very good. Once more, I would turn to God and read His words, which seemed to be written especially for me. I could hear Him say, "Lynne, give me your fortuneteller's hat. Trust me with your future, '… for I know the plans I have for you… plans to prosper you and not to harm you, plans to give you hope and a future'" (Jeremiah 29:11). My wife hat? I didn't even fight God for control over that one. I knew it would take a miracle for my marriage to be mended.

Through faith, I was able to relinquish all of my hats to God. It was one of the most challenging times of my life, but also one of the most rewarding. I was able to have peace in the midst of a hair-raising, hat-dropping roller coaster ride. People are skeptical when I tell them that, but it is true. I even came to a place where I could pray for my husband, in spite of the painful choices he was making, and my prayer was that he would come to have a renewed faith in God. I knew that if he did, his life would change forever.

Eventually, my husband did put his complete trust in God. We reconciled, and God was able to work the miracle we needed in our marriage. If I hadn't put my faith in God and trusted him with my hats, my children, my husband, my marriage, my life, well, I would have missed all the good things God had for me, including a restored marriage. Instead of living like the Mad Hatter with a false sense of control, I have now found a peace and faith "which transcends all understanding" (Philippians 4:7).

In the midst of joy and blessings, we have experienced loss and sorrow, like everyone else. No, we are not promised a problem-free life. But we are promised that when we put our faith in God, He will never leave us nor forsake us, whatever we go through. He is now my counselor, my comforter, my controller, and He sits beside me on every roller coaster ride that life brings my way.

~Lynne Leite

72

Fear, Faith, and Trust

Fear and courage are brothers.
~Proverb

"How many fingers am I holding up?" The cornea specialist had asked me this question every day for weeks. Once again, in despair, I whispered, "None." Then I cried, "I'm living my worst nightmare!"

"Don't give up hope," he said. "You WILL see again, I promise you." Only later would I discover that he'd been lying and didn't really believe my vision could be restored.

Due to complications from an illness, I'd been struck blind. In spite of various treatments, my inflamed corneas would not heal.

"Continue the steroids and eye drops," the doctor instructed. "And be careful not to touch your eyes."

I was frustrated, but most of all afraid. Even worse than the searing pain stabbing at my eyes were the terrifying "what ifs." What if I rubbed my face in my sleep? The slightest touch could cause irreparable damage. What if I would never see to drive my car, read a book or watch a sunset? In despair, I questioned, "Why, God?"

I'd become skittish about anything near my eyes. I needed Valium to be coaxed into the examining chair. Still, I soaked it with perspiration. And when the doctor announced that I needed another surgery, I responded, "I'd rather have my legs amputated!" But I had no choice.

That night, as I lay awake, I discovered the meaning of the saying by Dorothy Bernard: "Courage is fear that has said its prayers."

When life was easy, I hadn't thought much about my faith. After all, who needs faith in good times? Faith is for troubled times, and now I needed it. As I listened to a radio station playing soft music with Bible readings, I begged God to increase my trust.

I'm not sure what caused my sudden feeling of peace. Maybe it was knowing that God had heard my prayer. Maybe it was remembering that others were praying, too. Or was it the soothing music? I believe it was the power in God's Word.

I felt the anxiety draining from my mind and body. As the lump in my throat melted away, I took what felt like my first deep breath in weeks.

It was as if a fountain of fresh water rinsed away my fear. I remembered the words of Jesus: "Do not let your hearts be troubled and do not be afraid" (John 14:27). I could either let myself be troubled or let myself accept His peace.

Suddenly, I trusted God's wisdom and love completely. "It's in your hands, God. Your will be done." I realized that's what faith really is—finding comfort in trusting God with every detail of my life. I knew that if He didn't heal me, He had a good reason. I also knew that He would provide all the strength I'd need to endure whatever happened.

The surgery went well. My vision grew clearer over the next few months. I had defied all odds, and doctors said it was a miracle—but I already knew that.

Actually, God gave me two miracles. He restored my sight, but He also transformed my attitude and increased my faith. Like a plant bursting from a dead seed, a peaceful trust in Him blossomed from fear. Perhaps that was the greater miracle.

~Marsha Mott Jordan

73

Backseat Driver

As your faith is strengthened you will find that there is no longer the need to have a sense of control, that things will flow as they will, and that you will flow with them, to your great delight and benefit.

~Emmanuel

Bless me, Father, for I have sinned. It's been one hour since I grabbed the reins and took control... again!

I confess. I am a planning, anal-retentive, organizing perfectionist who likes to make lists and be in control whenever possible! So, basically, I am a Type A personality, if you haven't already guessed.

I don't know how long I have been this way, whether by birth or created out of life circumstances, but I do know that it has made me who I am today and has been my cross to bear. Maybe it began when I was seven and discovered, rather harshly, that I had a learning disability. Maybe it was throughout grade school as I taught myself how to overcome and cope with my learning disability until it became barely noticeable. Or perhaps it was during high school when I graduated in the top ten percent of my class. My life is a variable bread-crumb trail of experiences that point to my excessive effort to control life's situations and circumstances, in my own effort to find peace and comfort. What I do know is that my life spiraled out of control during my freshman year of college.

Discounting the plethora of changes that occur during that transitional phase in a young adult's life, I developed a severe eating disorder. I was unhappy with my campus life, and what little school "family" I did have was wrapped up in crew (rowing). I dived head-first into the crew team and found my niche at school. Life was perfect—until I blew out both my knees during a placement test that determined boat position. I ignored the pain at first, wincing through the training sessions and competitions. I couldn't lose this; what would I do? Besides, I could overcome (control) this. It wasn't until I couldn't make it up the stairs that I had to face the problem. After months of therapy, doctor consultations, and cortisone shots, it was determined that surgery was out of the question, it wasn't severe enough, and I would no longer be able to row. I was devastated. The coach let me stay on as coxswain, but it never felt right. I began my lengthy descent into the valley.

It wasn't long before the eating disorder took control, although I thought I was the one holding the reins. Eventually, I had to admit that I needed help. I called home, withdrew from college, and entered rehab. It was one of the most awful times in my life.

Rehab, however, was worse. Of course, I was completely and utterly out of control. It was a nightmare. I had no say in what I ate, when I ate, what I did, when I did it, or free-time activities. I couldn't even work out, which I needed for my sanity. But just when I thought things couldn't get worse, a yearning developed from deep within, and a faint light began to glow in the distance.

It was then that I saw Jesus and met Him again, although it felt like the first time. During my sixty days in rehab, I was alone, truly alone, for the first time. I had no choice but to look within myself. I began to relish my daily time of reflection, and soon began to pray and foster my newfound relationship. And, before I knew it, I was out of the valley and back on the mountain path. But this time, I had a travel guide.

I have been through various other mountains and valleys over the years, and they haven't always been easy or pretty. Our relation-ship with the Lord isn't a promise of smooth paths; in fact, sometimes they are rockier. What He does promise us is that we will never travel it alone or in complete darkness. There will always be a lantern, map, and guide to traverse the winding and shaky terrain with us.

I admit, I still like to be in control, but these days I have an easier time recognizing it and calmly, although sometimes half-heartedly, handing the wheel back over to God. As the tried-and-true analogy states: You are driving in a car with Christ. He is at the wheel, and you are in the back seat, taking it all in. Worries, troubles, headaches, and problems come and go, but with Christ in control, you never have to worry because He knows exactly how to run the show. And, you know, I've found that I like the back seat—the view is great, the responsibility nil, and the conversation superb. I just hope He takes pit stops; my bladder isn't what it used to be.

~Francesca Lang

74

Love Is Near

What lies behind you and what lies in front of you,
pales in comparison to what lies inside of you.
~Ralph Waldo Emerson

I look around at my family that I love so much. We are sharing a Christmas season breakfast at a local pancake house. The Christmas feeling surrounds us with its sounds, smells and sparkling decor. My two daughters are discussing menu options with my four grandchildren, while my husband and sons-in-law are discussing last night's game. How blessed I am to have my family, and how fortunate that I can be there for them now. How thankful I am for my health and for my career as a counsellor and health care assistant, which enables me to assist so many of the vulnerable in our society. I am so very grateful.

Things were not always like this. In the 1970s, when very little was understood about depression, severe postpartum depression robbed me of precious time with my girls, family and myself. The pain and feelings that accompany a clinical depression are overwhelming, and for me no physical pain has ever been as bad. I hated the fact that I could not think my way out, and I felt guilty and angry.

Thankfully, things changed on one cold gray day. The day matched the cold grayness of my life at that time. I was alone and lonely. I stood by my window and looked out. Without thinking, I cried, "Oh, God, what am I going to do?" I had not thought about God for a very long time. I stopped and wondered what in the world had made me think of God. I thought I had rejected that belief along with many others from my childhood. That day, though, I was convinced the path I was on was going nowhere at all. I was desperate. There had to be another way, so I decided to try asking for help.

"Okay," I thought. "God, Universe, whatever you are, if you are there, please show me another way, because what I am doing is not working. Please help!" I looked at the dark clouds outside my window and imagined my request floating up into a vacant sky where it might not be noticed. But from deep inside me I felt a response. It came very subtly, a shift or a slight stir from somewhere that brought a feeling of peace.

To help maintain this peaceful feeling, I began to practice meditation as a way to calm my mind. I was totally unprepared, as I meditated one day, when a door seemed to open inside me, and a loving, warm energy enveloped me in a moment of oneness and spiritual connection. The word "connection" definitely describes this profound experience. It was amazing! I recognized that what I had been searching for had been there all the time. Things began to change. Outside, the world was the same, but the way I viewed it was changing. It was as if I was looking at the same scene, but seeing it from a different perspective, from another window that let in much more light.

My faith began to grow, and my belief in this higher power sustained and guided me—and still does. Life began to change for the better as I took responsibility for choosing my own path. At times, it was not easy to follow and still isn't, but the difference is that I know it is my path!

Now, I live my life more from the inside-out, instead of the opposite. I still have many lessons to learn, but I have found that my faith, self-love and increased awareness are much better tools than the ones I had before.

I enjoy spiritual gatherings, but I can find a sacred connection from a bird flying serenely across the sky, or by the stillness and tranquility found in a forest or by the love I feel for my family.

As I bring my attention back to my family and the Christmas

breakfast we are enjoying together, I am so glad that I asked for help, and found my faith and another way to live. So much good has come out of the darkest, most painful experience of my life. I realize now that love was always so very, very near!

~Elizabeth Smayda

75

The Promise

Let God's promises shine on your problems.
~Corrie Ten Boom

The surf rolled ten feet over my head, and the surge pushed me back into the deep. A beginner scuba diver, I panicked, trying to crawl as fast as I could, and forgot to plant my fingers into the sand when the next wave came. This time, the surge rolled me onto my back and pushed my mask and regulator off my face. The weight of the oxygen tank and weight belt on my back made it impossible for me to turn over to climb out of the surf. Thinking this was the end for me, I pledged that if God got me out of this mess, I would commit my life to serving Him. As the waves tossed me around, I thought of my kids on the beach waiting for their mom, and felt helpless.

My scuba instructor came to my rescue. He dropped my weight belt and called to people on shore to help. It took seven men to pull me, the panicked woman, out of the surf and back onto Monastery Beach. As I lay exhausted on the sand, I thanked God for returning me to my children and promised to go back to church and straighten out my life.

Although my children and I went back to church, my life didn't change that much. My cravings for more of everything brought me no satisfaction, and my bad choices led me down an emotional path of destruction. The kids grew up and moved away. Two divorces and several crumbled relationships left me alone and depressed. I thought about God and my broken promises. In my despair, I cried out to Him, "I don't want to go on anymore!" He heard my cry and whispered into my ear, "Could you make it today if I stay with you?"

How could the God of the universe care about me? My parents brought me up to love, trust and obey Him, but strong-willed and stubborn, I chose my ways over His. I don't know why He showed me love that day, but I'll never forget how He made me feel. It was as if He put His arms around me and kissed away my troubles, the way a loving father would. I've never wanted to be outside of the love I felt, so I picked up my Bible and started reading it every day before I went to work. It seemed as if every passage spoke directly to me, and I began to pray. Sometimes, I didn't know what to pray. All I could say was, "Thank you, Jesus. Thank you, Jesus." I said those words over and over again. Sometimes I cried myself to sleep saying those words, so thankful that the God of creation would love even me.

When the kids left, I moved to another city. On a sunny Sunday morning, I picked up my Bible and went to the church near where I lived. Something didn't feel right. I longed to be a part of the church family as I had before, but the people all seemed perfect. I felt like an outsider. I had made such a mess of my life and didn't know how to make things right. The next day, I called the church office and made an appointment to talk with the pastor.

"I've loved attending church and being part of the family for so many years, but I am not worthy," I said.

The pastor wrinkled his brows. "No one is worthy."

"You don't understand. I've walked away from two marriages and other broken relationships," I said. "The people here look like they have their lives together, while mine is a total failure."

What the pastor said next changed my life. "We live in a world of sin, and there is no way we can be here without it touching us. The good news is that Jesus died for sin. You can accept what He did on the cross for you or you can keep beating up on yourself."

I walked out of the pastor's office a changed woman. It was a gift from God—a gift I could never earn. Jesus forgave me as He did his adversaries from the cross. He picked up the shattered pieces of my life and crafted something beautiful. He filled the void that once held restless cravings with deep longings for more of Him in my life.

Walking with God hasn't taken away pain or suffering or trials, but the difference is that I have a friend who comforts, counsels and empowers me to persevere. He gives me strength to face each day whether I experience joy or loss. He brought hope out of my despair by letting me know He is always with me. I can't describe the peace that comes from knowing I'll never walk alone again.

~Sue Tornai

Lost in Life

In order to find yourself you need to get lost in the forest of life.
~Mike Dolan

My years as a field forester spanned three geographical states—from California to Oregon to Washington—two marital states—from single to married—and, on one particular day, two physical states—from lost to found. For four years, every workday began largely the same way. I'd load my boots, my vest, and my hardhat into the company truck, stop at the office for a co-worker, my paperwork, a cup of coffee and a doughnut if I was lucky, and then head out for whatever corner of the company's land holdings I was to work in that particular day.

At the end of the day, everything went back into the truck for the drive home and a run-through of the events of the morning in reverse. The duties of each day varied depending on my job title, office location, and the season.

Some days I found difficult, such as the one on which a controlled burn lost that status when it jumped the fire lines and turned into a raging forest fire. I hated working in the bone-numbing cold of snow and hiking on terrain so steep that I had to hang on to the brush I was pushing through to keep from catapulting down the hillside.

But there were many more moments I loved, such as coming over a ridge onto the heart-stopping beauty of tree-covered hillsides stretched out before me, the heart-dropping thrill of helicopter rides with herbicide applicators who needed to be shown boundary lines, and the depths of friendship that developed between co-workers who got through all the moments together somehow. Yet few days stand out in my mind as forcibly as the day I got lost in the woods.

It began like so many others. Armed with the tools of our trade, my co-worker and I headed out to find the stand of trees we were supposed to work in that day. The morning seemed to go smoothly, but at some point in the early afternoon we noticed that our maps weren't lining up well with what we were seeing on the ground. The more we tried to get back on track, the worse the situation became until we realized we were hopelessly turned around; in short, we were lost. For hours, we trudged in one direction through thick brush and open tree stands, up one hill and down another, hoping to intersect with a road of some type that would give us a clue as to our whereabouts.

I remember the heat and physical exhaustion of the trek and our overwhelming disappointment each time we reached the top of a ridge only to see more hills and valleys before us with no logging trail or access road in sight. But mostly I remember my incredible thirst. Our water supplies emptied hours earlier, we looked in vain for refreshment in dry streambeds on a warm end-of-summer day. Weary, soaked in sweat, and incredibly cotton-mouthed, I can't describe our relief when we finally stumbled across a road, determined our location, retrieved our truck and were headed home at last.

It was a humiliating experience at best, one that required multiple explanations over the days that followed to an inquisitive boss, interested friends, and (supposedly) sympathetic spouses. Mine just thought it was funny, and the longevity of our marriage is due in part to the fact that he quickly learned to quit bringing up the subject for laughs in social gatherings. The people around me focused on the fact that I got lost. Yet what made it memorable to me was the absolute joy of being found—the relief of finally coming across a road, the gratitude for the directions we were given, and the satisfaction of finally drinking my fill.

Shortly after this incident, I discovered that I was as lost in life as

I had been in the woods that day. My job had been going along fine until a transfer to a new city left me lonely and vulnerable. A few missteps in the wrong direction knocked me seriously off course until I gradually came to realize how desperately I longed for a way to get myself back on track. I was tired of waking up each morning to more of the same questions, problems and difficulties, the answers I sought having eluded me once again. I didn't realize how spiritually thirsty I had become. Desperate to find a way out of my situation, I sought help from a fellow traveler in the guise of a Sunday school teacher who answered my questions and pointed me in the right direction, a path that led to the foot of the cross. I remember the absolute joy of walking out of the room much as I walked out of the woods that day, having moved from lost to found, a huge smile framing my face.

One more detail from our Bad-Day-in-the-Woods: When we finally found a road and had decided which way to head on it, we came upon a small house. My co-worker knocked on the door to get directions, but I spied something I needed more. A hose was curled underneath a faucet on the side of the building. Without waiting to ask permission, I ran to it, turned the spigot, and got the drink I so desperately needed. I drank, and I drank, and I drank.

Once you've discovered how lost and thirsty you are, you don't necessarily need to wait for the next available church service or to pray with a pastor to ask for a drink of Living Water, good though it is to get direction in those places. You can go straight to the Source and get what you need.

In my case, I found the Road, slacked my thirst, and have been happily heading Home ever since.

~Elaine L. Bridge

When God Doesn't Heal

Some of God's greatest gifts are unanswered prayers.
~Garth Brooks

It had been the most horrifying three years of my life. Being bedridden wasn't something I had ever thought about—until it happened to me. I'd been through a lot of surgeries but always recovered. But spinal surgery took me down. Prior to that, if I wasn't moving and doing something physical, you wouldn't have recognized me. I had owned a hair salon, played a lot of golf, and walked three miles a day. That was before, though. I often joke that I could hire myself out as a doorstop because there's not much else I'm good for these days.

My faith in God had grown exponentially during the years I spent in bed. Of course, I had assumed that being in close communication with my higher power would result in my healing. Long story short, that didn't happen. Some days, all I could do was get up and take a shower. Some days, I could have a friend over and sit and talk for a couple of hours. Going out to a store and walking around would mean that I'd pay for it for days and sometimes weeks afterward.

I had been home alone for three years in the most unimaginable pain when I decided that I should try to "get out of myself" and think of others. So, I started to volunteer at a local hospital for just four hours a day, twice a week. I ran the front desk in the lobby, telling people where to go. It made me feel like I was back in the swing of things even though standing on my feet for any longer than ten minutes at a time was a thing of the past. But even the four hours a day at the hospital proved to be too much for me. After a year of that, I landed back in bed for nine months.

At first, my faith was still strong. I believed God had something better in store for me, and that my healing would still come. But it didn't. After almost five years of believing, I gave up. I was lying on the floor and talking to the air around me. "God, if this is who you are, and this is how you work, then I don't want any part of you." I meant it. I was mad. I had had it.

I confided in a friend I had met while volunteering at the hospital. "I feel so isolated and out of touch with the outside world." I told her I didn't want any part of God. "If this is how He works, then I'm not giving Him any more of my time." I cursed Him up and down. I was in a seething rage.

She didn't say anything, but her tears spoke volumes. She understood. She had gone through a similar experience, but she had healed. I saw something in her tears, in the way she looked at me — a quiet wisdom. She had a love for Him like I never saw before — a close relationship that I didn't understand. Our visit ended with a warm hug, and I went back to lying on the floor.

Suddenly, I felt something grab my heart with a gentle strength. I must have had a look on my face like I was trying to do calculus because it was so hard to comprehend the magnitude of what I was experiencing. I knew it was God who was holding me. He gave me an intimate knowledge of the fact that He is in me and I am in Him, and that He runs through everyone, making us all connected. I had heard people say that we are all one, but until this holy moment, I didn't really understand. His touch on me that day was the purest form of compassion I had ever felt. It was clean and light and not tainted with pity, like so much of my compassion is. He grabbed the center of my being in a way that changed how I believe in Him.

It's been fourteen years now since my spinal surgery, and I'm still not healed. I still get mad, but now I know. I know without a shadow of a doubt that He's with me. He's here with all of us. And for whatever reason He chooses not to heal me, I have to believe that He knows something that I don't. He knows that I'm better off with this physical limitation. Perhaps it saves me from running around and screwing up my life. I feel like He's taming a wild horse and showing me that I don't always have to be in control. I can rest, because when I look back over the years, I can see that He's always given me what I needed, when I needed it, whether it is the right people or resources, or His grace. I can let Him guide my life in the way He knows. It's sufficient. It's enough. And I'm blessed.

~Marijo Herndon

Chapter
9

finding my faith

Finding Faith
Through His Word

There is nothing more essential to our lives than the Word of God.

~Jack Hayford

All Things

But Jesus looked at them and said to them,
"With men this is impossible, but with God all things are possible."
~Matthew 19:26 (NKJV)

I was raised in a strong Christian home. It was a home where, on a Tuesday, a stomachache could earn me a day home from school. But on a Sunday, I wasn't permitted to miss church unless actual vomit was involved. At my house, church was serious business.

But it wasn't just church. God played an active role in our lives. We read a chapter from the Bible after dinner each evening. Contemporary Christian music played frequently in our home. We prayed about big things and little things alike. My siblings and I not only attended youth group, but we were invited to be on the leadership team.

My dad made strict rules about the movies we watched and the boys we dated. Dad was a deacon in our church, and his expectations were high. He kept our family on the right path, and throughout high school, I made good choices because more than anything, I didn't want to disappoint my dad.

That's why it was so heartbreaking when my parents split up after almost thirty years of marriage. My dad, who'd always been a man of honor, had done some very dishonorable things.

I was crushed.

I blamed Dad for being weak and not caring about me the way

he should have. I was angry with him, and I was also angry with God. How could He have allowed my family to fall apart? Didn't He love me?

I felt rejected and abandoned by my father—and my Heavenly Father, too. Somehow, I'd allowed my faith to become all wrapped up in not disappointing my dad, and when he disappointed me in the worst way possible, I just gave up.

What was the point of living your life to please someone who was just going to let you down anyway?

For the next decade, I lived my life the way I wanted to. I didn't worry about my relationship with my dad—or with God. I got married and had a couple of kids. I slept in on Sunday mornings and didn't think too much about my faith—until my nine-year-old son, Jordan, found my old Bible. It was the one I'd used in high school, when I'd read it daily with a pink highlighter in my hand and an earnestness in my heart.

"Whose Bible is this, Mom?" Jordan asked.

"It's mine," I said. "I used to read that book all the time."

"Why don't you read it anymore?"

I swallowed. "I don't know."

"Do you still believe in God?"

"Well, yeah, I still believe."

"So what's your favorite Bible verse?"

"Wow, I haven't thought about that in a long time," I said. "I used to have a lot of favorite verses."

Jordan handed me my Bible. It felt strange in my hands. "Can you show me?"

I thought for a minute, trying to remember a verse that used to mean something to me. After a moment, I flipped to Matthew 19:26 (NKJV) and read it out aloud, "But Jesus looked at them and said to them, 'With men this is impossible, but with God all things are possible.'"

"That's a good verse," Jordan said. "I like that. What other ones did you used to like?"

I turned some pages and read another of my old favorites,

Romans 8:28 (NKJV). "And we know that all things work together for good to those who love God, to those who are called according to His purpose."

"Got anymore?" Jordan asked.

I flipped to Philippians 4:13 (NKJV). It had always been my very favorite verse. "I can do all things through Christ who strengthens me."

Jordan smiled. "Those are great verses, Mom. How come you never read them anymore?"

I sighed. "It's complicated, buddy."

Jordan gave me a funny look. He knew my family background was a little mixed-up, but I'd never told anyone how deeply it had affected me.

"Is it okay if I read this?"

"Oh, yeah, that would be great," I said, suddenly feeling tears in my eyes. Although my faith had waned, I still wanted my kids to be close to God.

"Can you mark the pages of your favorite verses? I want to write them down."

I did as he asked, and he took my Bible into his bedroom.

A bit later, he came back, holding a notebook in his hand. "Hey, Mom," he said. "When I was writing down your favorite verses, I noticed something pretty cool."

He sat down next to me and pointed to the verses, now written in his own handwriting. In all three verses, he'd underlined the same two words: All Things.

"Your three favorite verses have one thing in common, Mom," he explained. "They include the words 'all things.'"

I nodded slowly, realizing the poignancy of Jordan's observation. With God, all things are possible. God uses all things for good. And we can do all things through His strength.

Not some things. Not even most things. But all things.

All things.

A parents' divorce. A dad's failure. A daughter's heartbreak.

With God, it was possible to renew my long-lost faith. God could use my pain for good. And through His strength, I might even be able to forgive my dad.

I bowed my head and thanked God for never giving up on me, even though I had walked away from Him. I thanked Him for His word, and the reminder to come back to the faith I had so desperately missed.

I thanked Him that Jordan had found my old Bible. I promised to spend more time reading it and to introduce my children to its truths.

"Thank you, God," I murmured. "Thank you for loving me through all things."

~Diane Stark

The Peace I Never Knew

But seek first his kingdom and his righteousness,
and all these things will be given to you as well.
~Matthew 6:33

I sat on the edge of my bed crying. With one hand, I held the phone to my ear while trying to sort laundry. "No, Mom," I said with a lump in my throat, "you don't need to bring dinner." I swallowed hard. "I'm okay."

I lied. I wasn't okay. My life had turned upside down, so unexpectedly, so unfairly.

"Mommy, I want a drink," my three-year-old called from the kitchen.

God, why did this have to happen to me? Why now? I brushed my tears with the back of my hand. The pain weighed heavily on me, and I stood slowly. With shaking hands, I reached for the dresser and followed it to find my way to my little boys in the kitchen.

Only a few months earlier, I could still see a little. And in desperation, I had prayed, begged and pleaded over and over again to God so He would keep me from going blind. I sobbed inwardly during sleepless nights.

In vain, my husband and I had visited retina specialists and healers, and tried New Age methods, natural herbs and anything anyone suggested.

With each month, my side vision closed more and more, until all I saw was what one sees through a keyhole. Weeks later, the day

I dreaded came. I blinked, looked to the right and to the left. I saw nothing. My vision had closed in completely. No shadows, no shapes, just a gray nothing. The incurable retinal disease won, leaving me numb with fear.

I never wanted my sons to have a blind mommy, nor my husband to be married to a blind wife. My future had shattered. Without sight, I'd never be able to be productive or accomplish anything.

Feeling useless, ugly and discarded, I shook my fist at God. His punishment was undeserved and His silence cruel.

My husband, unprepared to face this trauma, grew distant. And I grew bitter. Only nine years into our marriage, my blindness was destroying our future.

"I don't think I can go on with our marriage," he announced one evening.

His rejection seared. I sank further into self-pity and fought the urge to give up.

"Mommy, he's hitting me." My little boys' antics never let up as their voices echoed in the house. And while despair filled my heart, I cared for them following mindless motions. My nights were long, and my days were dark.

One afternoon, the phone rang. With my fingertips, I followed the kitchen wall to find it.

"We're having a special service at our church," my friend said.

Church? Service? God was not on my list of those I wanted to visit.

"Some people are healed," she said.

I sighed in my gloom. With a tiny amount of hope for a miracle, I accepted.

I sat beside my friend in that Christian church while Bible verses, singing and testimonies poured toward the congregation. But there was nothing for me. No healing. No miracle. No hope.

The next week, my friend called again. "I'll pick you up."

My days at home were getting harder to cope with, so I went. And this time, seated in the same pew, while I dabbed tears with a wrinkled tissue, I heard something that whispered into my broken heart.

"But seek first his kingdom and his righteousness, and all these things will be given to you as well." It was a Bible verse from Matthew 6:33.

Seek God first? I was seeking to see again. Hoping to be normal again; longing to win my husband's love again. Those were my priorities.

"God," I cried out in my heart, "how do I seek you? I'm lost, and I'm dying inside. Will you show me?"

With a headset on, I listened to the Bible, soaked in His Word and delighted in His promises. I then took the step, the bold step, to invite Jesus to be my Lord and owner of my life. And how beautiful that life became!

In the same way that I got to know my husband when we dated, I got acquainted with Jesus. I spent time with Him, listening to passages that spoke of His miracles. The stories where He healed thousands. The episodes that recounted His unending love for the unlovable. The instances where He restored sight to the blind. And how He died a cruel death just for me. But what made our relationship a forever union was the fact He wasn't dead, but alive. Always vibrantly active in moments when I tripped over a toy. When I groped my way through the kitchen. And in moments when I called people to help with rides for my son's Boy Scout meetings. He was always there, able to meet my every need.

He also knew the perfect order of those needs. Ever so gently, he scooped up the pieces of my broken heart, wiped them and put them back together. Restored and triumphant, I saw beyond my blindness. I was at peace and I regained my confidence.

I wasn't that scared and broken young woman anymore. With dignity in my heart and poise in my words, I called my husband. "I won't force you to stay," I said. "I have someone who will take care of me and watch over our sons; someone who will never leave me. I'm not afraid of being blind anymore. You're free to go."

Days later, he came home, and told me with conviction in his voice that he'd chosen to be committed to our family and devoted to me. We fell in love all over again. And now, after thirty-five years of marriage, I delight still in the sweet forgiveness that began on that day and continues to repeat the blessing he is to me.

Healing fueled my passion. And back then, as a mom at thirty-two, I didn't let blindness decrease my energy. "C'mon, guys, it's bath time!" I called out to my sons.

Learning to perform tasks at home—cooking, laundry, cleaning, helping with homework—were all achieved. I made mistakes. I washed dark clothing with white, used powdered sugar instead of flour, and knocked glasses of milk off the table. But there was never a mistake in what I had received: Jesus had set me free from my dark prison.

And in that freedom, Jesus didn't give me what I wanted, but what I needed—courage to defeat gloom and strength to venture out. He wasn't silent anymore. His voice leaped from the Bible to guide me to an award-winning Spanish-interpreting career. He was active in every detail, giving His direction for me to write books and to craft messages to help others see the best of life.

And although physically blind, with new vision I see—truly see—my life shining with contagious joy, the joy I never had, and the peace I never knew.

~Janet Perez Eckles

The Lie

The LORD detests lying lips, but he delights in people who are trustworthy.
~Proverbs 12:22

I am grateful that God would not let me rest when I tried to be dishonest. The burden of my guilt became so heavy that I could not bear it. It was a physical presence that I could not escape. But I tried. Oh, how I tried.

It began as a small, insignificant incident, then mushroomed beyond all intention or expectation, the way that lies often do. I was on a business trip with a colleague, driving a company car. We stopped for lunch at a delightful Cajun restaurant and were anxious to beat the crowd, in a hurry as usual. Jennifer alighted before me and rushed ahead to get a table. When I tried to open the door of the car, it stuck. I pushed harder. No luck. Taking a deep breath, I shoved with all my might. The effort was rewarded, and the door flew open, producing a sickening thud.

I had scratched the door of the car parked next to me. This was my first business trip, and Jennifer was so self-assured. I didn't want to admit my mistake to her, much less my boss. So, I decided to just ignore it. I figured no one would notice, not right away at least.

Lunch consisted of a succulent blackened red snapper, but tasted like straw to me. My heart sank upon returning to the car. Fluttering in the breeze under the windshield wiper was "the note." Jennifer immediately called the other driver a jerk. "Nancy, you would have known if you had hit his car. That scratch was probably already there, and when he realized we worked for a big company, he saw the chance to get some money." She pointed at the company logo on the side of the car.

"Yeah," I agreed. Thus, began the mushrooming. It was rather easy, for I had a witness who would swear I had not done it. It was simply a matter of our word against theirs. So, I lied to my boss, then to the risk management person, then to the accountant. With each lie, my burden became heavier. I tried to ignore my growing guilt, rationalizing that it wasn't important.

But it was.

My New Year's resolution had been to read the Bible through before the year ended, using the daily readings suggested in my devotional. When the lying commenced, my shame would not let me face our Lord, not even in His Word. So, on the day that my guilt became so heavy I could ignore it no longer, I was many days behind.

That day, I had been unable to concentrate. I was not capable of thinking of anything but The Lie. So, I finally confessed—to a dear and trusted friend. She sent me to The Word. I still resisted and offered some feeble excuse about not knowing where to start. "Just read what you're supposed to read in today's reading," she counseled. When I picked up my Bible at last, I simply began where I had left off.

This is how God spoke to me five times that day, knowing what I needed to hear, knowing where I would begin to read.

Deuteronomy 31:6: "'Be strong and courageous. Do not be afraid or terrified because of them, for the LORD your God goes with you; he will never leave you nor forsake you.'" I memorized this verse and repeated it over and over. Otherwise, I would never have the courage to confess to all the people I had lied to.

Luke 12:10: "'And everyone who speaks a word against the Son of Man will be forgiven…'" I had spoken a lie and that is against the Son of Man. But God promises to forgive me.

Luke 12:11-12: "'When you are brought before synagogues, rulers and authorities, do not worry about how you will defend yourselves or what you will say, for the Holy Spirit will teach you at that time what you should say.'" My translation: Be obedient to me, Nancy, and I will help you do as I ask.

Psalm 78:36-38: "But then they would flatter him with their mouths, lying to him with their tongues; their hearts were not loyal to him, they were not faithful to his covenant. Yet he was merciful; he forgave their iniquities and did not destroy them." Once again, God assured me of his forgiveness and his mercy.

Proverbs 12:22: "The LORD detests lying lips, but he delights in people who are trustworthy." Oh, how I wanted to be a delight unto the Lord!

I could not believe as I progressed from reading to reading that God had more for me. Each reading brought greater and greater assurance of God's presence. With His help, I could be honest.

The confessions were not easy. I cried. Jennifer said she still thought the guy was a jerk. The risk management person said she was glad to get the straight story and had no recriminations. The accountant just adjusted her records. My boss said he could not think of a better time (Easter) for a catharsis, a change of heart that allowed me to turn back toward God. He even said that he was proud of me for my honesty.

I thank the Lord for this experience, for allowing me to make this U-turn. I am grateful that He loved me enough to humble me. I know beyond a doubt that He is ever present in my life and in His Word, and will not forsake me.

~Nancy Baker

81

Pauper to Princess

If any of you lacks wisdom, you should ask God, who gives generously to all
without finding fault, and it will be given to you.
~James 1:5

College was a confusing place for me. I had been raised in a loving Christian home and had been sheltered from the harshness of life. I was a little too naive for my own good. When I unpacked my boxes and suitcases from home and pinned my posters on the wall, I chose to leave the faith of my childhood packed away. I was eager to find my own way and discover my own beliefs apart from my parents. Here, I would become an adult and I was eager to become wise and mature.

At the university I was exposed to many different philosophies and religious beliefs, and I studied them with great interest. I frequented every advertised lecture series that came on campus and was swayed by each prestigious speaker who took the podium. I boldly adopted new convictions and tossed aside the old. With each new idea, I broke through personally held barriers, both in my thinking and my actions. Everything was exciting and new, but I had an uneasy sense that my decisions were anchored in shifting sand and could change at any moment.

Art was my major and "eat art" my motto. I painted realistic portraits in watercolor and sculpted futuristic playgrounds in clay. I designed marketing pieces for business campaigns and experimented with abstracts. It was a very creative period for me.

My boyfriend of several years transferred from his college to mine so that we could be together. He, along with my new philosophies, pushed at my long-held boundaries. Because I no longer clung to the absolutes I had learned from the Bible, I was inclined to go along, but I began to feel used. I was losing something of myself and no longer felt loved and cherished as I had before. I felt very alone. In the past, I would have prayed for guidance, but I had tossed aside that practice, deeming it archaic.

One evening, feeling very conflicted, I decided to go to a local church service. I listened to the pastor speak and the choir sing, but I felt I didn't belong there anymore. Perhaps God had tossed me aside too. When the final prayer was said, I stood to walk back to my dorm, lost in my thoughts of desolation.

"Headed to the dorm?" I turned to see who had spoken to me. It was Ali, a girl I knew only casually. She caught up to me and matched me stride for stride. She mentioned the service and how she liked what the pastor had said. I didn't want to speak to anyone so I hardly responded. Oblivious to my lack of interaction, she pointed across the campus and commented on how beautiful the clouds were now that the sunset was tinting them amber and fuchsia. Barely lifting my head to look at the sky, I agreed, but again had nothing to add to the conversation. My heart was heavy, thinking of the poor choices I had made and how bad I felt about myself.

When we got to the steps of the dorm, I told Ali I lived on the third floor. She said she lived on the first, so I gave her a small smile and turned to part company. Ali smiled back and said, "Okay, see ya! And remember, you're a princess!"

Her words startled me to attention. I could not have felt less like a princess than I did right then. I wheeled around to face her. "What did you say?" I asked.

"You're a princess. You're a child of the King!" she replied, still smiling. I collapsed on the stairs leading up to my room, my body wracked with sobs.

Ali rubbed my shoulders, trying to find a way to comfort me. "I don't know what is wrong," she said, "but maybe you should read the 'Consider It Pure Joy Book.'" I had no idea what she meant, so she explained that the book of James in the New Testament talked a lot about going through trials and tough times, and how God would be there with me through it all. I nodded and sprinted up the stairs, still unable to speak.

Back in the privacy of my room, I dug under my bed and pulled out the suitcase that had nothing left in it but my Bible. I began to read the book of James. "Consider it pure joy, my brothers and sisters, whenever you face trials of many kinds, because you know that the testing of your faith produces perseverance. Let perseverance finish its work so that you may be mature and complete, not lacking anything" (James 1:2-4). I wanted to be mature more than anything else, and these words spoke to me as though written in a personal letter. I read on. "If any of you lacks wisdom, you should ask God, who gives generously to all without finding fault, and it will be given to you" (James 1:5). Here at college I was listening to teachings from various conflicting sources but God was telling me to come to Him for wisdom. I read through most of the night, stopping occasionally to wipe away tears and pray for understanding. The morning came with new hope, courage and joy!

I never told Ali what a difference her simple statement made in my life. In fact, I don't remember even running into her again the rest of my days at college. But she had reunited me with my best friend, Jesus. From that moment forward, I read the Bible and weighed each of my decisions against the Rock that doesn't change. I was reminded of how much I was loved and I knew that God, my Father, the King, was welcoming me back home.

~Lindy Schneider

82

The Jewish Believer

For there is no difference between Jew and Gentile —
the same Lord is Lord of all and richly blesses all who call on him…
~Romans 10:12

"Mommy, why don't we believe in Jesus?" I asked at about age six, startling my Jewish family. We'd recently watched the movies *Ben-Hur* and *Spartacus*, and it kindled my desire to know more about Jesus.

Actually, this is not an uncommon question among Jewish kids who've been exposed to Protestants and Catholics, either in their neighborhoods, on TV or in school.

Most rabbis and Jewish scholars acknowledge Jesus as a sort of rebellious Jewish teacher with a radical message, and that knowing Him as anything more is taboo. I was curious. To me, it seemed perfectly reasonable that one man should die for the sins of many. After all, when one child misbehaved in school, we all seemed to get punished.

When I was little, we were the only Jewish family in a predominantly Catholic neighborhood. One time, I traded necklaces with my best friend, Laurie—a diamond-studded, six-pointed Star of David for her gold cross. I'll never forget seeing our two mothers rush across the street to exchange them!

It's not that I didn't want to be Jewish. The sight of my grandmother lighting the Sabbath candles in a darkened room, the glow of candlelight on her face and a delicate white lace shawl on her head, is a beautiful and precious memory. I happily anticipated becoming the woman of a house so I could do it.

But other than my maternal grandparents, I seemed to be the only person in the family who believed the stories of the Torah. I loved Passover, and totally believed the story of Moses and the Red Sea parting.

At age thirteen, I was bat mitzvah'd. I stood in front of two hundred people and read the appropriate portion of the Torah for the season of my birthday.

After my grandparents died, my parents turned to atheism. I became a "closet believer in God." I forgot all about exploring any connection to a man named Christ because it was hard enough to even keep up the Jewish traditions. Slowly, my faith died completely.

Three years after my marriage to a Jewish young man failed, I met the man who would become my lifelong husband. He was from a family with Christian roots, but he hadn't attended church since his teen years.

While we were dating, his mother started going back to church, and he began having long conversations about God with her. A year after we married, he went to a church near our house. From then on, he went on a regular basis and studied the Bible daily. One day, he announced, "I've accepted Jesus as my Lord and Savior."

Having forgotten my girlhood desire to know Jesus, I thought his newfound belief was preposterous. How could a man be the miraculous "Son of God," die on a cross and then come back to life to "take away the sins of the world"? I feared his faith would lead to divorce for us. I still considered myself Jewish by tradition, as do many atheists and agnostics with Jewish backgrounds. So staying married to a Christian didn't appeal to me, even though we had other interfaith marriages in the family.

I decided to go to his church with him and prove him wrong. First, upon entering the church, I had to get past the feeling that God would strike me dead for sitting in front of a cross! I remembered all the bad things that my Jewish family and temple leaders understood happened to the European Jews during the Holocaust, and they felt many Christians were known to have looked the other way.

The people at my husband's church made me feel welcome and comfortable, and in fact were very excited to have a Jewish person among them. I learned their Bible included the Holy Scriptures from the Jewish Torah, and that you could read the Bible yourself, not just when the person in the pulpit was talking.

I began to see the old scriptures in a new light, and realized God could be in my life. Through verses like "The LORD is my light and my salvation—whom shall I fear?" (Psalm 27:1), I became acquainted with God as more than just the heavenly being who gave us the Ten Commandments. My eyes were opened to Him as someone I could talk with and pray to.

Because the prayers at the Jewish synagogue of my childhood were pretty routine, I never knew there was such a thing as having a "personal relationship" with God—bringing Him our deepest desires through prayer and considering Him as a father.

Over the next few months, I also re-discovered the fact that Jesus was from a Jewish family, and that he didn't come to start a new religion, but to bring both Jewish people and Gentiles into a greater understanding of who God was.

We studied similarities about the Messiah in the Torah and the Gospel, like Psalm 22:18 and Matthew 27:35. Other verses stunned me about Christ's followers worshipping the same God as the Jews, like Romans 10:12. The feelings of my childhood rushed back. Could Jesus really be more than just a man, a teacher, a radical? Could He be the Messiah? Could knowing Jesus fit in with being Jewish? But how could I believe in Jesus when it seemed to be a general understanding that His followers had hated my ancestors for centuries?

Then I remembered. The Jewish religion is entwined with the concept of redemption. Animal sacrifices were made in the temple for redemption from sin. Boaz was Ruth's "Kinsman Redeemer"—he rescued her from her widowed state. Plus, if biblical prophecy is to be believed, everything happens for a reason and is within God's control.

And so Jesus, Yeshua in Hebrew, is the ultimate Redeemer who could save me from my own disbelief to live a new life for God.

I became a Jewish believer in Jesus in 1987. As a wonderful serendipity, my Jewish faith has grown! I've gone back to appreciating my Jewish roots and believing the old Bible stories are true, not just legends I learned as a child. There aren't many of us Jewish believers in the world but we feel assurance in our hearts that God's hand inspired all the scriptures, both Old and New.

Today, I help Christian churches learn about the Jewish holidays and how to celebrate them within tenets of the Christian faith. After all, when Jesus was conducting what would become known as the Last Supper, He was celebrating the Jewish Passover.

~Sheryl Young

I Will Give You Rest

"Come to me, all you who are weary and burdened, and I will give you rest."
~Matthew 11:28

Life as I knew it had become hectic. Between my full-time job, our three boys' homework and sports, keeping up with household chores, and making sure appointments were made and kept, I had definitely lost sight of who I was. It was the summer before my fortieth birthday, and I was struggling with all the things that I thought I should have accomplished by this age. I was being pulled in so many directions that I just started going through the motions. I was emotionally and physically tired. I really couldn't handle anything else on my plate. And then the phone rang at 4:38 A.M. on July 3, 2010.

"Daddy's not breathing. The ambulances are here."

Daddy was only sixty-three years old, and he and Mom had just retired a year earlier. He had his first heart attack nine years before, and over the years, five stents had been put in to relieve blockages. We knew his heart wasn't the strongest, but he had just gone to the cardiologist the Monday before to do a stress test because he had been feeling more tired than usual. The doctor called on Friday to say he'd passed the test, meaning there wasn't any significant blockage to cause alarm. He died in his bed less than twenty-four hours later.

Daddy was the foundation of our family. Sunday mornings, we would often get a call that Daddy was in the mood to barbecue or cook a gumbo, and all three of us children, three spouses, and six grandkids would stop whatever plans we had to spend the afternoon with them. When Hurricane Rita threatened our little corner of Louisiana and we had to evacuate, we all called Daddy to see what his plan of action was because wherever he was going, we were going, too.

In the months that followed Daddy's death, I found myself retreating from life. I longed for my pajamas and my bed. I just wanted to escape. I was overwhelmed and exhausted. The music at Sunday Mass made me emotional, and my boys kept asking if I was going to cry every time we went. I didn't want their memories of their Pawpaw to be of their mom crying all the time, so we quit attending church. I came home from work every day, got into my pajamas, and mindlessly watched TV. I remember telling my husband and friends that I just wanted to get away. I wanted to drive my car down the interstate until it ran out of gas, check into a hotel, and sleep for forty-eight hours straight. I just wanted rest.

In December, our church had a signup to attend a women's weekend retreat to be held at the end of January. I had heard of this retreat before, but always had a reason not to attend. The boys were busy almost every weekend year-round with sports. I didn't see how I could spare the time for myself. However, this retreat was to be held the last weekend of January, which was about the only month of the year that the boys did not have a full schedule of activities. So, I signed up.

It was time for me to find my roots again. My parents had raised us in a little Catholic church in the country. We could be found every Sunday morning in the second pew from the front on the right side of the church. Daddy sang in the choir, which was seated at the front on the right side of the church. He could see when Mom had to nudge my brother to sit up straight, or my sister and I to pay attention instead of giggling at whatever gave us the giggles that morning. Mom and Dad were strong in their Catholic faith and remained an intricate part of this little church even after we were grown and found churches of our own. To this day, Mom can still be found in the same second pew every Sunday.

On the first night of our retreat, the theme was unveiled to us in the form of a scripture verse and a picture. The leader of the retreat asked us to close our eyes and imagine our "safe place." Since Daddy's death, my safe place was crawling into my husband's lap, resting my head against his chest, and listening to his heartbeat to calm me. As the cloth was pulled from the picture, I couldn't believe my eyes! It was a portrait of Jesus holding a young girl who was resting her head against his chest. It took my breath away! If I had any remaining doubt that I was meant to be on this retreat, it quickly vanished when the cloth was removed from the board that held our retreat scripture: "Come to me, all you who are weary and burdened, and I will give you rest" (Matthew 11:28). Rest! That is exactly what I had been searching for. That weekend, I found rest in the form of my faith. I came away from that weekend with my faith renewed, and instead of tears flowing during Mass, I would sing along and sway to the music with a warmth in my heart that I hadn't felt since long before Daddy's death.

In the months that followed the retreat, I managed to attend Mass weekly, whether it was on Sunday with my family or alone during the week at the Catholic church near my office. About mid-March, I was having what I call a "Daddy day." I was missing him and feeling low, so I decided to attend noon Mass. I arrived about five minutes before the service started and decided to do a little reading. I picked up the missalette and read the gospel from the weekend before as well as the gospel for the following weekend. It then occurred to me that since Daddy died on a Saturday, the one-year anniversary of his death would fall on a Sunday. I figured we would all go to Mass with Mom at her church and squeeze our families into that same second pew.

I decided to flip forward in the missalette to the gospel that we would hear on the one-year anniversary, Sunday, July 3, 2011. As I began to read, I felt this calmness come over me. It wasn't until I read the very last sentence in that gospel reading that I understood why: It was from the book of Matthew. Specifically, chapter 11. The very last verse read as follows: "Come to me, all you who are weary and burdened, and I will give you rest." Once again, my faith was renewed!

Later that day, I found out that the gospels in the missalette are on a three-year rotation. What are the chances that the one-year anniversary of Daddy's death would fall on a Sunday? What are the chances that on that particular Sunday, the very scripture verse from my faith-renewing retreat would be the gospel reading for that day? Coincidence? I think not.

~Tracie David

84

Look Who's Knocking at My Door

I would rather walk with God in the dark than go alone in the light.
~Mary Gardiner Brainard

The knock at my back door came one late afternoon in fall. It was my mom. "Here, Marisa. I thought you might like this. Someone dropped it off at the rectory today, and it's in large print. Perhaps it will be large enough for you to read."

Taking the weighted, very large Bible from her hands, I just laughed hysterically.

"Really, Mom? Do you honestly think that I am going to read that? It's only going to collect dust on my bookshelf. Take it back. I'm sure someone else would actually put it to use."

She handed it to me anyway as she left and insisted, "You never know; you just may be happy to have it one day."

"Yeah, right," I said sarcastically.

I was almost thirty and had taught at a Catholic school for years until my second son was born. Now, I was a legally blind, stay-at-home mom depressed about my sudden vision loss. I couldn't drive, for I had lost my sight literally overnight due to a rare genetic eye disease at the age of twenty-five. My children were truly my joy, yet there was something desperately missing in my life. Not being able to drive proved to be difficult, and at times I felt like a prisoner in my own home. I was angry at God!

Several months later, my girlfriend, Deb, called me up. "Hey, Aunt Dollie would like to take you to a women's Bible breakfast. She thinks it would be good for you, and perhaps you will even be healed." I welcomed the invitation and looked forward to spending time with some dear friends, even if it was at a religious function.

On a blustery cold Saturday morning, my friend picked me up and took me to the hotel for the conference. When we got inside, three women drew near to me.

"Can I lay hands on you? I feel the Holy Spirit's presence in you very strongly." Sera was the speaker for that day and was known for her intercessory healings.

"Sure, whatever," I said, but I was thinking, "Lady, you can do anything to me if you give me my sight back. But who exactly is this Holy Spirit that is so strong in me? And how did she know that?"

Their hands felt warm over my eyes and head. It felt as though electricity was running through my body. When they finished, I knew that something remarkable had happened.

"Deb, I can't sit still. Something's going on."

"Can you see again?" she asked with an anxious voice.

I squinted hard, trying to focus my vision, but that was not the something that was happening. I went into the restroom, and my spirit cried out as I spoke to God for the first time in years.

"Lord, I don't know what you are doing to me, but I do know that something happened in there. I will follow you and do whatever you want me to do!"

I walked out and joined the two hundred women who were sitting and listening to Bible scriptures. For the first time the words spoke to my heart. Later, I stood up in front of those ladies and was compelled to share several amazing stories about things God had done in my life. I had never before had the courage to speak in public. But that was it. I was zapped by the spirit of boldness. My faith, which had once been even smaller than that of a mustard seed, had grown taller than that of a skyscraper—enough to move mountains.

My heart was healed. My spirit was healed. Since then, I have carried my Bible every day, and it is tattered and torn. I was called into ministry as a religious education coordinator at my church four months later. A year after that, some of my vision actually improved, which resulted in permission for a restricted driver's license—a true miracle! Later, I even entered into seminary for pastoral counseling. Today, at the age of forty-two, I have my own women's boutique where we minister to women in need, crisis, and depression through "The Wall of Compassion" and sharing our faith stories.

I had been angry at God at one time for my vision loss, but later learned that I walk by faith and not by sight. His vision is perfect for my life! So, when you hear a knock at your door and someone hands you a Bible and you laugh, you'd better watch out—you never know who's really knocking and when you are going to need it!

~Marisa Balzafiore

85

Back on the Team

Cast all your anxiety on him because he cares for you.
~1 Peter 5:7

I think I've always believed in God. I figured that this amazing universe must have some great mind behind it, planning it, keeping it running. But there was a time in my life when I decided to opt out of being on God's team.

I was living in Indonesia in the 1960s, the wife of a State Department communications officer, with our four children. I was depressed about the poverty. At that time in America, we didn't have many people living on the streets, but they surrounded me in Jakarta. Rickshaw drivers, who left their village families to earn money in the capital, slept in their rickshaws. Whole families lived in cardboard shacks or pieces of tin cobbled together for shelter, their neighborhoods reeking of sewage and garbage. Raggedy, runny-nosed little kids ran wild in the streets, skipping school, perpetuating poverty.

When we ate in restaurants, we always ordered more food than we could eat, knowing it wouldn't be wasted. Children stared through the plate-glass windows and rushed in at the end of our meal, giggling. They scooped our leftovers into tin cans, then flew out the door before the waiters could shoo them away. My heart ached for them.

I decided that if this was the way God ran the world, I didn't want to be involved with Him, and I figured He wasn't much concerned about me, either. We were no longer on speaking terms. Without

God's influence, I lived an unwholesome life and began an affair with an Indonesian.

Then I contracted typhoid fever. I truly didn't care if I lived or died; I didn't care about anything!

Communists were trying to take over the country, and Indonesian President Sukarno was cooperating with them. Tanks rumbling in the streets strictly enforced a 6:00 P.M. to 6:00 A.M. curfew. One horrible night, we heard shots as soldiers massacred anti-Communist officials and fed them to crocodiles in a swamp.

The American State Department gradually evacuated dependents and non-essential personnel. My husband had to stay. I gave the children footlockers to fill with whatever they valued, knowing they would likely never see anything they left behind. They weren't scared so much as excited over a new adventure. Great kids! We flew commercially to Clark Air Base in the Philippines.

My depression continued. After I'd get the kids on the school bus, I'd go back to bed and pull the sheet up over my head. The longing to see my Indonesian friend drained my energy. Visions of starving children haunted my mind. Disappointment with God crushed my spirit. I was beyond sad; I was numb.

Then a new friend, Mary, invited me to a neighborhood Bible study. For several weeks, I made excuses not to go, but my friend nagged me and at last I surrendered. Thank God she was a nag!

Truth to tell, when I got there, I was most impressed with the food. Mary's helper was a great cook, and a beautifully iced cake and several kinds of luscious cookies filled an orchid-decorated table. I decided I could fit the Bible study into my "busy schedule."

At first, the actual Bible study didn't impress me. I'd heard it all before and I didn't buy it. God didn't care about people. He'd proved that in Indonesia. So why should I care about Him?

As the weeks went by, though, I began to really listen to the teacher. Dottie Hash was part of a missionary family sent to live just outside the military base to provide a wholesome, off-duty hangout for troops. Dottie was obviously smart, yet she seemed to believe that the Bible was a guide for modern living.

I was fascinated. I'd never known anyone really smart who believed like that.

When I was a teenager, I read about healings in the book of Acts. When I asked my Sunday school teacher about it, she said, "Back then, they didn't have doctors, so when people prayed, God healed them. Today, we have doctors, so God doesn't do that anymore."

But Dottie believed that if it happened back then, it could happen now. She pointed to the scripture that said God is the same yesterday, today, and forever (Hebrews 13:8). Interesting thought! My nerves were strung out from the typhoid fever, still making me nervous and jumpy. I wondered, could God make me strong again?

Dottie began to assign us homework, directing us to search out passages that would answer some of our questions. Because of her attitude, I began to read the Bible with a more open mind.

But what about all those poor Indonesians?

"Their country's leadership has made bad choices," Dotty explained. "Sometimes nice people get caught in the disastrous result. But it's not what God has planned."

Okay, I'd think about that.

One day, I told her, "I've done a lot of bad things. I've been away from God too long. What do I have to do to get back?"

"Just pray," she said. "Tell God you're sorry. Tell Him what you told me, that you want to get back with Him."

"That's all?"

"That's all."

I prayed. It seemed like cheating! I'd done so much wrong. I figured I'd surely have to prove myself, maybe start teaching a Sunday school class, clean toilets in the chapel, give a bunch of money to her organization. But no.

"Jesus did it all for us on the cross," Dottie explained. My depression began to lift. My nerves were less jittery.

Even though I'd come to see the Bible as an authority on living, so far I hadn't found anything that told me this healing was coming from God. I saw no scripture that said God cared about individuals. Did He really care about me?

One evening, the kids and I went to the chapel for an open house. In one of their classrooms, on the blackboard in bright, tall letters was the scripture, "Cast all your anxiety on Him because he cares for you" (1 Peter 5:7).

Oh, my! This was it, the Scripture I'd been needing.

As I copied down the verse, tears began to roll down my cheeks. "Thank you, God," I whispered. "I accept that."

Within a few days, the rest of my depression was gone and my nerves were steady. I've never again doubted God's love for me, nor His interest in my daily life. Sure, I'm still not perfect, but now I know how to set things straight.

Thank you, God. And thank you, Dottie, for being the right person at the right time in the right place for me.

~Elaine Olelo Masters

Chapter
10

finding
my
faith

Finding Faith
Through Miracles

Don't give up before the miracle happens.

~Fannie Flagg

86

My Miracle

*If we are ever in doubt about what to do, it is a good rule to ask ourselves
what we shall wish on the morrow that we had done.*
~John Lubbock

I had been waiting for just the right time, and this Friday night was it. Ever since I had brought my newborn son home from the hospital, I had been carefully watching to make sure that my parents were comfortable around an infant. They seemed so happy to have him around, never hesitating to hold or feed him, even changing his diapers voluntarily! I was satisfied that they could handle things.

Tonight's the night, I thought, as I sat at my desk at work. Tonight I'll swallow those pills and never wake up again.

I had saved up the pain pills they had given me in the hospital following a caesarean birth, and adding those to the prescription the doctor had given me upon discharge from the hospital, I now had sixteen little white pills to help me reach my goal. I wanted to spare my new son the misery of having only one very scared and lonely parent.

What should have been the happiest time in my life had turned into despair and loneliness. My husband had walked out during my seventh month of my pregnancy, and I was no more equipped to be a single parent than I was to fly to the moon. I just knew I couldn't possibly raise a happy, secure child when I myself was so alone and scared. But I knew who could — my parents. My brother and I had had wonderful childhoods. I would spare my son the struggle of a single-parent home and leave him in the loving, capable hands of my parents. I knew they would love and cherish him the way they had me, bringing him up believing in God and family and the joy of living. I thought all the joy had walked out the door with my husband a little more than three months before. I couldn't imagine giving my son a joyful life when I couldn't find any joy for myself.

"Wouldn't it be horrible?"

My co-worker's words cut through my quiet scheming, and I turned toward him with a blank look on my face.

"Wouldn't it be horrible… for your folks to have to explain to Danny why both of his parents left him?"

I stared open-mouthed as Wade stated the one thing I hadn't considered. How would my parents explain this to Danny? How could I possibly consider killing myself now? Right or wrong, that little boy would always think he wasn't loved—and heaven knew how much I loved that baby boy. He'd never believe I had loved him if I left him now. What I thought was a noble act on my part would really end up being just an act of selfishness.

My co-worker calmly stood, folded up the newspaper he'd been reading, and put it in the trash can between our desks. He turned to smile at me, and before I could gather my wits enough to speak, to ask him how he had known what I was planning, he was out the door.

I went home that night and asked God, the Perfect Parent, to help me raise my child with confidence and love and, above all, joy. Such peace flooded my heart that I knew with all certainty that Danny and I would be just fine.

I went in to work on Monday, anxious to thank Wade, my co-worker, for opening my eyes and to ask how he'd known I had intended to kill myself that Friday night. But when I finally spoke with him, he looked at me blankly and shook his head in bewilderment. He said, "I wasn't here in the office at all on Friday. I stayed at the main office in Brandon all day making collection calls."

I glanced down at the trash can. It was empty. There was no

newspaper there, no evidence that Wade had been there on Friday afternoon.

But God had been. He had known the only words that could save me and my son.

~Ginny Dubose

Found

The value of consistent prayer is not that He will hear us,
but that we will hear Him.
~William McGill

I had searched everywhere. Twice, I had driven back and forth from the office to the fabrication yard seeking the parts we needed to complete the crane we were to ship to a military installation.

As is usually the case with our contracts, a clearly defined schedule for delivery and installation of the bridge crane we were building had been mandated and accepted. There were serious penalties for defaulting. It was to ship in two days, and I could not locate some expensive and backordered parts essential for completing the crane before shipping.

The company I work for is small, but the equipment we build, deliver, and install is vital to the production and maintenance operations of the clients we service. My responsibility for the company is to complete fabrication on time, check quality control, and ship to various jobsites across the country. It is fascinating work, though at times the stress level is intense.

Before leaving for home, I went into the storage bay of our small office and began once more to search methodically for the missing parts. I checked every bill of lading. I inspected every box and barrel. Rechecking the file manifest, I confirmed yet again that the parts had been shipped as ordered and had been received at the shop where

I now stood in discouragement and near panic. But they were still missing. It was too late to reorder the items and still meet the critical deadline. Shaking my head, I locked up the shop and headed for home, trying to figure out how I was going to resolve the impossible problems ahead.

In retiring to bed, I said a quick and empty-hearted prayer and tucked in. I slept fitfully. About 3:00 A.M., I woke up and started thinking about the missing parts. Lying there in the dark, I listened to my breath going in and out. Every few minutes, I looked at the alarm clock, hoping that time would move along while wishing I could prevent its passing. I retraced well-worn steps in my mind, hoping that some little detail I had missed or forgotten would suddenly leap out at me and the parts would miraculously appear. It didn't happen, and I decided to get out of bed and start the day.

This problem was only a small part of a bigger one that had been nagging at me for some time. Sitting on the side of the bed, I looked down at the pillow on the floor that had been placed there to remind me to begin the day with prayer. My shoulders rose and fell in a long sigh. I didn't feel like praying. I had been consistent for some time, but lately I felt like nothing I said was getting through the sheetrock above my head. Suddenly, I felt very alone and hopeless, and realized I had felt that way for quite some time.

Fighting my stubborn attitude, I slid to my knees and began my morning prayer by asking my Heavenly Father if He had forgotten where I was. I waited and almost quit. I chided myself and began to focus on the blessings of my life in hopes that it would alter my mood. It did a little bit, and finally I heard myself getting right to the point and saying, "Heavenly Father, you know where those parts are, and I don't. Is there any way you could let me know… today?"

As I knelt there, it occurred to me that God hadn't moved away from me, and I pondered on what I might have done to move away from Him. The shower turned off in the bathroom where my wife had preceded me, and I quickly concluded my prayer and went about the business of the morning. The longing for God's companionship didn't leave me as I pulled my truck out of the driveway and headed for work. It was going to be a long day.

Unlocking the back door to the shop, I flipped on the light switch and plodded toward my office just off the storeroom. I glanced glumly at the boxes I had checked and rechecked the night before. Their silent presence seemed to drive home the futility of my situation. Setting my briefcase on the desk, I returned to the storeroom and stood there with my hands on my hips. A large box caught my eye. There was something not right about it. A thought crossed my mind—could it really be that simple?

I walked to the box and saw that the unusual look was the edges of an open box with its flaps sticking upright so that the box sitting on top of it looked to be the same box as the box below. Grasping the top corners of the top box, I lifted that box from between the flaps of the one below.

Nestled neatly in the box were the parts I so desperately needed. At that exact moment, I knew that what I could not see was seen by my Heavenly Father. He had answered my prayer as simply as that of a child who has lost her favorite doll. I was elated and grateful. As I returned to my office to notify the fabricators, the deeper meaning of what had just happened enveloped me, and I began to shake with emotion.

God had not just found my parts, He had found me. In the middle of all the eternal motions for which He has stewardship, He had found a way to let me know that He knew where I was and that I was important to him.

Sometimes in our surprise at small miracles and joy in big ones, we fail to see the less obvious but more important truth. God loves us, not just collectively, but personally. He tells us all the time... if we will listen.

~Edwin Smith

Voices

Courage is not the absence of fear, but rather the judgement that something else is more important than fear.
~Ambrose Redmoon

As an itinerant preacher, I was temporarily living in a small town in Southern Oregon. I arranged with the civic authorities and the Christian church groups to hold an open tent revival meeting. I soon had an ample number of volunteers eager to tell their story before an audience. The stories were all good, concise and to the point. But as I listened to each one recite his testimonial to me in private before the scheduled program, I knew I needed a final speaker with a message that would send the listeners away in a thoughtful mood... a pièce de résistance, if you will. And then came the letter!

It was written in a tiny, feminine hand and postmarked from upstate Oregon. The writer believed I might appreciate an experience she recently had, and she would be only too glad to bear witness at my revival meeting. The letter went on to give a concise account of what had happened to her. And although her narrative was simply expressed in the form of a matter-of-fact report, without any rhetorical embellishment, I could at once see that it was the emotion-stirring and thought-provoking experience I wanted for my finale. I dialed the telephone number she had included in her letter, and it was arranged that my son would furnish her transportation from her home to ours, where she would be our house guest for the interim.

As I watched her deliver her impassioned narration to an enthralled audience, I felt myself being caught up and swept along by the powerful current of her inspiration. This young girl, with whom my wife and I had spent the earlier part of that same day visiting and conversing, and who had appeared to be unusually modest, was now transformed into an inspired evangelist. Her story, as she gave it now, was the first time I had heard it from her lips, and under the spell of her articulation you could feel that she spoke the simple truth as she knew it in her heart.

"I want to tell you a simple story, an adventure that happened to me only two weeks ago right here in this state, not far from where we are gathered here tonight. It is a story so strange, so eerie, that you may find it difficult to believe, but it has had a tremendous impact on me, and came as a blessing to renew my faith in God, which I was on the verge of forsaking.

"I was attending a small college in the state, and occasionally my parents, my brothers and my sister would drive to my college town and spend the day with me, going to church and picnicking in the park. Those were special days for me, for I loved my family dearly.

"On one such Sunday, after an enjoyable day visiting with my family, we said our usual fond goodbyes and they drove away. That was the last time I ever saw them alive. A few miles out of town, their car was involved in a head-on collision with a truck, and they were all killed."

Her flow of words halted, her voice on the verge of breaking as the memory of that night swept back to her in all its poignant bitterness and grief. I saw her bosom swell as she took a deep breath, and her voice continued in an even, constrained tone after a moment.

"How I endured this ordeal, I do not know. It remains but a blur in my memory. I was trapped in some kind of stoic trance. Then came the day of the funeral. Standing there by the open graves, stark reality suddenly penetrated my benumbed brain. The sight of those five caskets containing what had been my whole life was more than I could bear. My mind shut out the world, and I collapsed!

"The weeks that followed became an interlude of frustration.

I became entirely dependent on pills to induce sleep at night and dropped out of college. My life had lost all direction. I would not pray, for in my wild grief, I blamed God for my misfortune. I believed that He had abandoned me in my time of trouble, and that He would not help.

"Then one night, about three months after the tragedy, as I was preparing for bed, I suddenly realized I had run out of sleeping pills, and I could not get to sleep without them. It was a mile to town and the all-night pharmacy. I was without transportation, but I was desperate. Donning a light jacket against the cool of the night, I set out on my journey. The way led along the edge of a country road that connected the town and the college campus where I still lived. With some uneasiness, I noted that there were no street lamps, but the moon periodically broke from behind a cover of heavy clouds, adequately showing the way along the road with which I was fairly familiar.

"The store was almost deserted and the druggist promptly filled my prescription. I was soon on my way back to campus, impatient to take the pills that would bring peace to my beleaguered mind. As I stepped from the haven of the pharmacy, a sense of foreboding seized me. Quickly reassuring myself that it was only my imagination, I continued on my way with a tentative reluctance.

"From somewhere out of the cloaking darkness, so near at hand that I imagined I could feel the breath of the speaker, a voice came to me. Instinctively, I knew it was not of this world. It was quiet and gentle, yet at the same time, strong and reassuring. 'Do not be afraid of what is about to happen. No harm will come to you. Believe!'

"The next moment, the moon flashed from behind a cloud, and the roadway was bathed in an eerie light. My eyes detected something in the roadway ahead that riveted my attention. Scarcely fifty yards away, on the opposite side of the highway, was the figure of a man walking rapidly toward me. I stood motionless where I was, unable to move. Was this what the voice had meant?

"As he came rapidly nearer, I could see some object in his hand that glittered in the moonlight. Panic struck at my heart, and I thought to run, but something stronger than my will held me where I stood. The echo of that friendly voice came back to me, 'Believe!'

"I could only stare in helpless horror as the man crossed the road and came directly toward me. There was no mystery as to his intentions. He was almost upon me when I did something that I had been unable to do for a long time: I began to pray. 'Dear God, be with me. I believe!' The man's evil face loomed in the moonlight. I closed my eyes and waited. And then once more there came a voice, disembodied as before. But this voice was vastly different, harsh, commanding and sinister. 'Pass her by. She is not one of ours.' And I knew who had spoken… just as I knew the other voice.

"I opened my eyes and saw that I stood alone. The man had veered away at the last moment, and his figure was receding in the distance. Somehow the night was warmer and less dark for the remainder of my journey home, for I was no longer alone.

"Since that night, I talk to God often, for I have learned how to pray. Every moment of my life, I am grateful to God for the opportunity He gave me to love Him. He saved my life, He saved my sanity, and ultimately He saved my soul!"

Several years have passed since that memorable revival meeting, and I still receive an occasional letter from someone who attended. The letters are filled with words expressing gratitude at having heard that message, and the wonderful change it wrought in that person's life. I always let my daughter-in-law answer such letters, for she, more than anyone else, knows the true meaning of that experience. For it was she who experienced it! Yes, my son married the lady in question. And no one is more grateful than I for that historic confrontation between God and the devil that night on a dark and lonely road in Oregon, and the ultimate triumph of good over evil.

~Patrick P. Stafford

Planes, Strains, and Automobiles

Faith by itself, if it is not accompanied by action, is dead.
~James 2:17

It had been a long two months of pre-deployment training at Fort Bragg, North Carolina, and all the soldiers were excited. Despite being told we wouldn't get any opportunities to see our families again until after our deployment to Afghanistan, we were all given four-day passes to go home over Thanksgiving week. As if this thrill wasn't enough, we had just found out that we would probably be released a day earlier than anticipated, fueling our enthusiasm and prompting everyone to find earlier flights home.

I began fantasizing about getting home a day early. It was so perfect: It would allow me an entire day more to spend with my family, and I would be able to watch an uninterrupted Green Bay Packers game. I hadn't been able to watch my Packers play since before the deployment began. Never had a "day off" meant so much.

I had just gotten off the phone with my parents and my girlfriend, Joanna, to tell them we could start booking earlier flights when my section sergeant burst my bubble. He told me I had to go to what's known as the in-processing station to complete some paperwork the next day, and that I wouldn't be able to get on a flight until I had finished. The last time a group went through to do this in-processing paperwork, they arrived at 8:00 in the morning and didn't leave until late that night. The last flight to Chicago was scheduled to leave in the afternoon, much earlier than I would be finished.

The bad news got worse when I got a phone call from my dad saying that he checked with the airline, and every flight was booked. There wasn't a chance of getting on standby. I hung up, downtrodden with my rotten luck. I tried brainstorming ideas to whip up a plan to get on a flight the next day when I realized something: This was a situation that was too big for me to handle. Realizing my feebleness, I came up with a different plan: I started praying. Within minutes, the still voice of God gently whispered to my heart.

"You will be home early… You will be home tomorrow…"

For the next several hours, I kept calling the airline to see if I could get on standby, but each time I called, they told me that it was impossible. My family and several soldiers encouraged me to just give up, but I refused to hear it—because I believed God refused to hear it.

The next morning, in-processing got off to a late start, which didn't help my cause. Whenever I had a free moment, I'd call the airline to see if they found an available seat. Finally, a single seat became available, but the last-minute change would cost hundreds of dollars that I didn't have. The airline representative asked me to fax in my deployment orders to see if they could use that to their advantage. I just so happened to have my orders on me, and so I got off the phone and began searching for a fax machine. When I got back on the phone with the airline rep after faxing my orders, she informed me that in the time it took to find that blessed fax machine, the one available seat got booked. I had hit the final brick wall; there was nothing more I could do.

Even though it looked like I wouldn't have my miracle flight, one piece of amazing did happen: in the eleventh hour, I finished the in-processing. I had tenaciously downsized an eleven-hour day's worth of paperwork and medical examinations into a three-hour gauntlet. I was given the green light to start my Thanksgiving pass, if only I could find a way home. I contemplated my options as my cell phone rang. I groaned when I saw it was my section sergeant calling.

"Oh, no!" I cried to myself. "The last thing I need is to be told that I forgot to do something and can't leave until it's done."

Knowing I was obliged to answer the call, I picked up.

"Sgt. Geist, how close are you to finishing in-processing?"

Here it was. He was about to give me a new task, grounding any chances I had of getting home early, as God had told me I would.

"Sergeant, I'm done with that. I just finished it."

"Great," he said. "I'm en route to your location. I'll pick you up in five minutes."

"Pick me up?" I inquired. Why did he need to pick me up? Was he going to shuttle me back to base for something?

"Yes, pick you up. You need a ride to the airport, don't you?"

Oh, my gosh. I had completely forgotten that I didn't even have a ride to the airport, which was at least thirty minutes away. This was an oversight that would've cost me all my efforts! As I waited for my section sergeant, I wondered what I was going to do once I got to the airport. Just when I resolved that I would covertly duct tape myself to the wing of a Chicago-bound airplane, my cell phone rang again.

"Mr. Geist, we found a seat on the 12:40 P.M. flight to Chicago."

Not only did a seat magically pop up, but the representative had decided to go out of her way by calling to tell me about it. I was bamboozled by this little piece of amazing, but it didn't amount to much of a miracle just yet. Could I even afford the last-minute change?

"Well, thank you, thank you very much. But, uh… how much is this going to run me?"

"Mr. Geist, we have waived all the extra fees for you. Would you like to book this seat?"

"Ma'am, you have no idea how much I would love that. Thank you so much. God bless you."

"God bless you, too." I could hear the smile in her voice.

Just as I ended the call, my section sergeant pulled up. I must've looked as stunned as a deer in the headlights. As we drove to the airport, I wasn't yet at a point where I could settle back and relax. After all, my flight was leaving in about an hour, and I was still a half hour away from the airport. That would only give me a half hour to print my tickets, check my bags, get through security, and find my terminal.

When we arrived at the airport, I went to get my tickets; no problem there. I checked my bags; there were no complications. I got in line to go through security; I stepped right through. I found my terminal; it was 12:20 P.M.

And then I was soaring through the air on a 12:40 P.M. outbound flight to Chicago.

On the flight, I was able to decompress and reflect on the day. I was reminded that "faith by itself, if it is not accompanied by action, is dead," according to James 2:17. I was so grateful that my faith hadn't been dead; when I felt God tell me I'd be getting home early, I didn't sit on my butt waiting for a chopper to land behind my tent on Fort Bragg. Instead, I acted on the faith that I had to put the miracle into motion. When else might I have to act on my faith to achieve something God has promised?

After the flight landed in Chicago, I walked out of the airplane and into the arms of Joanna, who had managed to get past security with my dad to meet me as I got off my flight. We stood there in the airport embracing each other, tears rolling down our cheeks. My dad gave me a warm welcome-home hug, and then we got into the car and drove home. Yes, I would be in dangerous Afghanistan in just a few weeks. But for one special holiday, I was home. God's promises are true and trustworthy.

~Sgt. Danger Geist

One Small Miracle

Desperately, helplessly, longingly, I cried;
Quietly, patiently, lovingly, God replied... "Wait."
~Russell Kelfer

I'd already had the final surgery. It was my last chance, after numerous failed attempts. One more painful doctor visit and I would know if I could have a child or not.

There wasn't anything I could do but plow ahead with my daily activities, wait for the scheduled meeting with the doctor to find out if the surgery had performed the magic it was intended to, and cry when the emptiness I felt in the interim overcame me. I prayed and pleaded with God to give me the gift that I felt too many took for granted.

While my friends and family reveled in their own joy, a growing child in the womb or a full nursery, I was left alone with my thoughts, my wavering faith, and fading dreams of motherhood.

In the other rooms of the house were the toys of my trade, sitting unused when the children I cared for during the day went to their own homes. A playroom. Crayon drawings posted on the front of the refrigerator. Echoes of laughter and tears bounced around the rooms searching for the children in their absence.

I pulled the comforting quilt around me in bed. I had been praying ad infinitum, and a long nasty-looking surgery scar on my stomach was all I had to show for what often seemed like my one-sided conversations with God. No answers had come. Darkness has a way of magnifying every sad or frightening thought.

I had put an old black-and-white photo of my mother holding me as a small child on the bedside table. It was a visual bond with the lady who had left the world without ever seeing me hold a child of my own.

But I knew that I was blessed to have known the great love and faith of an amazing mother. I longed to pass that same love and faith on to a child of my own.

The morning of the appointment finally arrived. My hands shook with fear. While I sat in the doctor's consulting room, the red vine-print wallpaper that always reminded me of tiny red blood vessels mocked me. "Even we have life flowing through us, but you don't," the vines seemed to whisper to me. I never did like that wallpaper. It gave me the creeps.

The doctor walked into his consulting office. I watched him sit down and open my file, knowing from the strained smile on his face that the news was not good. His normally energetic voice was suddenly consoling. "I'm sorry, Laurie. The scar tissue is too severe. The chances of you conceiving and carrying a baby to full term are almost nil." The silence in the office after he spoke felt as empty as my womb.

I drove home and arrived without even being aware of what route I had taken or what had happened as I traveled on the freeway across the city.

I walked in the front door and sat down on my favorite chair, numb, feeling as if I'd been swallowed up in a void. I couldn't hold back the tears. "It isn't fair. It just isn't fair. God, why me? That woman in the news drowned her own sons. The one on television, that drug addict, had six kids. She was popping them out like the pills she swallowed, and she wasn't even trying to have children. She didn't even want the last one. It isn't fair! You let them have children. Why not me?" I cried myself to sleep sitting up in the chair.

From then on, knowing how painful it was for me, friends and family initially held back telling me when they got pregnant. I was often the last to find out. I appreciated their sensitivity on the one hand, but on the other, the fear to share their joy with me made me feel even more left out and broken. I felt defective, like a factory reject from God.

I settled back into my daily existence and consoled myself with the fact that I had children in my life to take care of and love intensely, as if they were my own. And I did. But what I felt was my failure as a normal woman haunted me.

I had never thought about adoption before. When the idea came to me, alone in the middle of the night while my husband was on the night shift, my heart raced a little. I didn't say anything about it to anyone for months. I was afraid of that possible final "no" that would eventually seal my emptiness forever in a hollow tomb. I could picture my own future headstone, Beloved Mother of No One.

The agency research, failed adoption attempts, massive amounts of paperwork and endless meetings to adopt took more than a year. The call from our agency giving us the court date in Russia came on the seventeenth of December—the most amazing Christmas gift I ever received. I would finally be able to adopt a baby girl from Russia. I felt it was the perfect scenario for me, a person who had traveled her whole growing-up life, adopting a child from another country.

I had never completely lost my faith in all the years I had waited for a child. But it had waxed and waned in my emptiness and sense that somehow I was flawed, or that God was punishing me for some unknown transgression. I found it a little ironic that my mother, who had doubted the existence of God until my older brother was born, had told me, "When I held him for the first time, I knew there was a God. My children are miracles."

On the other hand, I had started my attempts to get pregnant with a strong belief in God. I started to doubt God when my constant prayers seemed to be unanswered. The truth was that God had made me wait for the right child. He did answer my prayers. He just didn't do it precisely in the time frame or the way I had expected.

I came to realize He had his own ways that were often beyond my ken, and that faith meant believing even in the most doubtful times.

As I stood over my sleeping baby, I had no doubt that my own small miracle and the answer to my prayers was asleep in front of me, holding a knit pink bunny. He had heard me all along. He had simply saved the best for last.

I closed my eyes and repeatedly said, "Thank you, God. Thank you." The tears flowed while I prayed. They felt like healing waters to my soul.

~L.L. Darroch

Faith on the Night Shift

Hope never abandons you; you abandon it.
~George Weinberg

For many years, I wondered if God had rejected me. I'd been given permission to enter a monastery at the age of sixteen. My mother had given consent, and my father, away at sea, indicated that he would sign on his return, which was the night before my scheduled entrance day. Instead, the night before I was to board the plane, he said he had decided not to sign. What made it more difficult was the way he grinned at me over his fourth bourbon-on-the-rocks, tore up my admissions document and threw it across the table.

In the decade that followed, I experienced terror and feelings of abandonment by both parents, forced sex, a hasty marriage to someone I hardly knew, two children in two years, brutality, hospitalizations and suicidal thoughts. Part of me lost faith. I'm not sure why I continued to pray, "God, please help me to understand. Please show me what it is you want me to do."

I had always believed that it was good to pursue your passions and use your natural gifts. But I had also learned that if you had to do something you felt to be against your nature, and yet you did it with as much diligence, dedication and devotion as if it were what you had always wanted, it had twice the value. So when the only job training available to me for the means I had available was to become a licensed practical nurse (LPN), I began to pursue it, even when I frequently fainted while performing tasks for which I felt ill-equipped. Somehow, I persevered.

I began my first job on the night shift at St. John's Hospital in Santa Monica, California. A series of events happened during that year that reawakened my hope that God had not forsaken me, and that, in fact, perhaps He was allowing me to somehow be of greater help to others. As a float nurse, I was frequently sent to different floors on different assignments. We picked up our assignments each night as we clocked in. One night, I arrived a few minutes late. The nurses had already begun night rounds and received their report. They were at the other end of the wing as I stepped off the elevator, and I noticed a call light flashing on and off at my end of the hall. When I went to investigate, a man was sitting up, blood gushing from a surgical site in his back. I called loudly for help, but nobody heard. So I propped the man upright, shoved a pillow behind him to help staunch the flow and went running for the other nurses.

Once the emergency was over, the charge nurse asked, "How did you know he needed help?" I told her I had seen his light flashing as I stepped off the elevator. "Impossible!" she snapped. "If you'd been here in time for report, you would have heard that he was scheduled for discharge tomorrow. He is the only patient we could put in that room until an electrician could come because his call light isn't working." When I insisted I had seen it, she marched me down to the room and pressed the switch again and again. The call light, true to her word, was not working!

A second incident happened just a few weeks later. This time, I misread my assignment and arrived on the pediatric wing, which was on the third floor. After we were given our assignments, I answered a little girl's call light. As I gave her a bedpan, I heard a scrape of metal on the floor outside, and the emergency exit door opposite her room opened and then clicked shut. Mystified, I went to see if a child had wandered out of this exit. As I opened the door, I gasped in surprise as a young man on crutches was climbing up on the fire escape. "Don't come near me, or I'll jump!" he said as I took a step forward, and the exit door closed and locked behind me. Immediately, I recognized him as the patient I'd heard about in report who had just won a football scholarship to college and then been in a tragic motorcycle accident that resulted in amputation of a leg.

I assured him that I would not approach. "But suicide is awfully final. Could we talk first? I'm only a few years older than you," I said, "and it would help me to help other patients if you would tell me your story." For nearly an hour, he sobbed out his grief while I stayed at a distance, listening. He decided he didn't really want to die and asked me to help him get back to his room. But the door was locked, and no one heard our pounding! Not knowing whether to laugh or cry, we clung to each other and began to climb down the fire escape to the floor below where someone finally heard us and let us in.

Mrs. Weaver, the supervisor, was on the floor and greeted us with the charge nurse. "Where on earth have you been?" she demanded. "I have been paging you for an hour. Apparently, you misread your assignment and went to the wrong floor. But why didn't you hear me paging you on the intercom? Go downstairs immediately. I want to have a word with you." When she had completed her interrogation and the young man had told his story, I could only stammer that perhaps it had been a lucky mistake, after all.

There were many other such events in the decades that followed, including a time when I worked among the Sisters of St. Francis caring for terminally ill priests. "I trust you as I would trust my own nuns," the nun in charge told me one afternoon. And many times, I witnessed amazing incidents as I carried out my duties.

I can't tell you why things happened as they did in my life, but over the years I have definitely felt God's presence. Faith happens sometimes in strange ways, and what I'd felt had been lost forever was regained in this most unlikely way. I am convinced now that nothing happens to us that cannot be used for good, even when we have felt the most abandoned. As I look back on my life, I realize that I had been chosen for a special purpose—I just hadn't realized it.

~Anne Wilson

92

Knowing God

The day which we fear as our last is but the birthday of eternity.
~Seneca

I knew about God after attending years of Sunday school and earning the attendance pins to prove it. Because I had subsequently taught Sunday school, I could recount Scripture stories. Prayers I had said since I was young rolled off my tongue mindlessly. But if you had asked me about my relationship with God or where God fit into my life, I couldn't have answered—that is, until after I died.

Following my graduation from college, I remained a Christian but changed denominations because I felt that God had called me to a relationship. The trouble was that I didn't have any idea how to form a relationship with the Almighty. I thought my new faith would clear up that mystery for me.

My boyfriend and I often attended church together and continued the practice after we married. We wanted a family and had two daughters three years apart. One day when our older daughter was five and the younger a year and a half, I suffered horrible abdominal pain and dizziness. The pain increased during the next week. My husband grew alarmed and took me to the doctor, who ordered me hospitalized for a simple procedure designed to ease my symptoms.

My surgery would be Monday morning. The dizziness continued all weekend in the hospital. When I told nurses about my lightheadedness, most said I shouldn't feel that way. Only one truly listened. As the time for my surgery approached, I told her I wanted to shower. She asked me if I was certain because I seemed so weak, but I insisted.

She accompanied me down the hall, where I collapsed. Suddenly, I was somewhere brighter than anywhere I had ever been. My nurse was not with me, but I was not alone. The light was so intense that I could not see whether the figure in front of me was male or female. Although I couldn't discern any features of that being, I knew I had nothing to fear. Despite not hearing any voice, I realized the being wanted me to look down. I saw at least four doctors in my room working on my still body. There was obvious tension as my husband stood against a wall looking distraught. Doctors shouted about no blood pressure. I felt completely at peace and experienced no pain for the first time in two weeks. Suddenly, the figure before me made it clear I could go no farther.

I awoke in my room with doctors surrounding me. One knelt on the floor and was hitting my arm.

"What are you doing?" I whispered, too weak to speak normally.

"I'm trying to bring up a vein so we can pump blood into you and get you to surgery." I told him to please let me go.

I couldn't summon the energy to tell him how beautiful it had been when I was in that place where I floated above my body. It was a place of no pain, only peace. I wanted to go there again.

Finally, the doctors judged that I was ready for surgery. Someone wheeled me away. Hours later, I awoke in the recovery room where a nurse called my name and told me to wake up. When I awoke, I felt disappointed that I wasn't in heaven.

Back in my room, I tried to sleep. But every time I closed my eyes, I felt a hand on my shoulder. I wondered if it was the nurse who had been so kind to me, but when I opened my eyes, no one was there. I decided to look around the minute I felt the pressure of that hand so I could see who was with me, possibly playing a trick. But my room was still empty save for me.

That's when I finally understood that I was feeling the healing and compassionate nature of God. It changed my life and deepened my faith. At last, I not only knew about God, but I also knew God intimately. I had felt His presence in my room, His hand on my shoulder.

In the next few days, I learned that I had suffered an ectopic or tubular pregnancy and had bled internally. I didn't even know I had been pregnant. Each day, I looked for that caring nurse who had accompanied me to the shower room. I assumed she must have summoned help when I collapsed. She never came back to see me. And when I talked about her, no one knew anything. My questions went unanswered. I now believe that nurse was an angel sent by God to save my life.

Before I left the hospital, I knew God wanted me to live for some reason. So I have dedicated myself to being a Christian writer, sharing my faith with readers I will probably never meet. For years at the beginning of each Advent, I went on a silent directed retreat. I talked to no one but my retreat director and God, filling my days with thanks and praise and establishing a deeper relationship with my Maker. I became active in youth and prison ministry to give back to God.

I still say rote prayers as a way to enter into prayerfulness, but I talk to my Life-Giver from my heart. I don't have to go to a quiet place to pray. I do it in my car, when I do household chores and in the quiet of the night. I tell the Creator about my fears and longings as well as my joys and gratitude.

Yes, when I taught Sunday school and even when I changed denominations, I knew about God. But now I know God and have experienced His mercy and kindness. Because of my experience, I have no fear of death as I go forward. It is faith that makes my life worth living.

~Sandy McPherson Carrubba

Chapter 11

finding my faith

Finding Faith
Through Service

Bread for myself is a material question.
Bread for my neighbor is a spiritual one.

~Nicholas Berdyaev

93

Blind Faith

For we live by faith, not by sight.
~2 Corinthians 5:7

My blind dog Sage and I walked slowly down the school's newly tiled hallway toward the boisterous classroom. The voices of seventy third-graders mingled with chairs dragged across a wooden floor. Sage paused in the doorway and cocked her head to listen. The children's whisperings grew louder, and when they saw her, their delight manifested itself in enthusiastic squeals and jumps on the hardwood floor. Sage flopped to the floor and flattened herself horizontally. I bent down and whispered to her gently as the classroom teacher calmly spoke to her students. A moment later, Sage rose again, stuck her nose in the air, took a deep sniff and moved two steps forward, her feet following her nose. Having been her companion for nearly nine years, I knew Sage's long black muzzle helped her understand her surroundings, capturing the multitude of scents filtering through this room, from the youngsters seated in chairs to the lunches in their backpacks.

I tapped my leather boot on the floor as I often did when we visited new places, helping Sage realize I was nearby and signaling her to move closer. She obliged, using her senses of hearing and smell to guide her. I had come to understand during the past nine years that a blind dog in an unfamiliar setting uses her other, more acute senses and her faith in her special person to conquer her fear of the unknown. After Sage sat next to me, I began my presentation to the students.

I often marvel at Sage when we visit classrooms or other new places. Blind for almost eight years, she hesitates only slightly when we walk into unfamiliar buildings, following the sounds of my voice and footsteps with trust. When we reach a classroom filled with strange noises, as we did on this particular day, Sage pauses in the doorway and uses her nose and ears for navigation. I keep her on a leash while in the classroom for, within a few minutes, fear of the unknown subsides, her curiosity peaks, and she explores. The strangers' voices, though somewhat loud, make her inquisitive—she wants to meet the people in the room. She trusts me to lead her through the crowd, avoiding head-on collisions with the sturdy desks or the children's bodies. She greets each child with a wagging tail and sometimes a nuzzle to a soft cheek. We walk among the crowd as I talk about disabilities and answer questions about my dog's blindness. This routine is repeated numerous times throughout the school year.

The journey began when a genetic disease robbed Sage of her eyesight at barely two years old. Trust increased as her vision decreased. The first ride on an elevator and the first night in a hotel room showcased her apprehension of the unfamiliar, but also her faith in me and in the words she had learned. I taught her words and phrases that I thought would help keep her safe, like "no," "sit," "come," and "stop," as well as "step up" and "step down" for navigating stairways and street curbs. Nearly a decade later, Sage still walks with confidence, trusting the one who guides, cares for, and protects her.

In many ways, Sage helped build my faith. Her trust and her perseverance have provided great lessons. Her faith in me as her guardian taught me more about trusting God, and her perseverance through numerous collisions with the furniture modeled for me patience through my life's obstacles. The first time I watched my blind dog leap from the floor onto the bed not only caught me by surprise, but reminded me of the numerous times God has called me to a leap of faith. Fear can prevent us from stepping into the unknown, yet

Sage courageously jumped from the solid floor into the air to land on a piece of furniture she could not see.

My blind dog constantly shows her faith in me as her caretaker. She cannot see me, yet she trusts me; can I also trust the One who cares for me yet I cannot see? Wading through uncharted waters of economic stress, stumbling amidst uncertainties in job situations, fumbling around dark caverns of loss in the death of special friends, and wavering among the new realities of my aging physical body, I need to trust that God is all-knowing, all-loving, and all-providing. Yet, I often doubt, I often question, and I often become discouraged.

Biblical writers remind us that faith is not in what we see, but in what we do not see. The author of Hebrews says, "Now faith is confidence in what we hope for and assurance about what we do not see" (Hebrews 11:1). Sage embodies the idea of blind faith. Her sightless eyes cannot see the one who feeds her, walks her, or pets her, but she trusts me completely when I guide her down the steps, along the sidewalk, or through the hallways of a school. She trusts me to care for her well-being and her safety. And she bravely walks down a sidewalk and leaps onto a bed she cannot see.

When I allow life to discourage me through fear, suffering, loss, and other hardships, I need only to look as far as the sightless dog lying at my feet to be reminded of the importance of blind faith in the One who really loves me.

~Gayle Mansfield Irwin

94

His Messenger

If you can't feed a hundred people, then feed just one.
~Mother Teresa

She came to me — a small, dark-eyed girl. She was God's messenger, but I wasn't perceptive enough to grasp it. Not then.

My story begins when I was an un-churched, forty-something woman from the suburbs. For most of my life, I had bowed to the god of goals, who demanded higher levels of achievement for my own glory. I bought into the intellectual formula for happiness: Earn good grades, so that you can attend a good college, so that you will land a good job with a large company, so that you can earn a good salary, live an affluent life, marry a successful man and live happily ever after. At no time did I consider the cost of that path or entertain the possibility of failure.

Single and childless, I achieved career success, but I did not find peace. I had affluence, but no gratitude. I traveled the world, restless. My pride drove people away. My self-centeredness led to loneliness. My remorse drew me to my knees. I dropped to the floor of my shower and wept. In the steam on the glass door, I wrote: "God help me."

Months after my "baptism" in the shower, I went to a local church and waited in the last row for the worship service to begin. A steady stream of unfamiliar people passed by, so I grabbed a bulletin and started to read. I hoped that I would remain unnoticed, but that was not to be.

God sat next to me and invisibly tapped my shoulder. I saw an invitation for a two-week mission trip to the Dominican Republic. I experienced a sudden desire to go to a place I had never visited, to serve people I had never met. Several months later, I was on the way to a divine encounter.

Everything about my first short-term mission was unfamiliar. I didn't know the people's culture or needs. I didn't know what to say or do. Most importantly, I didn't know God or His intentions. I had stopped attending church when I was nine years old. I read the words of the Bible as if they were poetry from dead saints—beautiful, but not relevant. Intense heat assailed my body and wilted my confidence as we traveled in a bus across the Caribbean island. I watched the view change from crowded city street to deserted highway to dirt road. Families lived in shelters made out of dried sugarcane stalks and banana leaves. Our guide pointed to children playing in muddy water.

"More children die every year from drinking bad water than will die from any other cause," he said. "Fresh water is a precious commodity."

I hugged my filtered water bottle like a security blanket.

We bunked with a Christian relief organization and gathered in the morning for a project overview.

"We're going to the village of Los Robles to help build an elementary school," the leader explained. "We provide one meal per day for every child who attends our school, and we give free meals to as many others as we can. We'll bring some gifts to give the children. We can't eliminate poverty, but we can show them love.

"One more thing: Don't give anything away if you don't have enough for the crowd. You could start a riot, and people could get hurt." He paused before adding, "Pay attention. God will meet you somewhere as you work."

Curious children ran through our project with more confidence every day. Young girls carried baby siblings with the poise of an adult. Dirt covered their naked bodies, but couldn't hide their natural beauty and gentle spirit. I was surprised to hear their constant laughter and see their joy.

On my third day in the village, a young girl approached and smiled. Her braided hair was fastened with rainbow-colored ribbons. A too-large dress hung unevenly to the tops of bare feet. She pointed to the bottle of water tied to my waist. Her dark eyes sparkled with anticipation.

"*Agua?*" she asked.

I looked at her, and then at dozens of other children playing nearby. I remembered the instructions not to share anything with one child that I could not share with all. I remembered the warning about fresh water and feared for myself. I yielded to the loud voice in my head, not the soft whisper in my heart.

"No *agua*," I responded and kept working.

Her dark eyes lost the sparkle, but she did not give up. She stepped closer and asked again.

"Sandy. *Agua, por favor?*"

"No," I answered and turned away.

I started to cry. I was powerless to help all the people, but why had I declined the opportunity to help just one?

"Why am I here if I can't even provide a drink of clean water?" I shouted at God. In kindness, He remained silent.

In the morning, our pastor taught from the gospel of John. I heard the story of Jesus and the Samaritan woman at the well. Her story sounded like the events of my prior afternoon.

Jesus asked the Samaritan woman, "Will you give me a drink?"

Not yet aware of who was standing before her, the woman did not offer the stranger any water. She offered Him questions. He spoke about eternal life through faith. He already knew her checkered past, but still promised her the hope of God's forgiveness. The woman believed the stranger and went back to her village infused with joy.

After that teaching, we brought big jugs of fresh water for hundreds of children in the village. Within minutes, our supply was depleted, and the children returned to their homes. Ten days later, I returned to mine. I remained haunted by the look of disappointment in the little girl's eyes.

Months later, I remembered that my employer offered a line of well pumps in a different part of the company. I approached a senior manager and asked if he would help secure a donation for a tiny village. He agreed to assign help with the specification and installation process. When I learned the name of the project manager, I was amused and amazed: Jesus Rodriguez was assigned to help me. I exchanged regular e-mails with Jesus.

Less than a year later, fresh water flowed to thousands of villagers in a third world country. At last I had peace.

I discovered the truth of God's merciful love in a third world country. His young messenger asked me for a drink of water, and exposed my hard heart. Undaunted, God demonstrated the distance He was willing to go to help a child believe in forgiveness. I finally understood that I was the child God wanted to bless, so I too could become a messenger of grace.

~Sandra Wood

95

A Daughter's Prayer

Gam zu l'tovah. (Everything is for the best.)
~Jewish Saying

I remember as a kid thinking it so odd when my parents and their friends asked each other where the time went. Now I understand. Life goes by in a blink. And people die so young, some of them never getting a chance to feel as if they mattered in this world or made a contribution to society.

My mom died at the age of fifty-four. She was forty-eight when they diagnosed her with choriocarcinoma of the breast. She was one of those people who died thinking her life never mattered.

After undergoing surgery, radiation and chemotherapy, Mom had four years of a relatively pain-free and active life. In her sixth year of survival, we went to the mall one day. After a lovely lunch, my mom suddenly turned to me and asked me who I was and where we were, and then she cried and asked who she was. The cancer had metastasized to her brain.

She died within three weeks. Everyone said to pray for a miracle. The only prayer I could say was, "Please, God, don't let her suffer. If you have to take her, do it fast, without pain."

During that three-week period, my mom made me promise that she could die at home. Being a nurse, I figured that should be easy enough. And, actually, it was. I went to my charge nurse at the hospital where I worked and told her what my mother wanted me to do.

"Take whatever you need," she said. "Do you need help figuring out what to take?"

With her help, I had boxes of necessary supplies. I started the IVs myself and inserted a catheter. It never occurred to me to ask someone else to do these things for my mother. When Mom did develop pain, I called her doctors for a prescription.

Dr. Yoshida brought it over after work that night. He lived a few blocks away. When he came into the bedroom, I remember him sucking in his breath and looking at me with astonishment. "You're doing this all by yourself?"

I nodded.

He wrote his phone number on a piece of paper. "You call me any time of the day or night if you need me."

I sat for hours on end, holding Mom's hand, and begging God to end the torture. She died within forty-eight hours of that visit. After her body had been taken to the funeral home, I finally collapsed and slept. It was a sound sleep with no remorse. I had fulfilled my mother's dying wish. I had made sure that she died comfortably and with dignity and, most importantly, without fear and at home surrounded by her family.

A week after I returned to work, a co-worker of mine who had chemo the same time my mom did, pulled me aside.

"You know I have breast cancer, right?" she said.

"Yes, Flo, but your chemo is going well."

Flo shook her head. "It's only a matter of time. Listen, all of us patients are talking about what you did for your mom. You did a great thing for her, and it's the way I want to go, too. I want you to do that for me."

"I don't know how I can, Flo. I broke a lot of rules."

"Exactly. That's why the doctors in the chemo clinic want to see you after work. I've talked to them about this. They want to figure out how to make it easier for their patients to die like that at home. It's what most of us want."

That night, I sat for hours with Dr. Yoshida and my mother's other doctors, as well as Flo's wonderful minister. She had told him about my mother's death and what she had asked me to do for her. He wanted to be a part of this.

We talked about my mother's last days and how difficult and overwhelming it had been for me. Until that moment, I had not realized what an incredible stress my improvised palliative home care had been. I've never regretted it, not once, but I did not want anyone else to have to go through that horrible stress alone. But I prayed that something good would come out of my experience with my mother.

During that initial talk, we realized what an incredible need our community had for a hospice centre. Windsor has one of the largest cancer rates in Canada, as well as one of the best chemo and radiation centres. We were looking at a monumental task to have the hospice dream fulfilled.

After weeks and months of discussion, planning and fund-raising, we indeed had a hospice unit led by an amazing nurse, Jean Echlin. Hospice cared for patients in hospital, at home, and as outpatients. Now families had somewhere to turn to for guidance and help. Again, my prayers had been answered.

Over the years, our hospice has grown into a multimillion-dollar organization that treats thousands of dying people a year. We even have an "inn" where patients and their families can go in the final days before their deaths. Other communities and countries come to see and learn from our wonderful organization.

It's been thirty-four years since my mother died, and I have been able to look back and see how much God has been by my side, giving me courage and determination that I never knew I possessed. I only realize now how much blind faith I had in God. All these years later, I can see how He performed so many miracles in order to influence and encourage the thousands of people who made this hospice a reality.

God made my mother's life matter more than she could have ever hoped. And Flo's life, too. He gave me faith and the understanding that things happen for a reason. The Jewish phrase *gam zu l'tovah* comes to mind—everything is for the best. Or, as I interpret it, God is here. Have faith.

~Pamela Goldstein

96

A Hand on My Shoulder

As the body without the spirit is dead, so faith without deeds is dead.
~James 2:26

A panel truck stopped for a red light. The driver got out, whacked the side of his truck with a big stick, got back in, and drove to the next red light. After watching him do this at several intersections, the fellow driving behind him finally leaned out his window and yelled, "Whaddya think you're doing?"

Giving his truck another whack, the driver shouted back, "I've got two tons of canaries in a one-ton truck, so I gotta keep half of 'em flying!"

I chuckled when I read that joke, but basically that's how I've managed to juggle fifty-four years of marriage, author eight Christian books, help my husband raise our four kids, write a weekly newspaper column for twenty-three years, sell hundreds of photos, contribute to *Daily Guideposts* for sixteen years, grow a big annual garden, preserve, pickle and freeze the produce we grow every summer, and stitch together more than fifty patchwork quilts. If it sounds impressive, it's because I've been on the road with my "load of canaries" for forty-nine years now, and along the way I learned how to juggle priorities so they didn't all land at once.

Life has been good. It is still fulfilling.

But it wasn't always like this.

Back in 1962, married for five years and the mother of two little boys, I had become indifferent in terms of my Christian faith. Telling myself I had no time for Bible reading and even less for prayer, I had become stunted in my spiritual growth. To make matters worse, we were living in a remote area where the nearest Bible teaching church was at an inconvenient distance, especially in the middle of a Canadian prairie winter. At least that was how I tried to justify not going. And so, although I was a Christian, my faith was languishing for want of proper nourishment and exercise.

But then we moved back to the city and my husband insisted on searching for a church "home." We began making the rounds, and on one particular Sunday, at the close of the service, I felt a gentle hand on my shoulder.

"Would you by chance be available to teach Vacation Bible School next week?"

How did this friendly woman with the warm smile even know I was a Christian? And how could this church be so short of workers that someone would approach a total stranger to teach? With such thoughts running through my mind, I politely declined her request that Sunday, but her hand on my shoulder seemed to be the very hand of Christ.

"I need you," He seemed to be saying. "It doesn't matter that you haven't had training, that you don't know the Bible very well as yet, that you have all this guilt about your indifference these past few years. Yes, there are others far more experienced, but I need you. Are you willing to get involved in service for me?"

I sensed a calling unlike any other I had ever experienced. God needed me. You know those time-exposure photos that show a flower rapidly bursting open into full bloom? That's how it felt in my soul when, deep down in my heart, I responded to God's invitation to serve Him. My Christian walk just seemed to blossom thereafter.

Within weeks, there were opportunities popping up where I could be of help in various ministries. And each and every one demanded more and more Bible knowledge. How could I teach in the weekly children's club if I wasn't familiar with the stories? How could I present a devotional at the mission society meeting without praying for direction? How could I influence my family without setting a good example? In short, how could I continue to serve others without going spiritually deeper myself?

I signed up for a Bible correspondence course, and then another and another. And the more I learned, the more opportunities to serve God came my way. "Faith without deeds is dead," we read in the book of James. Compared to those earlier years when I took no time to get to know God better or serve Him, my faith was alive and growing in ways that were both enriching and satisfying. I led neighborhood Bible studies, directed not-so-neighborly kids in a weekly club, donned a clown suit as the church summer school mascot, warbled alto from the choir loft, decoded the preacher's hieroglyphics as church secretary, and scrubbed toilets when the caretaker failed to show. I also taught an adult Sunday school class and served in one capacity or another on the executive committee of our local Christian writers' association for thirty years.

Although supposedly "retired," I am still freelancing, doing photography, gardening, quilting and staying involved in our church seniors' group. In retrospect, I doubt if any of these pursuits would have come about had it not been for that one encouraging person who was actively seeking potential workers whom God could use. It so happens that she and I are now both members of the same church. She is still encouraging people to serve, and I am still grateful for her hand on my shoulder so many years ago.

~Alma Barkman

97

My God Moment

God may not always come exactly when you call Him...
but He is always on time.

~Lemon

Truth be told, when my congregation decided to send its first ever volunteer group on a mission trip to Appalachia, I didn't want to go. It's not that I didn't fully support our decision to participate in such an undertaking, it's just that I had no desire to be there when it happened. Instead, I was perfectly content to work behind the scenes making sure that those who'd be doing the actual hands-on volunteering would be prepared for their undertaking. But, as so often happens, God apparently had other plans for me.

When one of our adult chaperones backed out, a replacement was quickly needed. Suddenly, I found myself seven hundred miles from home, lying on my back beneath a dilapidated trailer and working with others from my congregation. I was hot and tired. My clothes were filthy and sticking to my skin. But in spite of the litany of personal complaints that I suffered in silence, and much to my own surprise, I found that I was thoroughly enjoying the experience.

We'd joined a ministry whose purpose was the eradication of the substandard living conditions found throughout many sections of Appalachia. To accomplish this, existing homes were refurbished and made warmer, safer and drier for their occupants. Eventually, I'd become better acquainted with this ministry as a volunteer on future excursions. However, it was during one particularly sultry summer trip that I first reflected on the possibility of God's presence as we toiled for our Appalachian family. Months would pass before I'd revisit these reflections and ultimately arrive at a conclusion concerning them. And, oddly enough, all it took for me to achieve my personal epiphany was a late November's bitter wind.

My crew and another from our church were assigned adjoining jobsites—two trailer-homes. There was a third in this hollow and between them lived sixteen children. The work we needed to do was fairly basic—and yet so vital to the people living in these homes. An addition was begun for one while insulation was added to the floors and lower walls of the other. In the end, the fruits of our week-long labors would produce significantly improved living conditions for these families. What mattered most to me, though, was the impact that our efforts would eventually have on the lives of the children.

On our next-to-last night in Appalachia, everyone staying with us at the volunteer center gathered to share some of our jobsite experiences. A staff member posed an interesting question: Had any of us experienced a "God moment"? He described this as when we truly understood our purpose in Appalachia and the moment when we felt God's presence. I considered my week and quickly realized that I had a plethora of potential experiences to choose from—any one of them capable of fulfilling at least one of the two requirements needed to achieve the moment. Still, no single experience stood out above the others seeking special recognition. Besides, the big qualifier—experiencing God's presence—was the one requirement that I'd failed to achieve—or so I thought.

One by one, volunteers began sharing their responses. Many involved simple things—the smile of a child tasting an orange for the first time; newborn puppies and kittens held close; the satisfaction of making a difference in someone's life. But as my turn approached, I still searched for something to say. So, I told everyone that I hadn't experienced a God moment. I quickly added that I was certain mine was yet to come. I said that someday, maybe in the coming months when the coolness of a late autumn afternoon gives notice of the approaching winter, I'd recall a hot and dusty week in July. I'd remember being sweat-covered and struggling with itchy insulation. I'd think about our jobsite and all of the children. And I'd find comfort in the knowledge that sixteen kids were living in much improved conditions because of what we accomplished months earlier. I concluded by saying that when this happened, I might then experience my own God moment.

A few days after Thanksgiving, I was walking across my backyard for firewood when a chilly wind whipped the fallen leaves into a swirl about me. All at once, a flood of Appalachian memories came rushing back. I remembered the families we'd helped and all of the children—certain that they were warm now because of our efforts the previous summer. I was certain of something else, too: He had been with me then, and He was with me still, right there, in my own backyard. Suddenly, it was there after so many months: my very own Appalachian God moment, realized at last.

~Stephen Rusiniak

98

Finding God on a Warship

The true peace of God begins at any spot
a thousand miles from the nearest land.
~Joseph Conrad

When I wake up in the morning, I am surrounded by pictures of my friends and family. It looks like a collage of snapshots featuring special memories and smiling faces of the people I love most. Directly over my head, in the middle of all the pictures, is a small, flimsy dry erase board my mom and dad mailed me. On the board, I wrote, "Thank you, Lord, for today."

I'm a sailor on deployment in the U.S. Navy. I sleep in a "rack," which I like to say feels more like a shelf or a cubbyhole. When I lie in my rack and close my curtains, that's pretty much the only alone time or "me time" I get.

Being on deployment brings out the worst in people at times, even me. When we haven't hit port in a while, tempers really start to flare. It seems like everyone is irritated or having a bad day, every day. It's hard to not get drawn into the gossip and drama that goes on, especially when you're cut off from the "real world," as I like to call it. It's so frustrating when people talk loudly and show no respect for the nightly broadcast of the evening prayer. In fact, many times I look around and find myself the only one paying attention, and bowing my head during this time. I catch myself thinking, "How disrespectful."

To combat the stress, I attend church in the forecastle when I can get someone to cover my shift on Sunday. The service is quite different from any I have ever attended. The pews are replaced by folding metal chairs. When you go in, you have to walk around the huge anchor chain. Many times you can feel the boat moving, and the chaplain is constantly interrupted by the loud noises of the catapults shooting fighter jets off the boat or landing them. Our Sunday best is replaced by our working uniform of the day, and I'm pretty sure the altar is a foldout table. Either way, we still shake hands, say hello, and sing our hearts out. On some days, you can really feel the Holy Spirit. Sometimes, when I close my eyes, it almost feels like I'm in church back home.

Nearly every day, I long for the moment when I can crawl in my rack and close my curtain. I long to look at all the people I love and miss taped up in my rack, and the flimsy dry erase board that reads, "Thank you, Lord, for today." I shut off my personal light and say a prayer.

This is my favorite time of my day, right before I fall asleep. This is the time when I feel most at peace and the most loved. I know God is here with me, watching over me and everyone else on this ship. If I can find God on a warship in the middle of the ocean, then I know I can find Him anywhere. He is always with us. This blessing is what sustains me through deployments.

~Nicole Corene Stout

99

Contagious Christian

In about the same degree as you are helpful, you will be happy.
~Karl Reiland

As a teenager, I was filled with a lot of anger because my father had left when I was five years old. People saw a happy person, but I was miserable on the inside. I started to hang out with the wrong people and do the wrong things. I drank a lot and became fluent in two languages: English and profanity. I was very selfish, ignorant and prideful, among other things. But one of the things I remember fondly during this difficult time was coming home from a night of partying and opening the door to hear my mom playing Christian music on the piano. It gave me a warm feeling, but on the other hand it really made me feel bad about myself. My mom did her best to bring us up in the church, which planted a seed early in my life.

Isn't it funny how some of us only start to pray when we are in need of something? As I became older and found myself in need of God, I started to pray. My daughter, Maiah, was born with Erb's palsy and I didn't know what to do. She also had an extreme case of jaundice. The doctors told me that because her jaundice was so high, she could possibly have brain damage. She needed a complete blood transfusion. Scared to death, I started to challenge God. I told Him, "If you are real, then hear my prayers and help my baby girl!" Within a couple of months of praying over her daily, she began to move her arm and heal. She is now twelve years old and a straight-A student.

But even though this experience showed me how powerful and awesome God really is, and how He answers prayers, I'm sad to say that I soon forgot about God and went about my usual selfish ways.

It wasn't until my parents suggested that I attend a spiritual weekend called the Walk to Emmaus that I truly committed my life to Christ. Finally, He was not just in my head, but in my heart! I felt a need to serve Him and give back what was given to me. I wanted to be His hands and His feet. No more drinking, no more cursing, no more selfishness—only a commitment to serve. I wanted others to know Him like I had come to know Him.

For the past two years, I have been involved in the Kairos Prison Ministry. Sometimes, I feel that God has a real sense of humor—I tried to stay out of prison and now that's where He has called me to be. God has placed me there to let the inmates know that if I can change, they can change. It gives me great joy to see those who are so lost realize that there is a hope for them. I have witnessed to guys with multiple life sentences who have now given their lives to Christ and are serving others within the prison walls.

God is constantly putting people in my path who are seeking guidance. I guess you can call me a "Contagious Christian." Contagious means something that can spread from one person to another. It can be as little as a smile, a kind word or an ear to listen. And I challenge everyone to be Contagious Christians… not only in your words but in your actions.

~Matt Arnold

God Is Real

Pay attention to your dreams—
God's angels often speak directly to our hearts when we are asleep.
~Eileen Elias Freeman,
The Angels' Little Instruction Book

I stood on a busy sidewalk in the capital city of San José, Costa Rica. My mission team gathered outside a glass high-rise bank. Its portico sheltered us from the blazing sun. Bronze-skinned pedestrians scurried around us on a late-morning workday. I noticed their curious glances as they passed. As an obvious foreigner with my fair complexion, I imagine I looked as lost as I felt.

I asked myself, "What in the world am I doing here?" Fresh out of chiropractic school and in a foreign country for the first time, the thought of examining my first patients gave me butterflies. A trickle of sweat rolled down my spine from the tropical heat. Adding to my discomfort was the attention our team of twenty attracted. I grew impatient waiting to receive our marching orders for the day's work.

In that awkward moment, to summon courage and confidence, I reminded myself why I came. God made our bodies in His image. He designed them with a will to survive and self-heal. I had the humble privilege to facilitate in the healing process. This philosophy motivated me to travel a long distance and provide a natural form of healing to the sick, to the less fortunate who couldn't afford any form of health care, and to the remote villagers who didn't seek conventional treatments.

Our mobile clinic created a stir, and lines formed. I examined the spine and posture, and used a portable, handheld instrument to measure each patient's nerve pressure. Then I instructed the patients on how to position themselves on the adjusting table. With my hands, I applied a quick and gentle specific adjustment to the upper cervical spine. As word spread about our presence in the city, patient lines grew even longer, and I worked non-stop for hours. At one point, I paused to drink from my water bottle and looked out at a city plaza packed with waiting people.

Members of our host church worked alongside us to share the gospel. I knew Jesus, but did not feel compelled to tell others about Him. My faith was new. I didn't fully understand the enormity of my own decision to accept Him—the eternal fate of my soul and a fulfilling relationship. At this point in my spiritual walk, I recited a genuine prayer and my soul was reborn, but life continued as usual.

On one particular day, our team of doctors split into groups. Some doctors went to the schools and some to the hospitals. My group stayed in the city plaza. I adjusted a woman and her baby. In Spanish, I suppose she thanked me, but I didn't know. No *habla español*.

An hour later, she and her baby returned to me, frantic. Speaking quickly and waving her arms, her urgency was apparent. I found the interpreter and asked her to translate. The woman said she had come back to deliver a message from God.

I wondered if the lady was crazy. How did she know she had a message from God? How did she get the message? She proceeded to tell us that God knew the sacrifices we had made to travel to her country. He knew the families we left behind and the money we spent. She said God blessed us and our families, and He would reward our actions. Then she prayed for us. The woman, tearful by that point, finished her message and left, obviously relieved, as if someone had removed a heavy load from her shoulders. I was skeptical. I doubted God spoke in such a literal sense and questioned how the woman could be so sure it was God talking.

On Wednesday, our host church held a vibrant evening service.

People danced, laughed, and clapped. I had never experienced that type of worship and was hesitant to join the fun. A redheaded missionary woman from the United States hugged me tight, and whispered in my ear. "God wants you to know He is real."

Bewildered, I wondered what in the world was going on. First, the crazy lady on the street, and now this woman.

Another day in the city and a short, middle-aged Hispanic woman approached our group. She wore a yellow sweater, and two men trailed behind her. I saw the commotion from a distance. Then a stranger in the crowd pointed to me.

In broken English, the woman told me she was looking for a medical doctor.

I said, "I'm not a medical doctor. I'm a chiropractor. But can I help you?"

She said, "I have a message for you from God."

It wasn't the message I remember, but her explanation afterward that rocked me. When she finished speaking and I saw that familiar burden relieved, I asked her a question. "How did you know the message was for me?"

God had told her in a dream that she would see a group of American doctors, and she should deliver the message to the woman who said, "Can I help you?"

I stood there stunned as she recounted the remaining details of a dream I already knew. I didn't know whether to be scared or awed. A couple of months before, I had had the exact same dream as this woman standing before me now. I hadn't told anyone this dream. In fact, I had forgotten it until that moment. I didn't think it mattered, and I certainly didn't know it would have meaning connected to events during this mission trip.

My dream was brief, more like a snapshot than a video. In a sterile and stainless-steel operating room, three doctors in white lab coats stood around a surgical table staring down at a lifeless body laying on it. I was one of those three doctors. A Hispanic woman wearing a yellow shirt walked into the operating room. As she approached the table, I asked her, "Can I help you?"

God was real, and now I knew it. He was not some far-off entity, but intimately involved in my life and orchestrating events to demonstrate that fact. Three separate bizarre events proved it to me. God became tangible.

I returned to my home soil a believer in God's presence, His power, and His pursuit of those He loves. This first mission trip sparked a deep and growing relationship with God. My mission now is to share His love and deliver the message that was whispered to me: "God is real."

~Dr. Theresa Anderson

Too Old,
Too Stubborn,
Too Proud

You give but little when you give of your possessions.
It is when you give of yourself that you truly give.
~*Kahlil Gibran*, The Prophet

Sighing deeply, I peered into the kitchen cupboards. I could have tomato soup and a peanut butter sandwich for dinner. I slowly closed the cupboard door as despair settled over me like a heavy cloak. I had eaten soup and peanut butter sandwiches three nights this week, and the thought of having it again made me lose my appetite.

A myriad of "ifs" floated through my head. If only Ben had not let his insurance policy lapse when his medical bills got so expensive. If only I had managed to sell our house before the bank foreclosed on it. If only it were possible for sixty-eight-year-old women to find jobs these days. If only I wasn't too stubborn to give up my freedom and move in with my daughter in Seattle. My stomach gave a great growl as if to remind me that "ifs" don't buy groceries or provide peace of mind.

I had reluctantly signed up for food stamps a few days before but I had not received my card yet. Until it arrived, I had to save my pennies to make sure the utilities got paid. In the meantime, I ate in front of the TV, trying to concentrate on the show and not think about what I was eating. When I bought a loaf of bread, a jar of peanut butter and a few cans of soup for my weekly fare, I hadn't realized how dismal it would be trying to sustain such a meager diet.

I made a cup of tea and sat down at the kitchen table to nurse it. I made each action I took last as long as I could, prolonging every moment. It was how I got through the long, lonely days without Ben. I did everything in slow motion. I sipped my tea and thought about how upset Ben would be if he knew the dismal shape I was in since his death. He always believed he would beat the cancer and find a way for us to be solvent again. He always did have more faith than I did, and what little I had seemed to vanish when I lost him.

Mae, the elderly widow who lives a few doors away, told me about the soup kitchen that she visits several times a week. "The food is good, and it sure beats eating alone every night," she said. I had dismissed the idea immediately. To me, that was just a step above begging, and I was far too proud to do that. The meals were served in a new, modern facility, and the sign over the doorway said "The Shepherd's Table" in reference to a shepherd feeding his sheep, I suppose. But, nevertheless, it was a soup kitchen, and in my day only the homeless, the beggars and the winos went to them. I thought of Mae, in her crisp, little housedresses and her white hair always shinning, and I knew I was wrong. Still, I couldn't bring myself to take the bus downtown and enjoy a good meal at The Shepherd's Table.

As the evening wore on and my hunger returned, I knew I had two choices. Stuff another peanut butter sandwich down my throat or swallow my false pride and make my way to The Shepherd's Table. I finally pulled on my coat, and after stuffing a pair of cheap gloves into my pocket in case it got colder, I walked to the bus stop.

When I arrived at The Shepherd's Table, a line of people was already forming in front of the building. I shuffled around uneasily, taking furtive glances at the people gathered around me. They couldn't be placed in a neat, predictable category. I saw faces from very pale to very dark and every shade in between; all ages from babes in arms to the very old and frail came to seek a hot, nourishing meal. The only thing they all had in common was the look in their eyes. A touching combination of desperation, fear, embarrassment and pride showed in eyes that darted about but never quite made eye contact except for the regulars who had come to know one another. I wondered if my eyes told the same story.

A middle-aged woman in front of me pulled her hands out of her coat pockets and began to rub them together. Her fingers were red and swollen and bore the knobby signs of arthritis. Our eyes met, and she gave me an apologetic half-smile. "I'd trade my dinner for a couple of aspirin right now," she said, looking at me hopefully.

I shook my head. "Sorry." I nodded toward the door of the soup kitchen. "Maybe someone inside will have aspirin."

"They aren't allowed to dispense medicines," she said. "Only food." She squared her narrow shoulders and jammed her aching hands back inside her pockets. "We should be grateful for that," she said softly, turning away from me.

Her words shocked me into reality. She was right. Instead of being ashamed and embarrassed to be standing in line for a free meal, I should be thankful that it was available for those who needed it. And I should be more like my precious Ben and believe that things would get better. He had faith until the end, and he would want me to have it, too.

I pulled the pair of gloves out of my pocket and tapped the woman on the shoulder. She spun to face me, the curiosity in her eyes melting into surprise when she saw the gloves I held out to her. "Maybe these will help."

I could tell by the look in her eyes that she wanted to take the gloves, yet she hesitated. "They look new," she protested weakly.

I grinned. "They are. Brand new from the dollar store."

She took the gloves and immediately put them on her hands. "They fit," she said, almost delightedly.

I shrugged. "One size fits all for a buck."

We both chuckled.

Tears welled up in her eyes. "You're very kind," she said. "My hands feel better already."

Suddenly, I realized that I felt better, too. My spirits were lifted, and I was no longer feeling sorry for myself. There were many people much worse off than I was. I had made someone happy by giving her a one-dollar pair of gloves. I knew what I had to do to take my mind off my own problems. I had to reach out to others and do what I could for them. It felt so good to know that others needed me. I had felt so useless since Ben's death.

After I finished my meal, I timidly approached the woman who appeared to be in charge of The Shepherd's Table. I told her I wanted to volunteer. That was the least I could do for my meal. She was a bit taken aback, but when she realized I was serious, she smiled broadly and took me to a room in the back where we could work out a schedule.

"We can never have too many volunteers," she said. "And I have never gotten a volunteer before from the soup line." She leaned back in her chair and looked at me squarely. "We ask this of everyone who volunteers. Why do you want to do this?"

The answer spilled from my lips without hesitation. "I just discovered a few minutes ago that you can't feel sorry for yourself while you're doing a kind deed for someone else."

I left The Shepherd's Table with a much lighter heart. I knew why Ben held fast to his faith until the very end. Faith brings hope, and without hope one lives in misery and despair. Like Ben, from this day forward, no matter what life brings, I will cling to my faith.

~Alice Hobbs

Meet Our Contributors

Linda Allen's time in the garden with her family inspired her to read and write about plants. Her Christmas books, *Decking the Halls — The Folklore and Traditions of Christmas Plants* and *Menagerie at the Manger*, tell the legends behind popular Christmas plants and animals. E-mail her at lindaeallen@pldi.net.

Kate Allt received her Bachelor of Arts degree with honors from Bradley University in Peoria, IL. She is a multimedia journalist in Iowa who likes to read, write, and travel in her spare time. Kate's favorite spots include Sorrento (Italy), London, and Dublin. E-mail her at kate.e.allt@gmail.com.

Dr. Theresa Anderson received her Doctor of Chiropractic degree from Life University in 2000. She is now a homeschooling mom of two and has a passion for all things real — whole food, natural healthcare, and a thriving faith. E-mail her at traanderson@gmail.com.

Amanda Arbia, a graduate of Moody Bible Institute, teaches high school English in Clearwater, FL. She enjoys shopping, writing, traveling and, most of all, curling up and watching TV with her husband, Mike. Amanda aspires to write children's books and devotionals for women. E-mail her at amandaarbia@gmail.com.

Ronda Armstrong writes from Iowa about family, faith, and fortitude. Her stories appear in varied anthologies, in addition to *Chicken Soup for the Soul* books. She rotates with other writers at thebridgemeditations.

wordpress.com. Ronda and her husband are ballroom dancers. E-mail her at ronda.armstrong@gmail.com.

Matt Arnold lives in South Florida with his wife, Candy, and their children, Maiah and Andrew. He is an avid sports fan and enjoys attending games, coaching his children's sports teams and going on trips with his family. The Lord has blessed him, and he loves sharing his testimony.

Esther M. Bailey is published in the Christian community and writes on assignment for two publishers. She has a strong passion to bless others through the written word. Bailey enjoys dining out and entertaining friends. Living in Scottsdale, AZ, she attends McDowell Mountain Community Church. E-mail her at baileywick@juno.com.

Deanna Baird is a wife, mother, and writer. Deanna coordinates programs at the library where she works and teaches ESL at her church. She has been published in *The Upper Room*, *Just Between Us*, and *Daily Devotions for Writers*, and is working on her first novel. E-mail Deanna at Deanna.baird@gmail.com.

Nancy Baker resides in College Station, TX, with her husband and Golden Retriever. After retirement, she pursued her lifelong dream of writing, and has been published in numerous anthologies and magazines. Her faith is her mainstay and the source of many of her stories.

Marisa Balzafiore earned her B.S. degree in 1992. She taught in several capacities and coordinated religious programs. Marisa has Stargardt's disease, prompting her boutique, which features "Seeing with Style" necklaces. She writes poetry, inspirational stories, and tween novels. Contact her at marisasboutique@yahoo.com.

Shinan Barclay, a passionate gardener, swimmer and writer, prefers solitude and silence to television and city life. Her stories appear in several *Chicken Soup for the Soul* books. She lives on the Oregon coast and is working on her memoir: *Arctic Lights: Coming of Age in an Eskimo Village*. Connect with her at www.facebook.com/shinanbarclay.

Alma Barkman is the author of eight Christian books. She has had numerous articles and poems published in a wide variety of periodicals. She and her husband live in central Canada where they raised their four children. For more info, visit her website at almabarkman.com.

Kathy L. Baumgarten, TSGT USAF (Ret.) received her B.A. degree in Social Theory, Structure and Change in 2005 (Empire State College). Writing professionally since 2004, she lives in the Adirondacks and enjoys restoring her home, time with grandchildren, and serving veterans. Learn more at www.strictlyaloner.com.

Pam Johnson Bostwick's articles appear in Christian magazines, newspapers, and anthologies. She is visually and hearing impaired. She enjoys her condo and its peaceful surroundings, but misses the beach. She performs with her guitar, mentors others, and adores her seven children and sixteen grandchildren. Pam happily remarried on 7/7/07. E-mail Pam at pamloves7@comcast.net.

Rose Lee Brady is the mother of five sons: Jason, Chris, Tim, Josiah, and Nathan. She has two granddaughters, Delana and Lorelei. Her grandson, Asher, is an account executive for Merchant Services Direct in Spokane, WA. Rose enjoys reading and writing short stories in her spare time.

Jan Brand is a freelance writer in Arlington, TX, and former Assistant Director of North Texas Christian Writers. She longs to see God honored in America again. Much of her fiction and nonfiction focuses on America's Christian heritage—remembering the past so we can build a better future.

Elaine Bridge worked in the woods on the West Coast as a forester before becoming a stay-at-home mom to her three boys. Now living in Ohio, she stays busy working in a grocery store, caring for her family, and writing inspirational material. E-mail her at elainebrg@ yahoo.com.

Cynthia Briggs embraces her love of cooking and writing through her cookbooks, *Pork Chops & Applesauce* and *Sweet Apple Temptations*. She enjoys speaking to women's groups, critiquing and reviewing books, coaching budding authors, and writing for family publications. Her website is cynthiabriggsbooks.com or e-mail Cynthia at info@ porkchopsandapplesauce.net.

Georgia Bruton lives in Florida with her husband, Steve. She has two beautiful daughters, two great sons-in-law, and three wonderful grandchildren. She is a published author of nonfiction, and her first children's/young adult novel, *Escape*, was released in August 2012. E-mail her at gjbruton@yahoo.com.

Sheri Bull is a nonfiction short story writer. She writes from true-life experiences, and her goal is to publish a short story book. Sheri lives in rural Illinois on a fruit farm with her husband, Vince. She has three grown daughters and one grandson. She enjoys gardening, singing, visiting her daughters, and playing with her grandson, Jake.

Darlene Gudrie Butts is the author of *Lessons from the Depression, Eliminating Debt the Old-Fashioned Way*, and *The Promise*. She is a motivational speaker on perseverance, finding your passion, and personal finances. Darlene has been married for twenty-nine years and has three wonderful children. E-mail her at darb2363@yahoo. ca.

Barbara Canale is a frequent *Chicken Soup for the Soul* contributor and Christian writer. She has authored several books and is a columnist at *The Catholic Sun* in Syracuse, NY. She is the mother of two grown children, and volunteers in her community and church. She loves to ski and garden.

Bobbi Carducci is an award-winning short story writer, columnist, and book reviewer. Her book for young readers, *Storee Wryter Gets a Dog*, published in April 2011, earned a gold Mom's Choice Award. Bobbi is the director of the Young Voices Foundation, established to mentor young writers. E-mail her at bcarducci@comcast.net.

Sandy McPherson Carrubba traded teaching for full-time motherhood. She is now a devoted caregiver to her husband of forty-five years. Some of her stories for children are used in third-grade reading programs. Her short stories, essays, and poetry for adults have won awards. Finishing Line Press published her poetry chapbook, *Brush Strokes*.

Judy Ceppa is a mother, grandmother, great-grandmother, and former high school history teacher. She writes while she and her husband live as traveling contemplatives, first on their Gold Wing motorcycle and now full-time in their motor home and touring on their Silver Wing mega-scooter. They travel as the Spirit leads.

Harriet Cooper is a freelance writer and has published personal essays, humor, and creative nonfiction in newspapers, newsletters, anthologies, and magazines. She is a frequent contributor to the *Chicken Soup for the Soul* series. She writes about family, relationships, health, food, cats, writing, and daily life. E-mail her at shewrites@live.ca.

Dan Cosby received his B.S. degree from the University of Alabama at Birmingham and a diploma in addiction studies from the NET Institute. As a pastor and addiction counselor near Tampa, FL, he enjoys his family, including five grandchildren, and writing about recovery and spirituality. Contact Dan at www.Erecoverychurch.com.

Kat Crawford, author of *Capsules of Hope: Survival Guide for Caregivers*, is known as The Lionhearted Kat. She is a freelance author published in sixteen anthologies and numerous magazines. Her lifetime gift is encouragement. She enjoys sharing stories of God's love. Learn more at www.lionheartedkat.com.

L.L. Darroch is a traveler and explorer, both by nature and nurture. She is hoping to fill up at least one bookshelf with her current and future published work. Join L.L. Darroch on her writing journey and visit her at www.darroch-meekis.webnode.com.

Tracie David is a wife and mother of three boys in Lake Charles, LA. She spends her spare time cheering on her boys at their baseball and football games and wrestling matches throughout the year. This is her very first published piece.

After being diagnosed with multiple sclerosis in 2009, **Yvonne deSousa** started a blog that uses humor to help cope with chronic illness. She is writing a book on the same topic, and also writes about her faith and the history of Provincetown, MA. View her work at yvonnedesousa.com.

Ginny Dubose graduated from Florida Southern College in 1980. She is happily married with two sons, living in Central Florida. She is the Business Office Manager for a local retirement community. Her hobbies include writing and watercolor painting. Her sons and husband are her joy and her inspiration. E-mail her at DijaNich@aol.com.

Although **Janet Perez Eckles** lost her sight, she gained insight to serve as an international speaker, writer, columnist, and author of a #1 bestseller on Amazon, *Simply Salsa: Dancing Without Fear at God's Fiesta* (Judson Press, August 2011). From her home in Florida, she imparts inspiration at www.inspirationforyou.com.

Shawnelle Eliasen and her husband, Lonny, raise their five sons in Illinois. Shawnelle home-teaches her youngest boys. Her writing has been published in *Guideposts*, *MomSense* magazine, *Marriage Partnership*, *Cup of Comfort* books, numerous *Chicken Soup for the Soul* books, and other anthologies. Follow her adventures at Shawnellewrites.blogspot.com.

Judith Fitzsimmons is a freelance business consultant and technical writer whose greatest joy is her daughter, Chelsea. She lives in middle Tennessee in a house of love, light, and healing.

Virginia Funk is retired. Her interest in writing goes back to her teenage years when she wrote a sports column for her employer. She also won a short story contest, which was published in a local, small-print edition. She has written a children's book that she hopes to publish in the future.

Heidi Gaul lives in Oregon with her husband and four-legged family. She loves travel, be it around the block or the globe, and reading is her passion. Active in American Christian Fiction Writers and Oregon Christian Writers, she is currently finishing her second novel. E-mail her at dhgaul@aol.com.

Sgt. Danger Geist was honorably discharged shortly after returning home from Afghanistan, and he now lives with his wife and dog in the Chicago area. To read more of his experiences in Afghanistan, visit www.BurningBridge.com and pick up a copy of his memoir, *I Am Danger; I Am Prisoner*.

Pamela Goldstein has followed her passion for writing for more than twenty years. She has completed three manuscripts and four plays, and has several short stories published, many in the *Chicken Soup for the Soul* series. Pamela is honoured to be part of the Chicken Soup for the Soul family. E-mail her at boker_tov2002@yahoo.ca.

William Halderson lives in Cookeville, TN, with his wife, Monica, and dog, Max. For two years, he has written a newspaper column centered on his life experiences with family, pets, and wild animals. He is a member of the Lay Salvatorians and works in several church ministries.

Teresa Hanly married her husband, Kevin, in 1977, and found time to write stories from her experiences while raising their six sons. She is now pursuing publishing her works. She enjoys ministry at the local prison near her home and loves camping, skiing, gardening, and hiking. E-mail Teresa at tesshanly@yahoo.com.

Melanie Hardy received her bachelor's degree from Spring Hill College and her JD from Concord School of Law. She is employed by Cunningham Lindsey USA. She enjoys volunteer work, cooking, and spending time with her family. E-mail her at rhardy212@charter.net.

Marijo Herndon's articles, ranging from humor to inspiration, appear in several publications and books. She has also developed stress management strategies that benefit the coaching programs for a leading health plan company. She lives in New York with her husband, Dave, and two cats, Lucy and Ethel. E-mail her at marijo215@nycap.rr.com.

Nancy Hoag is a wife, mother, and grandmother. She graduated with honors from the University of Washington in Seattle. She has seen 1,000 articles and four books published; received numerous awards for her writing, including an Amy Writing Award in 2008; and currently travels with her husband to build Habitat for Humanity houses.

Alice Hobbs lives in Fayetteville, NC, with her husband, George, and her two cherished Chihuahuas, Prissy and Tangi. She loves shopping and has an uncanny ability to find fantastic bargains.

Gayle Mansfield Irwin is a writer with a strong background in animal welfare. She has written several children's books, and she is a contributor to other *Chicken Soup for the Soul* books. She enjoys sharing her stories with others and talking about the pet/human bond. Learn more at www.gaylemirwin.com.

Marsha Jordan, creator of the Hugs and Hope for Sick Children foundation and author of *Hugs, Hope, and Peanut Butter*, says hope, joy, and love are "sticky" like peanut butter. Spread them around, and you'll get some on yourself. Learn more about Jordan's book and charity at www.hugsandhope.org.

Miranda Kendall spent her first twelve years exploring the Missouri woods. She was transplanted to Kansas eighteen years ago and is now firmly rooted in Plains soil. She and her husband, David, are blessed with two children, Sky and Grace.

Heather J. Kirk is a writer, photographer, and graphic designer. Recipient of a VSC Poetry Fellowship, her book is titled, *We... a spirit seeking harmony for a world that's out of sync*. She's contributed to various anthologies and journals. Her photography has shown nationally and can be viewed at www.heather-kirk.artistwebsites.com.

Sandra Knudsen is a widow who started writing when her husband passed away in 2008. Ray had been totally disabled for twenty years. As his caregiver, she learned many foundational truths. She hopes to encourage others through speaking, writing, and even worship. E-mail her at knudsen3@centurytel.net.

Kathleen Kohler is a writer and speaker from the Pacific Northwest. Her articles, rooted in personal experience, appear in books and magazines. She and her husband have three children and seven grandchildren. Kathleen enjoys gardening, travel, and watercolor painting. Visit www.kathleenkohler.com to read more of her published work.

Nancy Julien Kopp is a Kansan originally from Chicago. She began writing late in life, but has been published in thirteen *Chicken Soup for the Soul* books, other anthologies, ezines, newspapers, and magazines. Once a classroom teacher, she now teaches through the written word. Visit her blog at www.writergrannysworld.blogpsot.com.

Francesca Lang lives in Orlando with her husband, Richard, and son, Aiden, along with Bailey the cat and Jazmine the dog. She holds a degree in intercultural and organizational communications and sociology. She currently works for the Central Florida YMCA, and is working toward further degrees in exercise physiology and nutrition.

Carmen Leal is the author of nine books, including *Faces of Huntington's* and *The Twenty-Third Psalm for Caregivers*. She is a popular presenter at women's retreats, church groups, conventions, and conferences. To learn more about Carmen or to book her for your next event, visit carmenleal.com or e-mail carmen@carmenleal.com.

Lynne Leite is pursuing the dream she believes God called her to since childhood—to be a storyteller through writing and speaking. Her first love is God, followed by family, which includes her husband, daughter, son, and son-in-law. You can learn more about Lynne at www.CurlyGirl4God.com.

Jaye Lewis is an award-winning inspirational writer and frequent contributing author to the *Chicken Soup for the Soul* series and other popular anthologies. Jaye lives with her family in the beautiful mountains of Virginia. Visit her website at www.entertainingangels. org and follow her blog at www.entertainingangelsencouragingwords. blogspot.com.

Rayni Lewis has always enjoyed writing fiction. Rayni also loves to draw and paint, as well as play soccer. Rayni loves to spend time in the mountains by snowboarding, camping, and hiking. She also spends time with her friends, going to movies or to the mall.

Karen M. Lynch is a freelance writer from Connecticut. This is her third contribution to a *Chicken Soup for the Soul* anthology. Other stories of Karen's have appeared in *Chicken Soup for the Shopper's Soul* and *Chicken Soup for the Wine Lover's Soul*.

Shawn Marie Mann lives in central Pennsylvania with her family and two crazy cats. She is a writer and an amusement park geographer. When she's not researching Pennsylvania parks, she enjoys quilting and stamp collecting. You can send her an e-mail by visiting www.shawnmariemann.com.

Long ago, **Elaine Olelo Masters** was Director of Christian Education in St. Thomas United Methodist Church, Manassas, VA. She has since led workshops in Nigeria, Hong Kong, and Thailand. She now lives in Honolulu, HI, and attends Bluewater Mission. Her sixteenth book, *What the Witch Doctor Taught Me*, will be available in the fall 2012.

Betsy McPhee grew up in Ann Arbor and graduated from the University of Michigan. She now resides in Arizona, where she enjoys hiking and travel with her husband. Her stories have appeared in various magazines and anthologies. Visit Betsy's blog, The Storied House, at www.betsymcphee.com or reach her at betsymcphee@yahoo.com.

Peggy Molitor received her Bachelor of Science degree from Northwestern College in 1996 and her Master of Arts degree in religion from University of Dubuque Theological Seminary in 2005. She works as an office assistant at a jewelry store and as a freelance writer. Her goal is to write full-time.

Amy Morgan lives in Grand Island, NY, an island in the middle of the Niagara River. She's an avid reader, and loves writing and cooking. Her husband, Steve, and son, Abram, are her greatest sources of encouragement and inspiration. E-mail her at amy@amywrites.net or visit her webpage at www.amywrites.net.

Before retiring to New Mexico, **Margaret Nava** spent twenty years traveling throughout the Southwest, researching and writing short articles about nature, spirituality, and Native American traditions. Since then, she has written two New Mexico travel guides and three Lady Lit novels. E-mail her at angeladunn08@aol.com.

Mary Eileen Oakes received her Master's Degree in special education from Long Island University in 1994. She taught for twelve years prior to staying home to raise her three children. She has been a personal journaler for thirty years and is putting together an anthology of her best work in a memoir.

Linda O'Connell has a deep, abiding faith that everything happens for a reason. Linda, a preschool teacher and freelance writer, lives in St. Louis, MO. She and her husband, Bill, enjoy the beach and outdoor activities. Their grandchildren give them reason to be thankful. Linda blogs at lindaoconnell.blogspot.com.

Manny Patla received his Bachelor of Arts degree from Saint Xavier College, a master's degree in school psychology from Governors State University, and another master's degree in school leadership from Olivet Nazarene University.

Faith Paulsen is delighted to share another Chicken Soup for the Soul story. An earlier version of "The Silence Sings" appeared in *What Canst Thou Say?*, a quarterly newsletter for Quakers who have mystical experiences or pray contemplatively. Faith's writing has also appeared in *Wild River Review*, *Literary Mama*, and several other collections.

Jill Pertler touches people's hearts and funny bones with her syndicated column, "Slices of Life," which is printed in over 120 newspapers across the U.S. She is author of *The Do-It-Yourselfer's Guide to Self-Syndication*. Find her columns on Facebook at Slices of Life or visit her website at marketing-by-design.home.mchsi.com.

Kay Conner Pliszka is a retired high school music teacher. She and her best friend perform solos and duets for churches and community groups as the "SONshine Sisters." Together they share their testimony of faith through their music and stories. To schedule a performance, please contact Kay at kmpliszka@comcast.net.

Yvonne Riozzi is an LPN and works for the Commission on Aging in northern Michigan. She enjoys spending time with her husband and two daughters. She likes to decorate, take long walks, and work with the elderly.

Tammy Ruggles is a freelance writer living in Kentucky. She writes short stories, articles, screenplays, and audiobooks. Her first paperback book, *Peace*, was published in 2005 by Clear Light Books.

Stephen Rusiniak is a husband and father from Wayne, NJ. He's a former police detective who specialized in juvenile/family matters and now shares his thoughts through his writings. His work has appeared several times in *Chicken Soup for the Soul* anthologies. E-mail him at stephenrusiniak@yahoo.com or visit www.facebook.com/StephenPRusiniak.

J.C. Santos teaches middle school English and religion in West Seattle. He loves spending time with family, singing, traveling, and playing basketball. Besides inspirational stories, he enjoys writing poetry, folk songs, and fiction. Someday soon, he hopes to publish his first book. He'd love to hear feedback at santosjcl@hotmail.com.

Beth Savoie is a pediatric nurse practitioner at the Children's Clinic in Lake Charles, LA, and a fledgling author. She loves to be outdoors, reading, writing, and cooking. When not working with kids, Beth can be found at her blog: www.creatingwordlenik.blogspot.com.

Nikolas Schanzenbacher is a high school student in Pennsylvania graduating in the class of 2012. He enjoys playing many different forms of music and instruments. He also loves writing poetry and lyrics in his spare time.

Jeffrey Schmatz resides in South Texas. E-mail him at jschmatz@jsmedia.net.

Lindy Schneider is the co-author and award-winning illustrator of *Starfish on the Beach*, a children's book that encourages both adults and children to make a difference. A regular contributor to *Chicken Soup for the Soul* books, she is also a playwright and inspirational speaker. To learn more, visit www.LindysBooks.com.

Kim Seeley is a former teacher and librarian. She loves to travel, read, and write. She is a frequent contributor to *Sasee* magazine and has written several articles for the *Chicken Soup for the Soul* series.

Audrey Sellers is a Texas mama with three indisputable loves: God, family, and white chocolate frozen yogurt. She's married to a high school coach and can often be found chasing after her toddler son and sprightly pug, Chompers. E-mail her at audrey.m.sellers@gmail.com.

Deborah Shouse is a speaker, writer, and editor. She loves helping people write and edit books, and she enjoys facilitating creativity and storytelling workshops. Deborah donates all proceeds from her book, *Love in the Land of Dementia: Finding Hope in the Caregiver's Journey*, to Alzheimer's programs and research. Learn more at www.TheCreativityConnection.com.

Elizabeth Smayda has worked in the field of social services and health care for twenty-two years, working with a very diverse, vulnerable population. She also co-authored a study involving eating disorders that was published in December 2005. Elizabeth enjoys her family, work, art, and writing. E-mail her at brsmayda@shaw.ca.

David Michael Smith, of Delaware, renewed his marital vows with his wife, Geralynn, on their fifteenth anniversary in 2012, much to her surprise. He credits his successes as a writer to his wife and children (Rebekah and Matthew), the prayers of his church family, and to his Redeemer and King, Jesus.

Edwin Smith is the past president for the League of Utah Writers. His award-winning stories, articles, and humor reflect the joys and challenges of life. He lives in rural Utah, golfing, fly fishing, writing, and loving his family. E-mail Ed at efsmithwrites@gmail.com.

Patrick P. Stafford lives in Northridge, CA, and works full-time as a journalist, copywriter, and editor. He has written for AccessLife. com, *Wheelin' Sportsmen*, *Amateur Chef*, *Healthcare Traveler*, and *Northern Virginia Magazine*, and has sold many diverse writings to numerous publications over the past thirty years. E-mail him at marcelproust37@hotmail.com.

Diane Stark is a former teacher turned stay-at-home mom and freelance writer. She loves to write about the important things in life: her family and her faith. She is the author of *Teachers' Devotions to Go*. E-mail Diane at DianeStark19@yahoo.com.

After entering the United States Navy in 2009, **Nicole Corene Stout** completed Aviation Boatswain's Mate Equipment service training and is assigned to the aircraft carrier *USS Dwight D. Eisenhower*, where she has completed four deployments, earned the Enlisted Aviation Warfare Specialist insignia, and has been promoted to Petty Officer Third Class.

Michael John Sullivan is a novelist living in New York. *Everybody's Daughter* was published in 2012, while *Necessary Heartbreak: A Novel of Faith and Forgiveness* came out in 2010. Some of the material in the novels was written while Michael was homeless, riding the train in NYC. Contact him at MichaelJohnSullivan.com.

Pamela Tambornino is a member of the Cherokee Nation, Wolf Clan, and has published a book on her grandmother, *Maggie's Story*. She lives in Kansas with a wonderful husband, two dogs, and four cats. E-mail her at bookwormbugg2002@yahoo.com.

Carol Tanis is an award-winning radio and TV journalist who later entered the field of public relations. As a PR specialist, she has promoted everything from higher education to classical music. E-mail her at taniscarol@hotmail.com.

Ronda Ross Taylor lives in the Seattle area with her husband, Eldon, and a couple of parrots. She has two grown sons, two charming daughters-in-law, and a granddaughter who calls her Gaga. When she's not reading, writing, editing, or volunteering in school libraries, she can be found swimming laps.

Marla H. Thurman hopes to publish her first e-book later this year, featuring short stories from her life. She lives in Signal Mountain, TN with her rescue dogs, Sophie and Jasper. Marla spends far too much time surfing the net and can easily be reached at sizoda1@gmail.com.

Author of more than one hundred articles and stories, **Sue Tornai** lives with her husband, John, and dog, Maggie, in Carmichael, CA. They enjoy camping in their trailer, and fishing the lakes and rivers in Northern California. Sue enjoys reading, knitting, and teaching Sunday school. Visit her website at www.suetornai.com.

Christine Trollinger is a freelance writer from Kansas City, MO. She has been published in several anthologies over the years. She enjoys gardening and her family. She is a widow and has three children, two grandchildren, three great-grandchildren, and the love of her life... Gabby, a Bichon.

Pam Williams is a pastor's wife and Nana of three awesome grandchildren. Her stories appear in several *Chicken Soup for the Soul* books and many Christian magazines. She is the author of *Baccalaureate: Guidelines for Inspirational Worship Services to Honor Graduates*. Connect with Pam through her blog at www.2encourage. blogspot.com.

Anne Wilson was an LVN/LPN for many years, but today she teaches writing courses at the University of San Diego. Anne has written and published since the mid-1980s in various genres, including inspirational writing, poetry, and essays.

David A. Wollin lives in the Ocean State. When he is not putting fingers to the keyboard, he practices law in Providence, RI, and elsewhere. E-mail him at wollinfamily@cox.net.

Beth M. Wood is a mom of three, marketing professional, and freelance writer. Her work can be found in *Sasee* magazine and various *Chicken Soup for the Soul* anthologies, including *Chicken Soup for the Soul: Think Positive*. She is a devout reader, semi-fanatic editor, and not-so-great golfer. Follow along at www.bethmwood.blogspot. com.

Sandra Wood is a freelance author who writes stories about God's practical help and amazing hope in our daily lives. She enjoys capturing the beauty of sunrise, rainbows, and wildflowers with a pen, a lens or a song. Long walks with good friends are as delicious as chocolate.

Sheryl Young has been freelance writing since 1997 for magazines, newspapers, and websites. She's written two books, *What Every Christian Should Know about the Jewish People*, to improve relationships between Christians and Jews, and *God, Am I Nobody?* about living within God's will. She's happily married and lives in Florida.

Heather Zuber-Harshman is a writer, speaker, and legal writing professor. She is currently working on a mystery novel and short stories while posting stories about faith, cooking, traveling, and humorous experiences on her blog at www.HeatherHarshman. wordpress.com. Between writing projects, she enjoys bicycling, traveling, snowboarding, and camping with her husband, Dale.

Meet Our Authors

Jack Canfield is the co-creator of the *Chicken Soup for the Soul* series, which *Time* magazine has called "the publishing phenomenon of the decade." Jack is also the co-author of many other bestselling books.

Jack is the CEO of the Canfield Training Group in Santa Barbara, California, and founder of the Foundation for Self-Esteem in Culver City, California. He has conducted intensive personal and professional development seminars on the principles of success for more than a million people in twenty-three countries, has spoken to hundreds of thousands of people at more than 1,000 corporations, universities, professional conferences and conventions, and has been seen by millions more on national television shows.

Jack has received many awards and honors, including three honorary doctorates and a Guinness World Records Certificate for having seven books from the *Chicken Soup for the Soul* series appearing on the New York Times bestseller list on May 24, 1998.

You can reach Jack at www.jackcanfield.com.

Mark Victor Hansen is the co-founder of Chicken Soup for the Soul, along with Jack Canfield. He is a sought-after keynote speaker, bestselling author, and marketing maven. Mark's powerful messages of possibility, opportunity, and action have created powerful change in thousands of organizations and millions of individuals worldwide.

Mark is a prolific writer with many bestselling books in addition to the *Chicken Soup for the Soul* series. Mark has had a profound influence in the field of human potential through his library of audios, videos, and articles in the areas of big thinking, sales achievement, wealth building, publishing success, and personal and professional development. He is also the founder of the MEGA Seminar Series.

Mark has received numerous awards that honor his entrepreneurial spirit, philanthropic heart, and business acumen. He is a lifetime member of the Horatio Alger Association of Distinguished Americans.

You can reach Mark at www.markvictorhansen.com.

Susan M. Heim is a longstanding author and editor, specializing in parenting, women's and Christian issues. After the birth of her twin boys in 2003, Susan left her desk job as a Senior Editor at a publishing company and has never looked back. Being a work-at-home mother allows her to follow her two greatest passions: parenting and writing.

Susan's published books include *Chicken Soup for the Soul: Here Comes the Bride*; *Chicken Soup for the Soul: Devotional Stories for Tough Times*; *Chicken Soup for the Soul: New Moms*; *Chicken Soup for the Soul: Devotional Stories for Mothers*; *Chicken Soup for the Soul: Family Matters*; *Chicken Soup for the Soul: Devotional Stories for Women*; *Chicken Soup for the Soul: All in the Family*; *Chicken Soup for the Soul: Twins and More*; *Boosting Your Baby's Brain Power*; *It's Twins! Parent-to-Parent Advice from Infancy Through Adolescence*; *Oh, Baby! 7 Ways a Baby Will Change Your Life the First Year*; and, *Twice the Love: Stories of Inspiration for Families with Twins, Multiples and Singletons*.

Susan's articles and stories have appeared in many books, websites, and magazines, including *TWINS Magazine* and *Angels on Earth*. She writes a parenting blog at http://SusanHeimOnParenting.com and a writing blog at http://SusanHeimOnWriting.com. And she is the founder of TwinsTalk, a website with tips, advice and stories about raising twins and multiples, at www.twinstalk.com.

Susan and her husband Mike are the parents of four sons, who are in elementary school and college! You can reach Susan at susan@

susanheim.com and visit her website at www.susanheim.com. Join her on Twitter and Facebook by searching for ParentingAuthor.

Thank You

When our publisher, Amy Newmark, was reading through the manuscript of this book, she said, "These stories are really going to change lives!" At Chicken Soup for the Soul, we see firsthand the power of sharing our life stories and experiences. That's why we are so very grateful to our contributors, who courageously and generously pour out their hearts and souls. Your story will truly touch many hearts and give hope to those who need to know that God is with them on this incredible journey we call life.

And for those of you whose stories did not make it into this book, we want you to know that your efforts weren't wasted. We read every single submission, and all of them have a profound influence on us and affect the final manuscript. Many of our contributors have been published after numerous submissions haven't made it into a book, so please keep writing and sending in those stories!

A special thank you to Amy Newmark, who so generously shares her time, wisdom, and expertise to make sure that every single *Chicken Soup for the Soul* book is the best it can be. Thanks to her vision, Chicken Soup for the Soul is better than ever and continues to inspire readers around the world. We also couldn't do what we do without the brilliance of Assistant Publisher, D'ette Corona, who works very closely with our contributors to be sure that we are printing the best possible stories. I also want to thank Chicken Soup for the Soul editor, Kristiana Glavin, who read every line of the thousands of submissions we received for this book, pinpointing those that brought tears to her eyes or gave her goose bumps. Thanks to editor Barbara LoMonaco, also a cherished and integral part of our team, who takes care of our website and databases, and is always willing to provide assistance and insight with a smile.

We have been greatly blessed to benefit from the artistic talents of our creative director and book producer, Brian Taylor at Pneuma Books, who spends many long hours working on the wonderful covers and interior designs of our books.

Finally, we thank God. Every story in this book is a testament to how much He loves us and guides us in everything that we do. His presence was certainly felt as we read every story submitted and put together this book. God bless you all.

~Susan Heim

Improving Your Life
Every Day

Real people sharing real stories—for nineteen years. Now, Chicken Soup for the Soul has gone beyond the bookstore to become a world leader in life improvement. Through books, movies, DVDs, online resources and other partnerships, we bring hope, courage, inspiration and love to hundreds of millions of people around the world. Chicken Soup for the Soul's writers and readers belong to a one-of-a-kind global community, sharing advice, support, guidance, comfort, and knowledge.

Chicken Soup for the Soul stories have been translated into more than 40 languages and can be found in more than one hundred countries. Every day, millions of people experience a Chicken Soup for the Soul story in a book, magazine, newspaper or online. As we share our life experiences through these stories, we offer hope, comfort and inspiration to one another. The stories travel from person to person, and from country to country, helping to improve lives everywhere.

Share with Us

We all have had Chicken Soup for the Soul moments in our lives. If you would like to share your story or poem with millions of people around the world, go to chickensoup.com and click on "Submit Your Story." You may be able to help another reader, and become a published author at the same time. Some of our past contributors have launched writing and speaking careers from the publication of their stories in our books!

Our submission volume has been increasing steadily—the quality and quantity of your submissions has been fabulous. We only accept story submissions via our website. They are no longer accepted via mail or fax.

To contact us regarding other matters, please send us an e-mail through webmaster@chickensoupforthesoul.com, or fax or write us at:

Chicken Soup for the Soul
P.O. Box 700
Cos Cob, CT 06807-0700
Fax: 203-861-7194

One more note from your friends at Chicken Soup for the Soul: Occasionally, we receive an unsolicited book manuscript from one of our readers, and we would like to respectfully inform you that we do not accept unsolicited manuscripts and we must discard the ones that appear.

The **National Bestseller** with Real Stories from Real People

Chicken Soup
for the **Soul**®

Messages from Heaven

101 Miraculous Stories of Signs from Beyond,
Amazing Connections, and Love that Doesn't Die

Jack Canfield,
Mark Victor Hansen,
and Amy Newmark

When our loved ones leave this world, our connection with them does not end. Sometimes when we see or hear from them, they give us signs and messages. Sometimes they speak to us in dreams or they appear in different forms. The stories in this book, both religious and secular, will amaze you, giving you new knowledge, insight and awareness about the connection and communication we have with those who have passed on or those who have experienced dying and coming back.

978-1935096-91-7

Classics on faith

Life has always been filled with trials, including illness, job loss, grief, addictions, and much more. In this collection of 101 devotions, others share their personal stories and prayers that show God's presence and ever-present love during a time of trouble. During any of life's struggles, readers will find counsel and reassurance in these stories of faith, strength, and prayer.

978-1935096-74-0

Classics on faith

www.chickensoup.com